"**A hilarious book**—a rollicking-good ... irrepressible presence throughout, the ... reminds us of what we often try to cover up—our desire to be other than who we are, if only for a little while, to be unfettered, to let off steam . . . all in the legendary name of Dracula. **If this wonderfully odd, zany work is any indication, Paul Bibeau will be around to delight us for many years to come.**"

—Jonathan Coleman, bestselling author of *Exit the Rainmaker* and *Long Way to Go*

"**You could shamble around in the shadows of civilization for a thousand years and not find a tastier pop culture exposé** . . . a diabolically funny midnight romp through all things wampyr. The treatise on the dark evil of funnel cake alone was worth the price of admission."

—Keith Blanchard, former editor in chief of *Maxim* and author of *The Deed*

"**A work to sink your dayglo plastic fangs into.** Bibeau's vampire tour leads us through Romania, Hollywood, and Minnesota, with stops at all our subconscious fears and dark desires and plenty of laughs along the way."

—David Wellington, author of *13 Bullets: A Vampire Tale* and the *Monster Island* trilogy

"**One of the funniest and most fascinating books I've ever had the pleasure of reading** . . . a captivating journey through the absurd, moneymaking, hilarious, and sometimes frightening world of the entire vampire realm. **It doesn't matter if you're into vampires or not,** *Sundays with Vlad* **is for anyone wanting to be thoroughly entertained.**"

—W. Tray White, award-winning director and producer of *Impaler*

"An amazingly talented new comedic voice, with **bits of the best of Dave Barry and Bill Bryson married to a surprisingly keen reporter's eye.** If Vlad the Impaler were alive today, he'd disembowel Paul Bibeau and put his head on a pike to show the world the price for such insolence. But then he'd read *Sundays with Vlad* and have a good laugh."

—Charles Coxe, former editor in chief of GiantMag.com and contributing writer to *Rolling Stone*, *Men's Journal*, and *Maxim*

SUNDAYS with VLAD

FROM PENNSYLVANIA TO TRANSYLVANIA, ONE MAN'S QUEST TO LIVE IN THE WORLD OF THE UNDEAD

Paul Bibeau

THREE RIVERS PRESS • NEW YORK

Published in the United States by Three Rivers Press, an imprint of the
Crown Publishing Group, a division of Random House, Inc., New York.
www.crownpublishing.com

Three Rivers Press and the Tugboat design are registered trademarks of
Random House, Inc.

Portions of the material in Chapter One originally appeared in *Maxim*.

Library of Congress Cataloging-in-Publication Data
Bibeau, Paul.
Sundays with Vlad : from Pennsylvania to Transylvania, one man's quest
to live in the world of the undead / Paul Bibeau.—1st ed.
1. Vampires.   2. Vampires in mass media.   3. Vlad III, Prince of
Wallachia, 1430 or 31–1476 or 7.   I. Title.
GR830.V3B53 2007
398'.45—dc22   2007010839

ISBN 978-0-307-35278-1

Printed in the United States of America

Design by Maria Elias

10 9 8 7 6 5 4 3 2 1

First Edition

To Paul Francis McNerney.
Thanks for all the monster books.

Author's Note

Sometimes people don't want their names in print. In several minor cases I've given sources pseudonyms to protect their identities. Take Steve, the hard-bitten, conservative lawyer who gave me a quote about Ukranian hookers. His name is not really Steve, and I won't tell you what it is, because then he'd get in trouble. Some folks want their privacy, and it's my job to take that right away. But still, I try to be nice.

Contents

Prologue

Monsters on the Brain

*"You were really acting odd. You kept checking your
traveler's wallet, and you were starting to sweat.
It was unsettling."*

The guard, polite and menacing, stepped in front of us. He gripped a wicked-looking submachine gun. He seemed barely old enough to drive.

"Can I help you?" he asked. "Where are you going?" It was really a demand, not a question, and my wife, Anne, and I couldn't answer. We glanced at each other nervously. We seemed out of place, anxious, guilty of something. Like we were hiding a secret. And we were—it must have been obvious. Because soon a half dozen more guards swarmed us, all of them armed, and I was sure something terrible was about to happen. It was a bad way for a honeymoon to end.

We'd raced into the airport at Bucharest with no tickets, no reservations, and no idea where we were going. It was late in the evening, and we were practically the only passengers in the cavernous building. The departure board posted a single flight: to Tel Aviv. And when the guards spotted us, we were actually debating

I was a teenage vampire (fan).

whether to buy a pair of tickets and hop onto it. Hurried, out of place, and ridiculously early for a flight we weren't sure we were going to take, the guards didn't know what to make of us. They asked us what flight we were waiting for, and we couldn't tell them. They asked us where we were going, and we couldn't tell them that, either. Neither of us wanted to just say the truth, which was this:

Anywhere. Absolutely anywhere. We want a seat on the very next plane flying out of this stupid fucking country, and we don't care where it's going. It could be headed to Vienna, Djibouti, or one of those remote research facilities in Antarctica, where an alien life-form has just killed one of the staff and mutated into a hideous parody of him, and now it's picking off the rest of the terrified scientists, one by one. That would be a Cancun sunrise compared to this god-forsaken crapheap.

But you don't use words like "godforsaken crapheap" to talk about the country a nineteen-year-old kid with a submachine gun calls home. We couldn't tell them the truth, so my wife and I found ourselves sticking to the story that we were anxious, secretive travelers with no reservations who might be headed to Tel Aviv. Looking back on it, that may have been a mistake. But it was only the latest in a long series of screwups that began when my wife said we should spend part of our honeymoon at Castle Dracula.

I know you don't believe it was my wife's idea. Nobody does. When I tell people she suggested it, they look at me like I'd just said my wife suggested we have a Superbowl-themed wedding with the priest dressed as Ditka or decorate our apartment with inflatable furniture or have a three-way with a Hooter's girl. But it's true. Anne's an attorney, so before writing this book I had her draft something up to make sure the whole story was on the record. After you've read it you'll know I wasn't to blame.

In re the Honeymoon of Paul and Anne,
AFFIDAVIT OF ANNE BIBEAU

Pursuant to 28 U.S.C. § 1746, I, Anne Bibeau, state as follows:

1.   I wed Paul Bibeau on September 25, 1999.

2.   In planning for our wedding, we mutually agreed to honeymoon in Prague.

3.   I proposed that we consider visiting Romania on our honeymoon.

4.   Mr. Bibeau immediately agreed to this proposal and began charting our itinerary in Romania.

5.   Although I initially envisioned a brief visit to Romania, Mr. Bibeau planned a three-day trip, the focal point of which was the "castle" of Vlad the Impaler. Mr. Bibeau informed me that the "castle" was in beautiful, legendary Transylvania.

6.   I admit that I consented to Mr. Bibeau's itinerary.

7.   While my aforementioned consent was given freely, it was not fully informed.

8.   Specifically, my consent was given without knowledge of the following key facts:

- Vlad the Impaler's "castle" is not, in fact, a castle, but is more aptly described as two piles of bricks, one dating from the fifteenth century and the other from the 1970s.
- Vlad the Impaler's "castle" is not in Transylvania but is in the Romanian province of Wallachia, an economically depressed industrial region littered with failed construction projects and empty factories covered with moss, scrub brush, and what appear to be wild goats.
- Wallachia is also infested with feral dogs that roam the streets in packs and harass tourists and locals indiscriminately.
- Wallachia is also infested with beggars who roam the streets in packs and harass tourists and locals indiscriminately.
- Romanian hotel corridors are unlit after sundown, so finding your room involves blindly fumbling through narrow corridors.

- Romania has no restaurants except McDonald's franchises and pizza parlors that serve their dish with ketchup.
- Romanian train and airplane service could be described, charitably, as spotty and unreliable. Once one enters the country, finding safe passage out becomes extremely difficult.

9. Upon information and belief, Mr. Bibeau was in possession of the facts listed supra in paragraph 8 prior to departure from the United States. Nonetheless, he did not disclose said facts to me.

10. Had I been fully informed, I would not have consented to visit Romania on our honeymoon.

I declare under penalty of perjury that the foregoing is true and correct.

Executed on November 20, 2005.
ANNE BIBEAU

Okay, maybe that raised more questions than it answered.

My wife seems to have some complaints about how I handled this trip. I'm probably not the first husband to learn there were problems in his marriage from a legal document. But let me explain my side. I suppose we should start from the beginning . . . which means I need to tell you some things about sibling rivalry, Leonard Nimoy, and a set of plastic glow-in-the-dark fangs.

"Thoo? Ith that you?"

Even the power of Dracula is nothing compared to the power of a big sister. And my older sister Sue was more menacing than most. Don't misunderstand me. She's often used her powers for good. She's let me crash on her couch for months at a time and lent me serious amounts of money. But when we were young, she was the first baby in our family, and I was the second, who ruined everything. After she was starting to get older, less babyish, and more like yesterday's news, I showed up with my footie pj's and my adorable lisp, and suddenly it was my spray-painted macaroni art that went up on the fridge.

"What wath that? If thath you, you better quit it. Thoo?"

Overall, she's been great to me. A protector and a friend. I want to make that clear, so you won't get any misconceptions when I tell you what she did to me when I was nine. Because every big sister has a dark side. Your parents go out for the evening, leaving her in charge, and suddenly the house becomes like a banana republic after the coup. There are displays of force, random imprisonments, and, of course, human rights violations. And your parents, off having dinner, are as well-meaning and useless as the UN Security Council. Sure you could call them. But they're not going to leave the restaurant on their only night off to come get you out of political prison . . . which might be a clothes hamper with something heavy weighing down the lid.

But that's not all. Our house had a crawl space that led from the attic to just behind the wall in my bedroom. And my bedroom had a set of dresser drawers actually built into that wall—so, theoretically, you could pull out a drawer and crawl through to the attic. Or if you were a big sister who was really maliciously inclined, you could pop in a pair of Day-Glo plastic fangs and climb out into the bedroom by opening the dresser drawer from behind so there'd be a massive crash followed by the dim, barely discernable image of you sliding out flashing a mouthful of feral teeth—just like a vampire emerging from a crypt in the wall—with your baby brother looking on in absolute pants-pissing horror.

"Thoo?"

This was worse than the rope burns or the noogies or when she and my cousin made me wear a wedding dress and my uncle thought I was developing some kind of cross-dressing fetish at the age of eight. Having my sister turn into a Nosferatu and attack me altered my hardwiring a little bit. I've never been the same since.

I became the odd little kid who's in love with monsters. There's one in every neighborhood. My favorite book was *The Three Little Pigs* because of that wolf peeking from just outside the window of the brick house. I loaded up on books about vampires and werewolves at the school library. The grisly woodcuts of creatures loping through the medieval fields and lunching on peasants would keep me awake all night. In the morning, I'd take the books back, promise myself I would never read them again, and check them back out the very next week.

I didn't like novels about this stuff. They bored me. What I liked were books about the actual legends in eastern Europe—folklore, ancient court trials, and even eyewitness accounts of monsters. I knew they weren't real, of course. At least that's what I told myself when it was late at night. But I wanted to get as close to the truth as possible. Vampires didn't exist, but at a certain place and a certain time, people believed they did. They had rituals to kill them or ward them off. They accused real people of lycanthropy or witchcraft, tried them, and even executed them. And it wasn't something out of a story.

Then I discovered *In Search Of* and got hooked. For thirty minutes a week, from 1976 to 1982, Leonard Nimoy, the Man Who Was Spock, appeared in a smart-looking suit jacket and turtleneck and told me about Bigfoot, UFOs, and the Loch Ness Monster. He showed photos—actual photos of monsters!—and interviewed eye-witnesses. Nimoy would be shown standing in front of some desolate patch of woods, talking about how the creature, whatever it was, could be somewhere out there right at that very moment. I was almost afraid for him. Like just before the credits rolled, I'd see some unholy creature come charging out of the shadows and tackle Spock in a fury. The camera would reel, screams of the crew filling the air, then static. And we'd know they were all gone.

Then when I was ten, I found a footprint stamped into the cement outside a golf course near my neighborhood. And I knew Bigfoot was not only real . . . *he was in my neighborhood.*

"Someone probably did it before the concrete was dry," my dad said at the breakfast table. "Some guy got drunk and wanted to leave his mark on the world." But I knew there was at least a possibility that some super-massive creature made the dent in the concrete after it was hard, which meant Sasquatch was hiding out nearby, and I could find him and become famous.

At the time, we were living on Governor's Island, then a military base off the tip of Manhattan, which meant Bigfoot would have had to travel several thousand miles from the forests of the great Northwest, swim Long Island Sound undetected, and constantly dodge the military police driving all over the complex in their scooters. I admit it sounds far-fetched. But back then I was determined. I looked all over that military base for Bigfoot: I searched utility closets near the golf course and poked through drainage culverts in back of the housing complex. I monitored small locked sheds and mysterious doors or windows wherever I found them.

I never spotted the beast, but that didn't stop me—not even as I grew up. I became a failed ghost hunter, the guy who couldn't visit a new town without going to a bookshop or tourist attraction and buying the book about the local legends. And then I'd have to drag my friends and family to the places described in such a book so we could see a kitchen where someone once saw a cupboard door bang shut or the graveyard where someone photographed a weird light or the inn where someone felt a cold spot. Now, deep down in the rational, practical part of my brain that I suppress and only bring out when I see an oncoming car or someone who is about to rip me off for a large amount of money, I always knew I'd never find a ghost. I knew cold spots came from drafts, cupboards slammed shut because houses settled, and cameras leaked all the time, causing strange lights to develop on pictures. But I could never stop trying.

During high school, I took an independent study course for which I could research any topic I chose. I studied vampire beliefs around the world and gave a slide show at the local library. I had garish pictures of the Rakshasas of India, who sucked blood from feet sticking out of bedsheets, and the Ekimmu, which was so powerful it could just appear in a house and kill everyone inside. There were vampires that hung upside down from trees, vampires that floated through the air, and vampires that didn't even look like people—they appeared as birds or shadows. I put posters all over the area.

"Attend," the posters read. "You'll sleep safer!" No one came but a couple friends and one Goth girl whom I had a crush on. She brought her mom, who kept pointing out my mistakes throughout the whole thing—her mom knew more about vampires than I did, which gave me a disturbing insight into the Goth girl's home life. I received an A, but everyone got an A in independent study. For years after, while digging through old files, I'd occasionally find a tiny slide photo of a horrifying monster and chuckle.

After college, I landed my first job as the only reporter for a very small weekly paper in West Point, Virginia. This town had nothing to do with the city up north that produced some of history's finest military geniuses. All West Point, Virginia, produced was paper—the whole town was dominated by a huge paper mill that employed half the population and filled the air with an overpowering stench like getting a face full of skunk spray every single day of your life. (In fact, this may have been pretty close to the truth. I have heard the solvent a mill uses to create paper contains the same chemical as a skunk's musk. So it was exactly like some giant, industrial-strength polecat leveling its ass at the whole community every morning and giving it a blast.)

I lived in a one-room attic apartment over the bingo hall of Blessed Sacrament Catholic Church—my place was decorated with shag carpeting and furniture that looked like it had been stolen from *The Brady Bunch*'s rec room. But the job was great: I wrote about nearby Native American tribes and profiled local politicos. We even had our own tiny drug ring the cops would bust from time to time.

What excited me most, though, was the Cohoke Light, a glowing orb that came drifting down a stretch of local railroad tracks on misty nights. No one knew exactly what caused it—people told tales of ghosts from a Civil War medical train or even a woman who'd gotten decapitated by a rail car back in the 1950s. But everyone in that town had seen the light and photographed it many times. Supposedly, a team from some college even studied it. It came so regularly that teenagers used to crowd around the tracks, drinking beer and making out like the place was some kind of supernatural drive-in theater—before the sheriff's department started chasing them away. The light may have been swamp gas or ball lightning instead of a ghost, but everyone agreed it was real.

One October, I convinced my editor to let me cover it. So my buddy Kennan and I found ourselves staring down the long, lonely stretch of track in the evening. We'd brought a small jack-o'-lantern as a joke. But an hour into our vigil, the night was cold and dark, and we weren't joking about anything anymore. Our eyes tried to adjust to the absolute black with no streetlamps or town lights. There were no houses in view, and we began to glimpse things moving in the woods.

"Did you see that?" Kennan asked, trying to sound casual.

"What?"

"Oh . . . never mind."

"No, what? What is it?" I was hoping he'd spotted the light finally, but he just shook his head.

"Nothing, nothing. It just . . . Nothing."

"C'mon."

"It just seemed for a minute like I saw some kind of . . . ghostly white dog up ahead."

We were back in the car and gone in five minutes, and we didn't even stop for the jack-o'-lantern. I saw that pumpkin again a few days later—on the front page of a competing newspaper. Evidently, that same night, some time after we had left, a rival reporter came to the tracks. She spotted the light and got some great shots of it—along with a mysterious and creepy pumpkin she couldn't explain.

The week after, on Halloween, the mist came back. I went to the tracks alone, desperate to get a glimpse of that light. I waited there, determined that nothing would tear me away. Soon I saw lights—blue lights flashing off of the trees as a police car rolled up beside me.

"Paul," the sheriff said cheerily, with just a hint of evil. I was a nosy reporter and he didn't really like me. I figured it would just make his Halloween if he could give me a ticket for trespassing. But suddenly right behind him a bus appeared filled with friends of his, who'd all come to see the light. The sheriff had me, but I kinda had him as well. He gave me a pass.

"I'll tell you what," he said. "Why don't you drive up ahead, turn the car around, and we'll find a place for you to park?" I thanked him, drove off about three miles looking for a wide space in the narrow road, and then accidentally dunked my car into a ditch while trying to make a U-turn. There was no way I could drive that car out. In desperation, I even found myself yanking at the bumper and hollering, like I was going to turn into the Hulk and pull the thing clear in a feat of incredible strength. A pickup came by eventually, and the driver hooked my car and pulled it out. But as my vehicle finally made it to the road, that bus drove past again, this time with its passengers chattering and hooting excitedly.

"It was just as great as I remember," the sheriff told me with a grin as he rolled by. I went home and drank. I never went back, and today the police patrols are even thicker. I missed my chance, probably forever.

A few years later, I was living in New York City, and my girlfriend Anne and I were dating seriously. A blond, pretty, whip-smart lawyer, Anne is sensible and caring—and her ass looks great in a power suit. She's also my best friend. She's very understanding, but she also doesn't put up with too much of my nonsense, which is a good combo.

The day before Thanksgiving 1998, I asked her to marry me and she said yes. We planned for a wedding in September 1999 and wanted to take a trip overseas for our honeymoon. We're not really tropical-island-with-fruity-drinks people, mostly because she has a lot of Scottish and English ancestors and mine are Irish and French. So between us we have the pigment of one quarter of a normal person. We decided to go to eastern Europe—Prague, then Hungary, and possibly Vienna. It seemed perfect. And one day, we were idly looking through travel guides at a bookstore, passing them back and forth between us, when one of us paused at an entry for a tiny village in Romania called Curtea de Argeş.

"Noted for its monastery and the legend surrounding it," the guidebook read, "Curtea also serves as an excellent base for adventurers seeking Count Dracula's real castle."

Monastery! Legend! Count Dracula's REAL CASTLE!

"You know," said Anne (honestly, she's the one who said this), "as long as we're in the region, we ought to see it."

I'd known for a long time about the historical Dracula. I couldn't say how I'd first learned about him—it's possible Spock told me about him during an episode of my beloved *In Search Of.* But since I was a boy, I'd heard the stories of Vlad's impalings, intrigues, and wars against the Turks. I was haunted by the crude drawings of him dining next to forests of dead guys on stakes. The historical Dracula seemed like the last chance for an absolutely true horror story. He wasn't a vampire, but he existed nonetheless. If I could see his castle, it would be like sneaking back to take shots of the Cohoke Light. It would be like finding Bigfoot cowering in a toolshed on the Governor's Island golf course. It would be like scaring my big sister.

There were other items in that guidebook: something about the castle being about 20 miles away from town and "a steep climb" of "1,500 steps zigzagging endlessly up a mountain." Oh yeah, and somewhere in the paragraph the author described the castle as "partially restored ruins." I was thrilled that Anne wanted to go, and maybe I should have read that guidebook more carefully. Maybe I should have explained these finer points of our trip. But I figured there'd be time on the plane.

A couple days after our wedding, we were off on the greatest adventure a failed ghost hunter could hope for. What could possibly go wrong?

We took an all-night direct flight to Prague, and with the time difference it felt like 3:00 a.m., but it was eight in the morning. We stumbled out of the metro, blinking in disbelief at the sunlight that shouldn't be there and the people bustling off to work. We spent the next couple of days wearing off our jet lag by wandering around this beautiful city and loading up on beer, puppet shows, and various kinds of cooked meats.

Prague Castle, a thousand-year-old structure, dwarfed the land-scape, and it looked like something out of a fairy tale. I kept doing a double-take every time I saw it. Being an American, I had, up to that point, seen exactly one real castle in my life—an imposing, butt-ugly keep in southern England—but I'd seen all kinds of movie palaces and amusement park attractions. I couldn't look at this real, honest-to-God seat of government without wanting to see a roller coaster nearby with some swing rides and a stall where bored teenagers would sell me T-shirts and soft serve in waffle cones. The whole dis-trict around it seemed like a bizarro Busch Gardens where the staff was required to chain-smoke.

Before we left, we visited the church in which the Infant of Prague is kept. The Infant is a tiny three-hundred-year-old statue of the baby Jesus that thousands of pilgrims visit every year. A group of nuns care for him there, constantly taking him out of his little glass case and changing his clothes. And in the church's upstairs rooms, you can see his many costumes. He had outfits in all kinds of different colors and styles, and I almost thought we'd see a Jesus Dream House where he could hang out with Barbie and Skipper.

"I wonder which of the suits makes him fly?" I asked Anne, who chuckled, but clearly wanted me to shut up before the nuns heard us.

Over the next couple days, we took a train across the Czech Republic and through Slovakia, which is romantic and wild. Then, we explored Budapest. That city is much less touristy—instead of jackasses like me from the West, the trains all seemed to be filled with locals going about their business.

We went south and east, the area getting noticeably poorer. As we moved deeper into eastern Europe, the buildings got flimsier and the toilet paper got harsher. In Prague, the toilet paper seemed like the utility-grade stuff you'd use in your college dorm, and most of the buildings of Prague seemed sturdy and well-kept. Hungary's offices and apartments seemed danker and more prone to collapse, but its TP was hardy and unrelenting as a Magyar horde. And nothing could prepare us for Romania.

During the flight to Bucharest, I read the *Lonely Planet* guide over and over to get prepared for the place. The guide convinced me we were going to get robbed, beaten, stripped, and left for dead—probably as soon as the plane touched down and the stewardesses could get their shanks out of their cute little carry-on cases.

"This is a poor country, so it's unwise to display your wealth," the guide read. "Keep to well-lit streets and look purposeful. If you are attacked, don't expect much help from bystanders or the police."

"Actually, there was nothing in the guidebook that was all that scary," Anne said recently. "People get robbed in eastern Europe. It's a fact of life. You were just getting paranoid." We've argued about this since. I can't find the passage now, but I'm sure there was something in it about stewardesses who shank you before you get off the plane. Anyway, I'd never traveled to any place as poor as Romania, so I wanted to be prepared.

The guide told me how to bargain with the locals: If I always said "prea mult" ("too much") no matter what they told me, I could eventually dicker them down in price for everything. Even though we had the money, I figured if I didn't bargain enough, they'd sense some weakness, and they'd be on me like lions on a gimpy gazelle.

We spilled out of the plane and I was muttering "prea mult, prea mult" and clutching my guide like a Bible to ward off evil as we looked for an exit. We stepped out of the airport and were instantly mobbed with cabbies shouting at us and waving to their cars. One of the cabbies stepped forward and began to bargain with us on behalf of the rest. He was a big bearish man with a movie-quality hunch, and one of his eyes was covered by a milky film. And he wasn't taking *prea friggin' mult* for an answer.

I kept trying to bargain with him, writing down price after price on little pieces of paper and shoving them under his nose, but he wasn't budging for me. At some point, he decided Anne and I weren't worth the effort and shrugged with finality. I suddenly realized that I was in no position to bargain at all. I was being stupid. But then one of his buddies pointed out a bus nearby—they'd had enough of us—and Anne and I raced for it.

We got on, the driver started the vehicle, and it roared off. Anne and I found ourselves traveling through completely dark countryside. I looked around nervously, my *Lonely Planet*-fueled paranoia growing, and I began to realize that the driver could easily whack us over our heads and steal everything we had, and he'd probably split his take with the stewardesses.

"You were really acting odd," Anne said to me afterward. "You kept checking your traveler's wallet, and you were starting to sweat. It was unsettling." Maybe so. But perhaps it was my cat-like readiness that the driver noticed, and that made him think twice about his highway robbery scheme.

Okay, that's not how it happened. Not only didn't the driver kill us, he drove out of his way to bring us right to the front door of our hotel and smiled at me blandly, and when I tried to give him a tip out of guilt, he waved me off. I felt like exactly the kind of jerk who gives American travelers a bad name. I just needed a fanny pack and one of those hats with the beer can attachments.

We got out and walked to the front door of the Hotel Triumf, a slightly rundown, romantic building in an overgrown, tree-lined section of the diplomatic area.

"Isn't this great?" I asked Anne. "Isn't this beautiful?"

I thought I'd just cheated death. Because I felt so relieved, the Triumf wasn't just beautiful anymore—it was suddenly the best place ever.

"I thought this might be nice, but it's so cool. And the front desk people were so nice—and so was that bus driver. I really misjudged these people, and I feel sorry!" I rattled off at Anne, who smiled warily like she was wondering whether I needed meds. "This is *great!*" I had this problem for the rest of the trip: being hungry and out of sorts and suffering from a massive caffeine withdrawal—instead of coffee, they serve a drink called *ness*, which is made with "vegetable extracts"—my blood sugar and adrenaline levels were spiking and diving while I went through wicked, asylum-grade mood swings: *Weeee! Gonna kill myself. Yippeee! Existence is futile. Having fun! Need a cup of coffee.*

The next day, we bought a ticket for a train that would take us into the country. Anne wasn't saying much. It was just dawning on her how this honeymoon was becoming a showcase of her new husband's bad judgment and terrible sense.

The Bucharest station looked like it was in the middle of some kind of renovation or possibly an artillery barrage. We needed to pick up Romanian currency—we only had American hundreds in our money belts, which was as terrifying to me as if I were smuggling dope in my colon. So we followed a sign that directed us down a dark, narrow hallway that zigged and zagged, turning one corner after another until I expected to look in a doorway and see Christopher Walken playing Russian roulette while hordes of people screamed and threw money around a table. Instead, we got to a tiny booth, and some guy gave us a clump of Romanian lei for our bills.

We bought first-class tickets, which were just coach seats. It made me wonder what coach class would be, and then I saw a car in which people rode with livestock. I thought that might be cool, but it would result in divorce proceedings when we made it back to America.

The train rolled out of Bucharest and into the Wallachian countryside, flat scrub fields with farmers holding wooden tools that looked like they were made centuries ago. We passed mammoth factories that dwarfed the landscape. They were big as skyscrapers, but empty and rusted. And some of them were even half-covered with moss, grass, and vine—like they'd shut down so long ago that the land itself was swallowing them whole.

"So we're in Transylvania?" Anne asked amiably.

"Uh, no," I said.

"When are we going to Transylvania?"

"We're going near the Transylvanian Alps," I offered weakly.

"When are we going to Transylvania?" my sweet, lovely, and oh-so-patient wife asked, her sweetness and patience wearing thin.

"This is Wallachia," I said. "Dracula's Castle is in Wallachia."

"Oh," she said. Just like that. Nothing more. So really, I could have let her sit there and deal with the fact that she thought I'd taken her to the wrong region of the world, and that maybe if she'd married someone else, she might have gone to Vienna or to Frankfurt or even to Transylvania instead of this desolate post-communist backwater. Maybe I should have just let the conversation drop. With the benefit of hindsight and six years of marriage to this wonderful woman under my belt, I can now say with certainty that sometimes the best thing to do when your wife gives you that quizzical slightly annoyed "oh" is to keep your fool mouth shut.

But back then I didn't know that, so I explained that in the region right next to us, Transylvania, there was indeed a castle known as Castle Dracula, but it wasn't the *historical* Castle Dracula, and its name was Castle Bran. And even though it was a beautiful castle in its own right, featuring lovely and inspiring Teutonic architecture, it wasn't the real thing. It was tacky. It was touristy. It probably had nice hotels and nice restaurants and the countryside probably had lovely forests instead of these giant defunct factories and the rusted, smoky, dangerous-looking nuclear power plant we passed as I was yammering on, but that was all because it was built on a big, fat lie. And though we were exhausted, wore clothes that by this time smelled, and hadn't had a hot shower or a good meal in two days, our experience was so much better because it was real.

After that, she got very, very quiet.

We arrived at the transfer point at Pitești, where we had to wait for a couple of hours before the next train arrived. We walked around trying to find somewhere to eat. Pitești, a small city of about 300,000, was founded sometime before the late fourteenth century. It was the site of infamous prison experiments in the 1950s, when administrators forced almost two dozen inmates to assault one another repeatedly in an attempt to break down their loyalty to anything other than the Communist party. After five years, they cancelled the experiments and convicted most of the staff who'd participated. The town was also known for its tulip festival.

Pitești: Come for the flowers! Stay for the brutal prison beatings!

Pitești's name means "hidden" in Romanian, because it is hidden on the banks of the Argeș River. If it were up to me, the town would be hidden somewhere better, like the bottom of the river. The place looked like a large construction crew started building a city, stopped halfway through, and then just abandoned the place for twenty years. The area around the train station was clogged with debris. Buildings were constructed from the top down—I saw apartments that had finished rooms with people living in them perched atop completely bare steel frames. Some shops and restaurants were blacked out and empty, but with their doors hanging open.

We wandered down the sidewalk looking for something to eat or anything to do, and finally Anne sat down on the pavement and shook her head.

"That's it," she said. "I'm tired and hungry and I don't want to walk anymore."

"Do you want to leave?" I asked her.

She shook her head.

"I don't know," she said. "I don't know what I want to do. I don't know if anything is going to get better when we get to Curtea de Argeş, and I don't know if there's even a train back. And I'm scared."

"Why are you scared?"

"I just don't know what's going to happen to us."

We stayed like that on the sidewalk for a long time, and neither of us knew what to do. I felt terrible. It was my fault, and there was no way to pretend otherwise.

You know how some people say marriage multiplies happiness and divides grief? It's not true. Sometimes it's exactly the opposite. Things can take a bad turn, and a couple can become a little echo chamber of misery. My mood swings and crazy need to see this stupid castle and her fears combined to produce the worst tourist in the world. We'd known each other for years, but I realized we had a long way to go. I calmed her down. But I didn't know what we were going to do.

Finally, we went back and boarded the train for the second leg of our trip. We rattled on to Curtea de Argeş, and at some point a random chunk of the overhead luggage rack just detached from the wall for no reason at all and hit a passenger next to us. He was startled, but just brushed himself off and carefully put the metal bar back onto the rest of the rack like it was another piece of luggage. We sat there, and I couldn't stop thinking about how many thousands upon thousands of parts were working together to make that train run along without an accident, and if one of them could just break for no reason like that, what else could give? I wanted to get off as soon as possible.

At the same time, we didn't really know what waited for us in Curtea de Argeş. The guidebook had listed hotels in the city, but we weren't even sure they still existed. I was worried we'd climb down from the train in the middle of some field and find ourselves stranded. I didn't want to sleep in a ditch with Anne. I didn't want to get robbed. I certainly didn't want to end up wandering around in the dark wilderness just beneath Castle Dracula—that would have sounded really, really cool if I'd read about it back in New York, but here it was not a cheery thought. Most of all, I didn't want Anne to think I'd ruined our honeymoon.

But then a nice-sized town appeared from behind a corner, the conductor called out its name, and we realized we'd made it. Curtea looked cute and suburban. As we strolled down the tree-lined main street, we felt at ease. Families were out walking and chatting alongside us, and we even passed a wedding party at a community hall. Aside from the packs of wild dogs everywhere, the place seemed perfect.

The dogs were scruffy and vicious—they'd crowd around shops and restaurants, and the locals would swat them away with broomsticks, but it never worked. They'd back off and return, back off and return, always hovering near. And what was most disturbing was that they were so *cute*. Snarling and yapping and lunging at passersby, they were spaniels, beagles, and labs, and you wanted to put a bandanna on them and play fetch with a Frisbee, but you knew they'd take your arm off. One dog trotted by, getting idly humped by a whole pack without breaking her stride. It was just plain wrong.

We ducked into a restaurant called Pizza Montana to get away from the dogs. It was an outdoor café, but protected by some high hedges, and Britney Spears's music piped in over the loudspeakers. They served halfway decent pizza, but it came with a side of ketchup we couldn't figure out how to use. While we were puzzling over it, someone called out to us in a flat midwestern accent.

"Are you Americans?" a middle-aged man asked, walking up to our table with his wife. They were a friendly pair, missionaries, and thrilled to see someone from back home. They talked to us excitedly about their work here and the interesting traveling they'd done through the area. They seemed like exactly the kind of decent, kindly, thoroughly good human beings I was proud to have on foreign shores representing America and everything that's right, but within five minutes of talking to them, I was willing to put a fork in my neck to make it stop.

"This place is wonderful, just wonderful," the woman said to us, and they kept telling interesting anecdote after interesting anecdote about the Romanians and their delightful culture and how drawn they were to these people. They seemed so cheerful and sincere, I just . . . I just hated them. I'm sorry. I know that's bad. But I couldn't help thinking, "This is why they boil missionaries in big pots." There's something about someone so good and warmhearted that really pisses you off.

Anne and I nodded at them politely, trying to smile and laugh whenever required, both of us terrified the other would ask them to sit down. But eventually their stories tapered off, and they left to go cure cancer or cuddle crack babies or whatever they were here for—I wasn't paying attention. Soon it was dark, and we hurried back to the hotel, hoping we wouldn't run into any more stray dogs or friendly Americans.

We reached our hotel as night came. The place was almost completely blacked out, so we had to stumble through the halls looking for our room. But we managed, and we found the place roomy and fairly well-kept. There was just this enormous hole in the bathroom wall that led into a crawl space or possibly a lair for C.H.U.D.s—we couldn't tell which. Anne and I called it the Rodent Chunnel, joking about how it probably had thousands of Hungarian rats coming through on vacation where they were met by a Romanian rat in a jacket and cap who stamped their little passports and welcomed them.

We brushed our teeth using bottled water because by then we were convinced anything that came out of the tap would be like eating random items from a hospital wastebasket. We climbed into bed and lay there, huddled together for warmth and also out of fear. Because by then we could hear the howls.

More packs of dogs had gathered outside, and the howling was everywhere. Sometimes it would sound far away and mournful, but occasionally there'd be a bark or a yelp right near our window—a large picture window on the first floor.

"Jesus," said Anne.

"Jesus," I said back.

We laughed nervously in the dark, both of us sure we were going to die. Then a thought occurred to me: This was just like *Dracula*, with Jonathan Harker going deeper and deeper into the East. Weren't there passages in that book in which the author described Harker being unsettled by the howling of wolves and by the foreign culture long before he ever came across the Count?

I was nowhere near the location of the story—Stoker set Dracula's literary castle farther north—but somehow I'd found the heart of the novel right here. And I *was* Harker, I realized. I was a complete wuss, a pampered and arrogant westerner traveling into the wilds, making an ass out of myself with my worrying and my endless complaints that the food and the hotel weren't like home. And now I was surrounded by the children of the night and the music they made. Not actual wolves—more like rabid weimaraners with the odd toy poodle thrown in—but still, the similarity was eerie.

An Anglo-Irishman, Stoker may have been satirizing the English fascination with and fear of other countries. Was I the updated version? The Ugly American Harker? I turned it over in my head as

Anne's breathing became deep and regular. I couldn't make sense of it, and eventually sleep got the last word.

We woke and took the first cab we could find to the castle. On the way, our car passed dusty little farm villages and the driver tried to teach us some of his language.

"Vacha! Vacha!" he said, pointing at cows.

"Capra!" he added, as we passed a goat.

"Ceauşescu!" he said, farther down the road. Now, we had no idea what he was talking about.

"Ceauşescu! Ceauşescu!" he said again, like we were going to see that the Romanian dictator had faked his own death and was hiding behind some hay in a field. He kept talking animatedly, trying to point out some spot, but we couldn't piece his story together. But then I saw he was making gestures mimicking a helicopter going down. He was pointing out the place where Ceauşescu's helo pilot faked an engine malfunction during their escape. He landed it to give the locals a chance to seize his boss, which they did. I'd heard the story before. I had no idea if this was the spot, but he seemed sure.

We drove into a dense forest flanked by mountains. The brush was lush green—too thick to see where Vlad could have hidden his castle. But we reached a small parking lot, the guy got out, opened our door for us with a friendly gesture, and pointed into a tiny, narrow clearing in the trees. A rickety staircase of cement blocks with a metal pipe banister disappeared into the woods there. The cabbie lit a cigarette and smiled.

"You'll wait for us here?" I asked. Well, pleaded. He smiled gamely and waved us off, as if to say, "no worries," and Anne and I started climbing into the green nowhere.

We were huffing hard by the time the parking lot disappeared. The trail stretched away in both directions, and for a long time, we couldn't see all the way back or all the way forward. There was nothing but Anne and me and the woods and the stairs and metal pipe, broken in places.

After about twenty minutes I felt tired. After twenty more, I began to think this was some kind of college prank. But while we climbed and climbed, my mind was reeling: Somehow, there were no crowds, no tourists, and no ticket counters. No kiosks! No gift shops! No one selling capes and plastic fangs or bloodred freeze-dried ice cream! No lines! No red velvet ropes! *Nowhere to spend money!*

It didn't make sense to me. This was Dracula's real castle, and I kept thinking the trail would turn a corner, and suddenly we'd run into a miniature vampified Disneyworld packed with tourists just like me. But it never happened. We were completely alone, visiting the fortress of one of the most famous figures in history.

Finally, somewhere after the 1,400th step, the stairs came out of the woods and up a ridiculously tiny, narrow crag that hung hundreds of feet above sharp rocks. We crossed a tiny footbridge that would have gotten an F in high school shop class, and we were on top of a mountain, where a massive plateau held the stately, dark walls of the brooding Dracula's Castle—except for the fact that it didn't.

The castle was nothing more than a tiny clump of bricks—some of them big sand-colored blocks hundreds of years old and some of them bright red, out of place, laid during a failed renovation in the 1970s. They'd also installed a couple of spotlights, but the bulbs were all smashed and rusted.

The place was small, sad, and utterly ruined. We walked around for a bit, glancing off the plateau down a sheer drop that ended in a tiny silver river below. (According to legend, Dracula's wife leapt out of the castle and into this river rather than be captured by Turks. Francis Ford Coppola put a Hollywoodized version of the story into his Dracula movie. But it doesn't occur in Stoker's book.)

"Here," the guidebook said, "Vlad Țepeș and his successors were bold enough to sleep 9 m from their prisoners."

But how many prisoners could he have put in this place? I won-dered. *Three? How many henchmen and family members?* There couldn't have been more than twenty people here at any one time. I had this vision of the whole crew—friends, employees, and bitter enemies—camped out here in the winter, getting bored and stir-crazy, playing an endless game of Monopoly, and bitching because Vlad kept stealing the Utilities cards and making all the captured Turks share the Thimble. This wasn't a warlord's castle. It was a beach house.

In the least-ruined section, where the short, weathered walls almost approximated a room, there was a deep pit—a shaft that slid away into darkness. I looked down it and tried to figure out if this was the secret passage I'd read about. He had one of these babies, supposedly. But I couldn't tell. Anne was looking around at the scenery gamely, smiling and patient, like she was going to tolerate at least another thirty seconds of this bullshit that had cost us three days of our honeymoon. I knew we'd be in therapy years from now, and she'd use this to justify a string of affairs. I knew the therapist would look at me and shrug, and I wouldn't say anything.

Then a guy in a red and gray track suit appeared up the stairs—the only person we saw there. He was huffing and stretching his hamstrings like he'd just finished the most hellacious wind sprints imaginable. When we caught his eye, he waved and we shook hands. His name was Silvio. He didn't speak much English, but he made us understand racing up the steps of this castle was some kind of train-ing regimen. We said good-bye and left him there, cooling down and enjoying the summit.

We took the cab back, caught the next train to Bucharest, and raced to the airport, where we got into that tangle with security. Eventually they let us go through, and within a day or two we were in some museum in Vienna listening to a snooty guide get into an argument with an obnoxious tourist who'd obviously taken a college class on the Hapsburgs and wanted to tell the guide everything he got wrong. The guide sneered at us, the hotel people sneered at us, and the people in Vienna's wonderful pastry shops sneered at us. The guy who drove us around in a carriage sneered at us, and maybe his horse did, too. Everywhere we went, things were expensive and tacky, and people were happy to take our money and treat us with loathing. We felt reviled and sucked up to, and it was wonderful. I was in heaven. It was what I was used to. Having foreigners take my money and treat me like dirt is what I expect as an American.

For years after, however, something always struck me about our trip to Romania and what we found there. It wasn't the feral dogs. It was that in the heart of Dracula country, they seemed to have no use for tourists at all. In America, we've made an industry of him. But in his home, at the site of the closest thing to Dracula's Castle, they did not seem to make any attempt to cash in. Can you imagine Americans doing that? Can you imagine Graceland or Hollywood or the birthplace of Washington without a gift shop? I didn't know if they were crazy or if we were.

The castle ruins were a colossal disappointment, but lurking under all the myths I'd learned about Dracula was a real story that was even weirder than anything I could have imagined. The tale of how this medieval ruler became the most recognizable figure in the world without changing his image back home was baffling. And more than a story about vampires, it was about globalism, history, and national pride. About how cultures rub each other the wrong way. It wasn't what I had expected to find. But it drew me in nonetheless. I had to dig deeper.

Tragic Kingdom

A tiny part of Dracula's schlocky financial empire.

"This is Romania. They will drill a hole into the tree, put a lit stick of dynamite in there, and say, 'You've got about two minutes to unchain yourselves.' "

Every morning when you head out to squat in your little cubicle, sip burnt coffee spiked with foul creamer, and stare at a computer screen until your eyes hurt, know this: Somewhere in a beautiful medieval town in eastern Europe, it's already quitting time for Nate Gendreau. It was quitting time years ago. Right now, while you steal a game of Minesweeper, Nate's probably sitting down with a pair of cute female backpackers, tipping back a golden pilsner, and *laughing at you*. Nate's lived your life. He gave it up. He never looked back.

"By the time I was twenty-six, I'd worked at Circuit City for eight years, and I was completely burned out," he said amiably, with that belt-sander accent people from the Boston area have. Nate's a Lowell, Massachusetts, boy, but he had become a highly paid executive in a corporate office in New York City.

"I had the half-million dollar four bedroom out in Westchester with the white picket fence, a mortgage that was trying to bury me, and a sports car I could never get out of second gear because I was always stuck in traffic," he said. He was good with money, and his job paid him very well. But it was becoming a trap.

"It was quite a dilemma. Do you work until you're forty-five and take an early retirement when you're old and gray and fighting three or four ulcers?" At twenty-six, he decided to take a decade off and travel.

"People at the office were telling me, 'You're stupid. You're crazy. Most people work thirty years to get where you've gotten, and you're going to throw it away?'

"But I was getting up at 5:30 and working until nine at night."

Nate was spending all his time at the job or driving to and from his expensive home so he could crash for a few hours and do it all over again.

"Sunday was my day off, but I'd be on call. I'd have a beeper, a mobile phone—you could get me anywhere in the world. That's not a life."

Nate Gendreau liquidated everything he owned, gave his father power of attorney, and stashed the money into checking and e-trade accounts. And in 2001, he set out with a backpack and an ATM card for London. By August, he'd hitchhiked to central Romania. Unlike the southern region, razed by massive Communist building projects, the country's interior was still beautiful and pristine. Nate eventually found his way to Sighişoara. The site of a trading center that had existed since the Bronze Age, Sighişoara was founded in the twelfth century by Saxon merchant-knights to protect Europe's eastern flank from Turkish invasion. Its nine-hundred-year-old architecture with gilded steeples, tiled roofs, cobblestone streets, and an old clock tower had somehow weathered two world wars and a brutal dictator who made a point of flattening everything in sight. It was dominated by a massive church fortress with extensive catacombs—designed so the whole town could wall themselves inside it in the event of a raid.

Sighişoara was magnificent. It was just the place to escape a tough job and a bad time—because of the terrorist attacks of September 11, Nate had decided he'd duck out of large American cities for a while. But he needed a legal reason to stay out in the country. He needed a job, or something like it.

"The country has no hostels," he said. "So I figured what better way to stay here than having a youth hostel where I could meet fellow travelers and help people out?" Within two weeks he'd bought a place. Soon he was kicking back with hikers and enjoying his eastern European version of the good life. And that's when he ran into the environmental nuts.

There were four of them, Americans, and Nate Gendreau knew they could easily get themselves killed in Transylvania.

"They were really bad tree huggers," he said with a laugh. Back in 2002, they'd arrived in Sighişoara to protest the destruction of a grove of ancient oak trees. The kids were bragging they would chain themselves to the trees in protest. Gendreau listened politely, but he knew they were fools.

"I asked them, 'You realize that the police will go there and beat the shit out of you and not even think twice?' " Gendreau said. They sat there, mouths open, while Gendreau continued:

"This is *Romania*. They will drill a hole into the tree, put a lit stick of dynamite in there, and say, 'You've got about two minutes to unchain yourselves.' "

The next day, the Americans left without any tree-chaining. But it wasn't long before Prince Charles showed up as well.

"I saw Chucky with the big ears," he said. "He couldn't keep his ears in his own business. Gotta put 'em in everybody else's." *Ears in his own business?* Was this some New England thing, like "wicked"? Gendreau didn't say. He continued, talking about how beautiful the trees were.

"Gorgeous," he said. "They were ancient white oak trees—some of them three yards across and one of them dated to eight hundred years old." Everyone wanted to protect them, he added, most of all the Romanians. They didn't need outside help.

"There was a proposal in the mayor's office," he said. "They had a scale model of what they were going to build. They were going to put all the trees inside without cutting down a single one. Prince Charles didn't like that. He said it was going to destroy the *ambiance* of the trees. He kept arguing against it, and with all the negative press, the project was nixed."

The project Gendreau was talking about was DraculaLand. Proposed in April 2001 by Romanian tourist minister Dan Matei

Agathon, it was going to cost $32 million and take a year to build—and it would put a massive development with an amusement park, a disco, an imitation Gothic castle, and even an amphitheater in the middle of one of the wildest and least developed sections of Europe.

But that's not all. The park would have imitation medieval courtrooms, alchemy laboratories, torture rooms, and a vampire den, along with something called the "Institute of Vampirology," with "Dracula's secret library" and workshops for teeth sharpening, armor-making, and even an "Eccentric Vampire fashion house," where you could shop for . . . eccentric vampire fashions. Promoters also promised theme restaurants offering "blood pudding, dish of brains and fright-jellied meat." They hoped it would create 3,000 jobs and bring in $21 million a year to the economically depressed area.

It will "propel Romania to stardom," Agathon declared. "It will bring tourists and be a solution to all problems." Its detractors said it would bring congestion, pollution, and a legion of Satan-worshipping tourists to trample over the only town Ceaușescu forgot to bulldoze.

By 2003, the detractors had won; they'd chased the project out of Sighișoara. Soon it appeared in another location: Romanian authorities announced they would build the project at Snagov, the traditional site of Vlad the Impaler's grave in Wallachia. Newspaper headlines appeared announcing DraculaLand had "risen from the grave." But had it? The new project was much closer to the capital city, and it was going to cost three times as much. But authorities were vague on the details.

"They have the location, and they are discussing about the project," said Simion Alb at the Romanian National Tourist Office in 2004. "However the construction has not started yet." He couldn't say when it would begin.

"I'm not sure that they have the financing they need," Alb added. "They've got some money but I don't think they've got enough to start."

DraculaLand might have risen for a moment, but it had clearly gone back to sleep. A year after it had stalled for the second time, I was researching the story of how this potentially lucrative project got trashed. Maybe it was the money-grubbing Yank in me, but I couldn't understand why a struggling country like Romania would let this opportunity slip away from them. I had the same questions that had dogged me since blowing my honeymoon. After that episode, my wife for some reason hadn't left me or put strychnine in my coffee. In fact, while hunting down the details of how this park failed, I alternated between pounding Red Bull, making frantic, expensive phone calls to Romania, Germany, and Canada . . . and racing back to the bedroom to help with burping, diaper-changing, and chin-smooching duties. Our new son napped when he wanted and woke when he felt like it, and the rest of us had to work around his schedule. No one in the house was sleeping for longer than four hours at a stretch, and I was never talking to anyone who wasn't five hours ahead of me. And the story I uncovered was so absolutely off-the-scale strange, I was never quite sure I wasn't hallucinating from exhaustion, caffeine overdose, or the absolute terror that comes from being a new dad.

Anyway, here's what I found:

As of 2000 almost half of Romania's population lived in poverty, with millions more scraping by as illegal laborers through-out Europe just to send $200 a month home to their starving families. It was one of the only countries in Europe that actually had a *growing* population of farmers—because people were fleeing the cities and moving back to hovels where they could raise crops and live off the land. But the country also had a potential fortune—a character whose legend had launched a multimillion dollar media empire. Romania was like a homeless guy carting around one of those stolen supermarket carts filled with bags of aluminum cans, a pile of dirty laundry, a half-drunk bottle of Night Train, and a framed

Van Gogh original in mint condition. It just didn't make sense. Why couldn't the country cash in? I needed to ask more locals, so I started calling random hotels in Sighişoara. That's when I found Yonel. He didn't have all the answers, he said.

"I am just a simple receptionist," he told me. But he was happy to talk. And just as happy to tell me how much he hated the idea of DraculaLand.

"Keetch," he called it. "The Dracula park would be keetch. It would bring a lot of tourists and animation, and a lot of crazy people. It would not be Sighişoara. Sighişoara is a quiet town. Romania doesn't need a Disney World."

Sighişoara had already seen its share of Goths, he added, and locals wanted none of it. At a rock music festival a few years ago, it was mobbed with up to 90,000 people.

"They were junkies, all dressed in black," he said. "They were sleeping in tents and turned the town into a big toilet." What's worse, the rock fans actually scrawled pentagrams on the gravestones at the local church, said its pastor, Rev. Hans Bruno Froelich, a priest who ministered to the tiny, beleaguered, and dwindling population of Saxons still living there.

When Agathon selected Sighişoara for DraculaLand, Froelich and his fellow padres led a protest of two hundred people in town and sent a letter to Agathon promising: "Everyone involved in this project will pay for it on Judgment Day."

"It's spiritual pollution," Froelich told me. Speaking in halting English, he said he was afraid it would bring the same Satanists who'd defaced the gravestones at the time of the rock concert back to town.

Sighişoara had also been a target of this kind of thing in late 2001, when a Miramax crew filmed a series of movies called *Dracula Resurrection* there. Locals reported stumbling over fake-blood-soaked mannequins in their town square.

"My daughter was terrified," said one townie.

It wasn't hard to see their point. To Romanians Vlad was a national figure, not a vampire. Imagine foreigners coming to visit the Lincoln Memorial by the thousands—wearing stovepipe hats, false beards . . . and plastic fangs. They love Lincoln. They love how he can turn himself into a bat. How he freed the slaves and rises at night to suck the blood of the living. Imagine you know you could make major bucks off these freaks if you chiseled a pair of wicked-looking teeth on Lincoln's statue.

You'd have to be desperate to even consider it.

On December 25, 1989, Nicolae and Elena Ceauşescu were led to a large room in a military base in northern Romania. An anonymous man read off a list of charges against them.

"We are declaring you condemned to death," said the "judge." Soldiers tied each of the couple's hands with twine. Elena struggled.

"What are you doing here?" she shrieked. "You don't have the right to tie me up. Child, do not do this to me! Don't you listen?"

But her husband, utterly defeated, simply muttered, "Relax. Leave it be."

The soldiers dragged them to a back lot. Whether afraid that a secret police raid would drop in at any moment or merely out of rage, the firing squad didn't wait for any command before opening up.

Many Romanians thought Ceauşescu would be a force for moderation and independence when he first took power—that he would allow Romania to assert itself like Yugoslavia had under Tito. But by the end of his twenty-four-year rule, he'd destroyed the country. He put almost thirty of his family and friends in top government offices, and his secret police locked up 50,000 political prisoners, tapped all the phone lines, and had handwriting samples for more than half of the population. He tried to make women give birth to five children apiece to build a workforce—and ended up warehousing more than 150,000 orphans. During the last decade of his reign, he attempted to pay down his country's debt with mandatory food shortages and ended up starving 15,000 people to death. His goons seized whole neighborhoods in the capital that were filled with ancient architecture and destroyed them to build huge, garish buildings for the government.

"It's hard to describe how bad it was," said Mircea Munteanu, an associate of the Cold War History Project who grew up under Ceauşescu's regime.

"It was like living in the library," he added, "only with the books taken out. You sit there, and you can't talk too loudly, or say the wrong thing, or they'll take you to the Bad Place." And it was Ceauşescu who was nicknamed "Vampirescu" among his own people. After his reign, the country was sucked dry.

But Ceauşescu was only the latest in a long line of terrible political leaders. Romanians have been cursed with bad governments and a poor economy since they were conquered by the Roman legions in the second century A.D. Then the Goths—real ones, not the pentagram spray-painting kind—kicked the Romans out in the third century, and for the next six hundred years, the Goths were followed by waves of attacking Huns, Avars, Slavs, Magyars, and even Bulgars (were these people actually conquered by a strain of wheat?).

The Magyars, also called Hungarians, invaded again in the thirteenth century, only to be battled back by the Turks, who finally seized the land in the bottom of the sixteenth, with two men on base and an Ottoman stealing third. In 1861, the Turks granted parts of the region their independence, which lasted until 1863—two whole years!—when the government collapsed and the locals actually invited a foreign king to seize power. It might have been the very first example of outsourcing.

During the twentieth century, countries kept beating the snot out of Romania—the pace just picked up. In June 1940, the Soviet Army invaded, but they were booted out by the Nazis four months later, only to have squadrons of American bombers wreck the country's oil refineries in 1942 and then once more in 1943 for good measure. Then the Soviets started invading again in April 1944, and in June of that same year, American bombers flattened everything they hadn't gotten around to flattening the first time. The Soviets seized what was left, including the smoking remains of the oil fields, and installed a puppet government that ruled over everything. Then, in 1965, the lucky Romanians got Ceauşescu.

And unlike the rest of the Warsaw Pact countries that sloughed off their Communist governments in the late 1980s without too much mayhem, Romania's revolt to depose Ceauşescu and his family sparked bloody riots throughout the country that killed more than a thousand people. Romania has always been like the pretty girl with the string of bad relationships behind her—kings, sultans, warlords, and the odd Panzer tank division. You just know she could clean herself up, find Mr. Right, and settle down with a nice, comfy free trade zone. But she's never had the self-esteem for it. When the new government took power after Ceauşescu's rule, things were scarcely better.

"The value of the currency had evaporated overnight," Munteanu said. In September 1991, labor talks between coal miners and the government evaporated and five thousand miners went on a rampage through Bucharest, leaving three dead and nearly three hundred injured. The prime minister resigned. The government looked like it might collapse for the second time in two years.

Nicolae Paduraru was there for it all. Since before Ceauşescu took power, he had worked in the government's tourism ministry, leading groups of westerners through his native country. And even though he had a stable government job, by the time the Communist system neared collapse, he was begging for food on the streets of Bucharest.

"In 1988 or '89, my young son and I were going from restaurant to restaurant," he said. "I was asking people I knew there if they could spare just three or four eggs for my son." But his friends turned him away—eggs were too scarce, even to help a three-year-old. I talked to him by phone while he was leading a group of people on a weeklong tour through sites in Stoker's novel.

"I happen to be in the medieval city of Bistrița," he told me, sitting down to relax after a long day of touring. He filled me in on how Romania learned the value of its most famous son.

After the government changed hands, Paduraru briefly rose to become a top bureaucrat in the new regime, before going into private practice by forming the Transylvanian Society of Dracula (TSD). In 1995, he was planning an academic convention about Romania for the TSD when he got a call from the Minister of Tourism, Dan Matei Agathon.

"He asked me who was coming," said Paduraru. "I told him: 27 foreign television crews and 126 journalists." Agathon couldn't get any tourists to just visit Romania. But Paduraru's "Dracula convention" had CNN, CBS, and Agence France-Presse lined up.

Paduraru recalls Agathon's disbelief: "He asked, 'How much are you paying them to come?' I told him I don't have money to pay them. He said he couldn't believe it." Then Paduraru had another idea: A trade fair was coming up later in Berlin. Why not take the export crystal, the leather goods, the wines, and other supplies his country was going to showcase and stamp them all with a giant *D*? Why not relabel all of this stuff "The Treasures of Dracula"? That's just what they did. At the convention, they were mobbed.

"We had the best of everything of Transylvania," Paduraru said, "all bearing the dragon *D*, the mark of the Count. And we knew when the people with the corner of their eye glimpsed these treasures they would look for a brochure of Dracula nearby, and since they were there, they would also take a map and learn about the Black Sea, the beaches, and even the skiing in Romania." And it all happened just as he predicted.

"That is how the Minister of Tourism learned the powers of Dracula," Paduraru said. In 2000, Agathon began planning a theme park. If stamping a big, red *D* on a load of export goods generated interest and moved them off the shelf, why wouldn't a giant Disney World of the Damned set in the very land of the legendary vampire king draw a huge crowd of spoiled western punks eager to burn through their parents' credit card so they could rave with the undead? But Paduraru disagreed bitterly.

"I expected him to understand how Dracula should be placed at the tip of the spear of promotion. Under the name 'Dracula' we could have the other assets of Romania—many as they are and original and unique as they are," Paduraru said. "But he took it like a child. We thought that he would understand that Dracula can attract attention—because you can't resist it, can you? No, you can't. And the moment you are close, you pick up all the stuff about Romania . . ."

"But no," Paduraru added with a sigh. "He wanted to make a Dracula park." Agathon went to different groups, including Paduraru's TSD, to drum up support for his idea, but the TSD was not impressed.

"We replied there should be no Dracula park in Romania because the whole of Romania is a Dracula park," he said. "To see the historical Dracula you must see the southern half of the country. To see the supernatural Dracula, the vampire count, you have to see the northern part of the country. What do you want to do? Concentrate everything in one point? Then what happens to the rest of it?"

The great opportunity and the great problem was that the whole country was loaded with places where the historical Dracula ate, slept, and killed people, and the literary Dracula added an entire new layer of spots.

What if you're an American who shows up in the country, throws around a lot of hard currency, and asks to see a tourist-friendly Castle Dracula because you have a wife who isn't going to put up with some wild-dog-infested pile of rocks? You'd probably end up at Castle Bran—this was the castle I'd told my wife about during our trip—the massive Meatloaf-video-style monstrosity smack dab in the middle of Transylvania where tourists have been visiting for decades. You can find it by clicking on www.draculascastle.com. A webpage called Dracula's Castle with a little ™ loads, and scrolled across the top, you'll see a giant sign reading, "Welcome to Dracula's Castle." And the only problem is that it is nowhere near the castle in Stoker's book, and the historical Dracula didn't build it or live there. So, a castle, but no Dracula.

"I was at a conference over at Brasov one year," said Elizabeth Miller, a Canadian college professor specializing in Drac. "I challenged the curator of the museum there about it. He said, 'Blame it on the Americans. The tourists come over here, and they want to do all of Romania, Bulgaria, and Hungary in just three days, and this park is on a main road . . . So we gave them what they wanted.' "

Back in the mid-1990s, she wrote a paper on the "schizophrenic Dracula," which concerns Romanian attempts to capitalize on their most famous son.

"Basically, they don't know how to deal with it," she says. "On the one hand they're cash-strapped. Here they're sitting on something no other country has. They have this great myth that is so universally known—in every country, on every continent, Count Dracula is known—so here they have this opportunity. And they want to use it, but they don't want to use it."

Why not?

"Because of the damn connection" between the literary and historical Draculas, she says.

If you retraced Jonathan Harker's journey and showed up at the Borgo Pass, 4,000 feet up in the Carpathian Mountains, you'd find the Castle Dracula Hotel—with sixty-two rooms, TV hookup, and a good selection of Romanian wines—but no castle. If you wanted to visit the ruins of the palace from which Vlad ruled, you could head on down to Târgovişte, seat of Vlad's government and site of most of his famous impalings. Or you could visit the spot where he was born, in Sighişoara. But those places had no castles.

You can get the castle without Dracula or Dracula without the castle. You can get both if you are willing to give up on Transylvania altogether. Slains Castle in Cruden Bay, Scotland, supposedly inspired Bram Stoker during the writing of his novel. That's what Scottish tourism people have said, anyway. But it was probably not true—Stoker stayed nearby, but the castles looked nothing like each other.

But if you want to find the closest thing to an actual castle that the real, live historical Dracula actually built and actually lived in, you can follow my footsteps through that actual industrial wasteland filled with actual wild dogs and soon you will experience the real-life loss of your marriage and possibly an intestinal illness if you drink the water. Plus, you'd see bricks. Real bricks!

The Romanians compounded this problem because they spent years downplaying the connection between the real Dracula and the literary Drac, even while the whole world was watching his movies, reading his books, seeing his plays, and sporting black velvet on Halloween. Until after the 1989 revolution, the government banned Stoker's novel and its many movie versions, and it wasn't until 1992 that Romanians translated Dracula into their language. And because Bela Lugosi was from Hungary, their ancient rival, many Romanians have claimed that the original 1931 *Dracula* was nothing more than a Hungarian plot to humiliate their national hero by turning him into a creature of the night.

No one knew about this better than Jeanne Youngson, the ultimate Drac tourist. In the early 1960s, Jeanne Youngson was rich, Hollywood royalty, and bored stiff. She was married to Robert Youngson, Oscar-winning director and one of the most successful movie producers in the business (he had just finished making the *Golden Age of Comedy*). She found herself alone while he was off striking deals and hunting the Next Big Thing.

"He used to go to Los Angeles, and even though I'd always been nuts about Hollywood—I found there was nothing to do!" she said, in a cheerful, gossipy tone.

"You can't walk anywhere, for God's sake, and pretty soon I'd taken every single tour." Youngson would spend endless days sitting by the pool in the hotel, listening to Mel Brooks and Imogene Cocoa writing notes for a television show in the next cabana.

"These guys would congregate around their cabana," she said, "and I would sit in my little chair and listen to them. It got to the point where I couldn't stand it any longer." In the evenings, when Robert got back from his meetings at Fox and MGM, he'd come home to a frustrated wife. He knew he had to do something.

"Finally in 1964, he said to me, 'You can go any place in the world, as long as you're here when I get back,' " she said. "So I started traveling." She went to Europe, and by 1965 she found herself in Romania.

"I went on a two-and-a-half-week tour through the country," she said, "and the Intourist guide was wild about Vlad Țepeș. He'd talk about him and talk about him." But this wasn't the Dracula she'd heard about—this was some medieval prince. Her government guide took them through the northern part of the country and into a small church with a giant picture of Vlad Dracul, the father of the

Impaler. The trip was rough—Romania was mountainous and poor, and practically nothing was paved. But looking up at that stern visage in that tiny church halfway around the world from her cushy chair by the pool, Youngson realized she'd found her calling in life. Youngson has never been able to find the church again. But on the way back, she told one of her fellow tourists that she would create a Dracula society. And in June 1965, the Count Dracula Fan Club—the first of many Drac fan clubs that would start up throughout the world—was born. Since then, she's been on almost ten tours of Romania, hitting every major Dracula-related site, and her group grew to fifteen divisions in North America and Europe and took over the International Frankenstein Society, a Stoker memorial association, and the International Society for the Study of Ghosts and Apparitions in some supernatural version of a corporate merger.

But throughout the years, Youngson said, the Romanians were in denial that a guy named Stoker even existed.

"Even when I went back in 1974 with the Dracula society, whenever people would even hint at Stoker's *Dracula*, the guide would say, 'Oh no, no, you can't mention that. It has absolutely nothing to do with us,' " she said. "So it wasn't until several years later that I began realizing that the Romanians were finally catching on that they might have something that might make a little money for that very poor country."

Romanian tour guides always used the name "Vlad Țepeș" or "Vlad the Impaler" because Dracula had been corrupted by the book and the movies. But the ironic thing is that Dracula was in fact the most historically accurate name for the guy. As Elizabeth Miller writes in *A Dracula Handbook*, there's no record he ever called himself "the Impaler." That name was probably something his enemies thought up. However, he did sign most of his correspondence "Dracula." Westerners tacked the whole vampire identity onto the poor guy, and the well-meaning Romanians finished the job by giving him a name he didn't use.

Romania was in a bind. For forty years, people have been coming over from the West asking to see the castles, the coffins, and the vampire bats. Documentary crews have been making films about the secret connections among Stoker's book, the historical Dracula, and the peasant superstitions about vampires. These people were gullible and they had more money than God. What's a peasant to do?

By January 2002, after decades of fighting it, the Romanians decided to give vampire tourism a shot. Agathon's plan was in full swing, and people at the post office in Sighişoara were lining up to buy shares—the government put $5 million on the market, with each share costing about a third of a month's salary.

"Some locals thought the town would be ruined," said Nate Gendreau. "But a lot of people were all for it." Plus, Agathon was appearing on TV ads with Dan Petre Popa, the head of Greenpeace Romania, who said the project had his full support.

But then people began to notice that something wasn't quite right about "Greenpeace Romania."

"It had nothing to do with our organization," said Herwig Shuster of the actual Greenpeace. "He was just calling his organization Greenpeace. We had to take him to court to stop him using our name in late 2002." In addition, groups like UNESCO, and even Prince Charles, came down on the plan as well. Plus, a scandal broke when the Romanian newspaper *Ziua de Ardeal* reported that Romania's spy service was investigating anyone who opposed the project.

To make matters worse, the business plan looked weak: Sighişoara was far away from any major airport or city, and the "highway" that ran past it was little more than a two-lane road. How were all those people going to arrive, and where were they going to stay? According to Gendreau, locals were planning to build a group of large hotels outside of town to accommodate everyone, but the bad publicity killed it.

"They weren't sure what it was going to be," Miller said. "A museum dealing with Vlad the Impaler, or a vampire theme park? And it lost a lot of people who might have supported it if they had just stuck to one thing or the other."

"When they're still looking for investors after five years, you begin to wonder," she added. "If they hadn't gone to Sighişoara, it might have worked. Now, I don't know."

Hellfire-preachers, Prince Charles, and fake environmentalists were swimming through my head. It wasn't just the sleep deprivation and the fact that I had enough Red Bull in my system to kill a horse—this story couldn't get more surreal. But I hadn't counted on Lia Roberts. A feisty dark-haired middle-aged woman, she'd emigrated from Romania in 1979 to become an American citizen. She settled down in the Las Vegas area, and eventually she became head of the Nevada Republican party. But in 2004, she decided the situation was so bad that she had to go back and run for president of her homeland. Her chief advisor was Dick Morris, the former Clinton aide who resigned after the hooker-toe-sucking incident.

Roberts told me her theory on why DraculaLand failed: The Romanian government wanted it to. After all, she said, the Impaler himself frowned on corruption. Turning Vlad into a theme park fixture would be a constant reminder of how far the country had fallen.

"Everyone knows he had zero tolerance for corruption," she said. "They don't want a park for him because they're afraid to bring up the word."

She wanted radical reform. The current political parties are just offshoots of the Communists, she said, rotating the same people through different positions, while a sliver of the population got "richer than the Rockefellers" and the rest starved. She was running to tear up the whole system and start fresh. Did she have a chance?

"Being an outsider is one of my strongholds," she said. "I don't owe anything to anyone."

Translation: No way. By the election in December 2004, Social Democratic Party candidate Adrian Nastase won with a clear 41 percent of the vote. His opponent, Traian Basescu, trailed with 34 percent, and the next ten candidates split the rest of the vote up into smaller, more ridiculous portions of the tally. The absolute last place guy got 0.26 percent, which means his mom started out for the polls, thought about it, and decided not to waste her time. Lia Roberts wasn't even on the list.

And by then, the park was in a permanent coma. But maybe that was just as well. Because I learned a truly mind-blowing fact about Dracula: The Romanians didn't have a legal right to portray him. Dracula's image—the famous, fanged version most likely to attract westerners—is owned by Universal Pictures. Any vampire theme park that wanted to employ any of these elements—and naturally they would so that they could appeal to the largest audience possible—would have to fork over royalties to Hollywood.

"They stole their Transylvania and turned it into something from a late-night horror movie. They stole their hero from the fifteenth century, and turned him into a disgusting vampire," said Miller. "It's what Americans do when they come in and tamper with the local culture."

And even if they somehow got around that, and built the park at Snagov, they might be wrapping that roller coaster around a lie. At an academic conference on Vlad the Impaler in 2001, a professor from the Romanian Academy, Dr. Constantin Rezachevici, presented evidence that the crumbled unrecognizable remains buried in Snagov may not be the body of Dracula, as people had assumed for more than one hundred years.

"Then, what of the legend of Vlad Ţepeş' interment at Snagov, made up by the monks there in the second half of the nineteenth century?" he wrote. "Nothing, of course. Most legends dissipate under a closer scrutiny."

Painstakingly recounting Dracula's death, Dr. Rezachevici made the case that it's far more likely Dracula was buried at another monastery in the country, called Comana, many miles away. That monastery had burned down a long time ago, and its exact location was lost.

"Lacking a tombstone," Rezachevici added, "the grave on the southern side of the first church of the monastery, although set in the proper place for a founder can only hypothetically be attributed to Vlad Ţepeş. If this is not the one, then Ţepeş' tomb, located in the same church, may have not yet been discovered, or, even more likely, was removed, destroyed with the whole first church by the end of the sixteenth century."

Of course, what may have happened to poor Vlad's head is even weirder. It might be down at the bottom of some Turkish well or just off the coast of Istanbul, a skull in a pile of other skulls, identifiable only because it smells like a bowl of five-hundred-year-old Honey Smacks.

After the sultan's men finished decapitating the Impaler, they allegedly sent his head to Istanbul and had it put on a pike. And according to Kathy Hamilton, a Texan expat living in that city who wrote an article about local ghost legends, there is a neighborhood there called Yedi Kule where diplomats who crossed the sultans got imprisoned until "they were either beheaded or released."

"The decapitated heads were thrown down a well to be eventually washed out to sea," Hamilton added in an e-mail exchange with me. And if a special trophy head arrived from Romania in early 1477, would they have displayed it near here? Would they have chucked it where they chucked all the other heads?

"Heads were usually displayed in front of Topkapi Palace, the sultan's residence," she told me. "It is on the other side of the old walled city from Yedi Kule, which is about a mile from the palace. In those days it would have been easily conceivable that the head, once it started to get a little funky while on display, would have been taken to Yedi Kule and thrown down the well there." But there's a catch.

"Unfortunately, no one seems to know which well heads got tossed into." Plus, she added, the Turks have filled these wells in over the centuries. It's possible they chucked it into a well that *didn't* lead out to sea, and Drac's noggin is still down there. But why would it smell different from the other, local pates that the Turks popped off like so many bottle caps?

"It would be most likely that if his head were brought to Istanbul, it would have been preserved in a vat of honey, which was the usual way of preserving body parts back then. (It's amazing how many people had body parts taken here to be buried—usually royal exiles.)"

This is only one of the lost relics of the prince. According to accounts by historians Raymond T. McNally and Radu Florescu, there might also be a Toledo sword Dracula's father gave him that is still missing. There are legends that Dracula's minions even dropped bags of treasure down at the bottom of the lake in Snagov for safe-keeping.

I begin dreaming up my next great adventure. I could get myself a backhoe, a fistful of maps, and a GPS locator and head out to Istanbul or the Comana monastery site to make history. But which treasure to hunt for? And more to the point: Would I rather spend the next twenty years in a Romanian jail or a Turkish prison for trespassing and tearing up a national landmark? It's that second question that makes me rethink my whole scheme.

Instead I decide to hunt for something else: answers to the riddle of Dracula himself. Who is he and who owns him? Did the Romanians fail to market him or just decide not to succeed? Will they ever have the ability to show the world their Dracula, or will he always be cultural property of the West?

Let's dive into the story of how this obscure medieval ruler became a notorious villain, a literary giant, and then a movie star. Along the way, we'll chat with scholars, bureaucrats, Goths, geeks, and people who have a taste for blood. We will find our Drac in a puppet parade, a seaside carnival, a hotel conference room, the cobblestone streets of Salem, the costume shops of Manhattan, and in the endless, soul-crushing footage of some of the worst movies imaginable.

And finally, we will chase Stoker's story back to the country that inspired it (or did it?). We will retrace Jonathan Harker's journey through the Budapest and Transylvania that appear in the first pages of *Dracula* on a quest to see what's really there. We will follow this trail back to the mythical Borgo Pass and take our own survey of a country hidden for so long.

But first we need a history lesson about Vlad and Stoker and everyone in between. And to do that, let's travel to an American land of monsters. This place is barely civilized and terrifying, but it contains some clues to unraveling our mystery. It is called by its natives . . . *Pennsylvania*.

Spirit of '76

*"They wanted all that money people were going to spend
on blow and Ukranian hookers."*

*Encased in a giant bulb of garlic, I'm stumbling near-blind through
the streets of downtown Philadelphia dodging horse crap. The bulb
is a monstrously heavy papier-mâché contraption that swallows my
upper body like a mascot costume for the world's lamest team: Coming onto the field is Clovey, trying to whip up the crowd and lead
State Agricultural's Fightin' Produce to victory! Go Produce!*

*The costume's wooden harness digs into my shoulders, and I
don't have enough headroom, so I can either stoop like Igor or stand
straight and let it compress my spine. Either way is ugly, so I alternate—stoop, spine; stoop, spine; stoop, spine—and I can barely see
through the tiny view hole as I follow the rest of the Dracula Parade,*

Hunting through the spooky lore for clues.

held every Halloween by the Rosenbach Museum and Library along with a puppet theater group called Spiral Q.

I'm dodging the horse crap because they shoved me behind an old gypsy wagon drawn by an animal that must have had a very healthy lunch. I can't see directly in front of my feet, and I skip to the left and then to the right, trying not to ruin my shoes as the musicians in the wagon play some creepy accordion tune over and over while the parade makes a meandering loop through the area. A bike messenger zips in front and the other garlic bulbs crash into me, jolting me off course. I turn around clumsily for a look, but all I can see is the giant sculpted head of Nosferatu behind me, his eyeballs twitching wildly as if he were drugged. His creator Beth told me she'd made him from a photo and never saw Nosferatu or even read Dracula. Beth used to be with the puppet theater, but she's on her own now, and she only comes back to do maintenance on her head. She's a short cute woman with brown curls and a strange orange jumpsuit that makes her look like she has just escaped from prison. She's also wearing a pointy cap that might be some kind of Transylvanian boyar's hat, but later I realize her outfit is just something from a thrift store that's supposed to be hip. And if an old guy like me can't understand what it is, it probably qualifies.

Early on the afternoon of August 1, 2000, police on horseback surrounded a warehouse that Spiral Q and other groups were using to store their supplies for massive protests against the upcoming Republican National Convention. Called the "Ministry of Puppetganda" by the protestors, the building held 135 cardboard skeletons for the prisoners President Bush executed while governor of Texas and "Corpzilla the Capitalist Pig," a giant cardboard hog dressed in a tuxedo and mounted on a 48-foot flatbed truck. The standoff lasted for hours, with police dropping onto the roof from helicopters. Finally, according to then-director Matthew Hart, the police told the activists that if they left the building, they wouldn't be arrested. So they left the building . . . and the police promptly arrested them. The case went to trial but the charges collapsed for lack of evidence.

"Puppetry is not a crime," Hart said to reporters during his trial.

After the incident, Spiral Q continued making giant puppets for protests—its most recent creations, for an anti-Iraq war rally, were oil derricks that appeared to pump blood. To this day, many people think the authorities targeted them to shut them up.

"*Of course they did it to shut them up,*" *says my friend Steve, a hard-bitten conservative lawyer who lives in Philly.* "*They didn't want them to fuck with the program.*" *But Steve doesn't think it was politics.*

"*It was for the tourism dollars,*" *he says.* "*They wanted all that money people were going to spend on blow and Ukranian hookers.*"

The vultures up ahead came from an earlier parade, Beth tells me, and I assume they used to represent something corporate or Republican. And glancing back at the Nosferatu head, I notice he kinda looks like Dick Cheney. If they haven't used him for Cheney yet, I'm sure they will. The woman up ahead is wearing a backwards baseball cap with a picture of Che Guevara on it. She's darting in and out, directing traffic, so every once in a while Che comes bobbing into view, and this annoys me. But I don't have time to ponder it.

"Left!" someone shouts from out of my vision, and I'm turning around wildly to see who it is and whether the person is talking to me. "Left! Left!" A garlic bulb slams into me, hard, and my whole papier-mâché world shudders.

"Stop!" someone else yells. "Stop!" I keep walking, hoping this person is not talking to me. Hoping I won't take a wrong turn, leave the parade, and get flattened by a truck. You can't die with dignity while wearing a garlic bulb costume. I guess I should have thought about this. My neck hurts. My legs hurt. My back hurts. And these commies are pissing me off.

"Garlic!" someone shouts, and now I know that this person is shouting at me, or maybe someone right next to me. Another bulb brushes me. I am seriously going to pick a fight with whoever this bastard is. But it occurs to me the crowd's just realizing what we are. I guess that squeezed between a troop of vultures and the giant Cheney-vampire (Dickula?), the little white puffy things with the weeds coming out of their heads must be a stumper to people. The onlookers take a beat when they see us before they figure out what we are, and then they shout something that sounds like it could be urgent instructions we need to follow so we don't get killed . . .

The gypsy wagon woman with the accordion has been playing that same goddamn tune over and over for about a half an hour, and now it seems like something they do to you at Gitmo to get you to talk. And by now, I would have given up.

We weave back into some familiar streets, and I start wildly hoping this thing is over because I'm sweating and the pain in my shoulders is unbearable. Finally, we make one final turn. The parade in front of me bunches up as people slow down, stop, and shuck their costumes. The crowd of parents, kids, and other onlookers spills into the alley to watch a shadow puppet show projected onto a sheet. It's the story of Dracula, except the vampire gets put in jail at the end. At first, I figure they want to make it less gory for the kids. But then after they jail him, they chop his head off. So maybe this is some statement Spiral Q is making about capital punishment. I half expect them to flash Mumia's face onto the sheet.

"What's a vampire?" one of the little kids asks, and there's an uncomfortable pause while the adults with her try to make some-thing up that won't give her wicked nightmares.

A corpse that rises from the dead to feast on the living? A blood-sucking demon? The Mora, the Vrykolaka, the Upir? A shape-shifting predatory count?

"A bat!" one of them says brightly, and the rest immediately cooperate in the lie like a corporate board under indictment.

"A bat!" "Just a bat!" "Nothing more!" "Nothing scary!"

And instantly I flash back to every lie my parents ever told me:

Santa, the Easter Bunny, twelve goldfish named Freddy scooped out and flushed in the middle of the night, and "Your mother and I just need some time apart. But we're still very good friends."

Steve the lawyer and I wait anxiously in the hall of the Rosenbach Museum for the tour to start. We're trying not to touch anything because it all looks valuable and breakable.

"Don't touch anything," the tour guide tells us. We've come to see two of the most important artifacts in the history of how Vlad the Impaler became Dracula, and how Dracula became a star.

Built in the 1860s, the Rosenbach town house is a narrow four-story building dominated by a winding staircase and stuffed with art treasures and antique silver. Its 350,000 books and records are a virtual history of the intellectual life of western society: manuscripts of the *Canturbury Tales;* Joyce's *Ulysses;* massive collections of Dickens, Conrad, and Lewis Carroll; the best-preserved copy of a first edition of *Don Quixote;* more than a hundred letters of George Washington; and, among Thomas Jefferson's papers, an early draft of the Declaration of Independence as well as a list of the slaves belonging to the man who wrote it.

Dr. Abraham Simon Wolf Rosenbach helped establish some of the greatest libraries across America, the tour guide tells us, like the Folger Shakespeare Library.

His brother, Philip, she adds, collected antiques. Our guide shows us his comb set, and Steve snickers.

Known as the "Napoleon of Books" or the "Napoleon of the Auction House," Abe Rosenbach made his first acquisition at the age of ten, and when he was still a college kid at the University of Pennsylvania, he acquired a rare first edition by Dr. Samuel Johnson for less than $4 and was mobbed by book dealers offering him thousands. So he drove over the book-buying world like a tank division, and his brother Phil . . . collected knickknacks. I begin to feel sorry for Phil as the lady walks us through each treasure that his more successful brother—who was more than a dozen years younger— obtained. Imagine being Phil! Imagine sitting across the dinner table, listening to Dr. Snotnose tell the whole room how just this morning he made a few grand rescuing some ancient mash note George Washington wrote to Martha—then everyone in the room turns to you, and you have to mumble something about finding a hairbrush.

"A really neat brush," you tell them. "It's gilded."

"It was Dr. Rosenbach who was doing the big deals," says one of the staff at the Rosenbach, "but it was Philip making sure the company was operating." Being Philip Rosenbach seems like the ironic punishment inflicted on the bad guy at the end of a particularly nasty *Twilight Zone* episode.

We climb the stairs to something that looks like a small, cramped New York City apartment—the collection of the poet Marianne Moore, whose belongings are laid out in an exact replica of her Greenwich Village pad. Then we tour spots filled with globes, busts, and overstuffed couches, all of it plush and expensive, coated with marble and leather, and eventually I get the feeling we'll turn a corner to find Professor Plum with the crowbar.

While the tour guide tells us about Abe Rosenbach's life, I'm jotting down notes in a little pad, and when she starts talking about how he drank a bottle of whiskey a day and eventually died from complications of alcoholism, I dutifully take that down, too.

"Don't put that down!" she says. "What's the matter with you? I don't want you to write that." I mumble something, and out of the corner of my eye, I see Steve sidle away from me, like I might get us thrown out of the place.

Finally, we reach one of the items we're here to see: a tiny hard-back book lighted and encased in glass. No bigger than a largish set of flash cards, it is the *Dracole Waida,* or *Voivode Dracula.* Printed in Nuremberg, it is one of scores of fifteenth-century anti-Dracula pamphlets, the only one of its kind in North America. (Even writing this I feel a small twinge of guilt that I'm still helping to keep Abe in the limelight. The *Dracole* was his find.) The *Dracole Waida* surfaced in Munich in the collection of a bookseller named Jacques Rosenthal. In 1930, during one of many buying trips abroad that Abe Rosenbach took, he purchased it and brought it back to his collection.

We finish the tour just in time for a show-and-tell kind of lecture about the notes Bram Stoker compiled while he wrote his famous book. We all file into a wide, shallow room and fill out the seats. In front of us, associate director Michael Barsanti, a friendly man with a cherubic face and round Lennon specs, is standing behind a long table. He takes Stoker's notes—each sealed in a plastic cover—and lays them out side by side while he talks. There are about 120 pages, typed and handwritten, along with photos and a newspaper clipping. One of the sheets is on letterhead from the Stratford hotel in Philly, where Stoker stayed briefly.

Barsanti stops talking and asks if there are questions. Someone raises his hand and launches into an extended analysis/group-therapy-sharing-statement about what *Dracula* means to him. He tacks a question on the end of it, just inviting Mike to agree. Mike nods amiably and makes some comforting noises. He calls for another question, and someone else lists everything she knows about the book. Barsanti nods again. Some guy hunched over in the back—enveloped in the kind of big puffy jacket that makes him look like he wraps his head in Reynolds Wrap to defeat the CIA mind rays—starts talking, and he doesn't even bother with a question.

Another person raises his hand, and then another. Mike is smiling, nodding, polite as ever, but there should be a point at which a

normal crowd would have their every conceivable question answered. But that's not going to happen, I realize with growing horror,
because these people are . . . different. I scan their faces—earnest,
articulate—the type who make C-SPAN lectures last twice as long as
they need to. They're the bane of the NPR call-in show. They don't
ask questions. They give speeches disguised as questions. I scan the
crowd, and I realize that everybody, *absolutely everybody*, in this
room has a little something to add. And one by one, we will hear
them all out.

The tour group are like Joy Division fans or *Star Trek* fans or
bloggers. They're smart and educated and they just can't shut the
fuck up. Mike's being really nice—decent and patient. And I have to
admit I hate him for that. Because he should just mock the very next
person who opens his piehole, cut everyone off short, and flee like
he's trying to catch the last chopper off the roof of the Saigon
embassy. I'm too far from the doors. I'm trapped.

Is there a fire alarm in the room? I could pull it, steal the papers
in the melee as the sprinklers turn on, and run out of there. I like
Mike, but I'll throw him to these jackals if I have to. Finally, there's a
lull, and Mike offers that whoever wants to can stay and ask him
questions one on one. I bolt.

Over the next couple weeks, I try to piece together the story that
these two documents—the Stoker notes and the fifteenth-century
Drac pamphlet—tell us. And it is a fascinating story. Underneath a
mountain of nonsense from the fans is a tale of how an obscure
medieval prince became one of the biggest cult icons in history. But
to tell that story, we have to start from the life of the man himself.

I've been able to piece together many of the details of Vlad's life from different sources, but the most detailed are biographies written by Raymond T. McNally and Radu Florescu, Boston College history professors who made their mark on the field of Dracula scholarship. I found many of the best anecdotes from the books they coauthored, like *Dracula: Prince of Many Faces* and *Dracula: A Biography of Vlad the Impaler.* But as we shall learn, aspects of their work are controversial.

In 1431, the same year Vlad Dracula was born in Sighişoara, his father was inducted into a military and religious order by the Holy Roman Emperor king Sigismund. It was called the Order of the Dragon, and its symbol was a dragon nailed to a cross, representing the heathen Turks who were battling Christian kingdoms along the fault lines of southern Europe. Approximately twenty years after Vlad's birth, the Turks would capture Constantinople, the ancient capital of the Eastern Roman Empire. And about eighty years after that, their armies would advance all the way to Vienna, leaving a trail of shattered coffee cups and half-eaten croissants in their wake.

To this day, the southeastern rump of Europe that Vlad called home is embroiled in the same battles between Muslim and Christian groups. The clashes between Serbs and Albanians in the late 1990s that prompted NATO air strikes and an occupation was only a reprise of the battles fought on the plain of Kosovo between Christian and Turkish armies in the fourteenth and fifteenth centuries. Vlad the Impaler's family, his political allies, and his enemies were fighting the same kind of ugly ethnic war that continues today.

Vlad's older brother and their father Dracul fought against the Ottoman sultan. But in the early 1440s, Dracul hedged his bets, pledged loyalty to the sultan, and even shipped off Vlad and his younger brother as Turkish hostages to cement the deal. And then after betraying his Christian allies, Dracul betrayed the sultan and his own younger sons—launching attacks against the Turks in a massive operation called the Varna Crusade alongside political rival John Hunyadi.

"Please understand that I have allowed my little children to be butchered for the sake of Christian peace," Dracul wrote to allies during the event according to Florescu and McNally.

For some reason, the sultan didn't kill Vlad and his brother. Florescu and McNally write that they were kept in court and trained by some of the best scholars of the day in the Turkish language, logic, math, and philosophy. The sultan wanted to hold them back as a bargaining chip to someday bring their father to heel. In addition, rumors have surfaced that Vlad's brother, Radu the Handsome, had become a—how do I put this delicately?—prison bitch for male and female members of court. The Turks treated him much better than young Vlad, and the two brothers hated each other intensely.

After having his dad and older brother trade him into slavery and do everything but send the sultan an invitation to kill him off, Vlad found himself being slighted while the Turks swapped his younger brother around for cartons of cigarettes. And by the time Vlad was released in 1448 and returned to Wallachia, enraged mobs had killed his father and buried his older brother alive. So Vlad probably had issues. And since there were no therapists back then, he worked through them by killing a whole mess of people.

Vlad ruled Wallachia for three short periods totaling less than a decade. He seized the throne in 1448 with help from his old friends/captors/teachers/sibling molesters the Turks, but local warlords quickly knocked him from power. Then he came back in 1456, but the Turks themselves chased him out of the country in 1462, and he was imprisoned in Hungary for fourteen years. He seized the throne once more in 1476, and this time it lasted . . . for a couple weeks, when peasants found his headless body in a forest. Next to Al Gore, Vlad probably had the worst political luck in history.

During this grisly career, Vlad the Impaler was famed for

murdering folks. According to the *Dracole Waida* itself, he had whole villages burned and his subjects "cut down like weeds" or "buried naked up to the navel and . . . shot at." The *Dracole* also says he boiled people, ground people to death with stones, and even roasted babies and forced their own mothers to eat them. Another German Dracula pamphlet that came from Strassburg in 1500 said he had victims "hacked . . . to pieces like cabbage."

As the Turks advanced toward Târgovişte in 1462 to expel Vlad, the Impaler's forces harried them constantly. McNally and Florescu described how Vlad used scorched earth tactics and guerrilla strikes against any of the sultan's men who'd strayed away from the main army. Some stories accuse Dracula of practicing a form of medieval biological warfare, sending members of his force who were afflicted with leprosy, bubonic plague, tuberculosis, and other fatal illnesses to mix with the Turks.

When the sultan finally reached Vlad's capital, he discovered who he was really dealing with—he saw over 20,000 mangled Turkish bodies impaled on stakes in a massive semi-circle around the area. Many of the corpses had birds feeding off them or building nests in their skulls. The sultan, who had conquered Constantinople less than a decade ago, promptly retreated.

But how many of these horrible, horrible tales are true? We have no idea. The stories originally come from the Turks or from the Saxons Vlad was constantly fighting as he tried to bring Transylvania under his control. Many of the Saxons got fed up and migrated back to Germany just when the newly invented printing presses started running. Other eastern European rulers maneuvering against Vlad lent their support to publish these stories as widely as possible— they made the rulers seem noble, keeping animals like Vlad in check. Every source of the legends was biased against the Impaler for one reason or another. It's not that the stories were all untrue, but it's almost impossible to figure out what's true and what's not.

The Nuremburg pamphlet that found its way to the Rosenbach Museum in Philly was not an objective news story—it was a political rant by a group of people who hated their subject. Of course, within three years after selling this catalog of medieval atrocities, Jacques Rosenthal's family witnessed modern persecution. According to a lecture given by Rosenthal's grandson Bernard, in 1933, the new Nazi leadership declared a boycott against Jewish businesses, targeting bookstores like Rosenthal's and marking them with anti-Semitic graffiti. The family escaped within a few years and settled in America. This book about Vlad, a chunk of propaganda telling nightmarish five-hundred-year-old stories of the persecution of a German group, was like a tiny reminder of our capacity for violence, for self-deception, and for turning the tables so that victims in one era become predators in another. It was churned out from Nuremberg, one of the ancient centers of publishing, an early example of propaganda that came from a town that would be known for some of the most virulently evil examples of propaganda in the modern era.

Now, don't get me wrong here. Vlad the Impaler was meaner and crazier than Courtney Love during an intervention. But as bad as he was, his real misfortune was picking on a group of people who had just invented the printing press.

"Remember there was no such thing as slander back then," says Steve the lawyer. "If you slandered somebody back then, the remedy wasn't to sue you. It was to beat your ass." As everybody knows, as soon as people invent a new communications technology, they use it for porn, crazy religious tracts . . . and for smearing the hell out of others. By the end of the fifteenth century, according to scholarly accounts, the German presses were putting out more anti-Dracula pamphlets than copies of the Bible. But as the years passed, the books dropped out of site—some of them squirreled away in monasteries in France and Switzerland.

It might have been inevitable that a document like the *Dracole*

Waida would have appeared in Philly because it has always been a book dealer's town. Along with Boston, Philadelphia was a publishing capital going right back to the Colonial era.

So this town is where old manuscripts come to molder, but it also has a connection to Bram Stoker. Stoker probably began sketching out *Dracula* in London, but while working on the project, he was also constantly traveling to Philadelphia with his boss, the famous actor Henry Irving. Irving's company put on plays at theaters like the Chestnut Street Opera House. Newspaper accounts at the time describe Stoker meeting business associates and running Irving's affairs from the Brunswick hotel in town.

According to another report, while Henry Irving was in Philadelphia in May 1894, the police department chaperoned him on a tour through their infamous Rogues Gallery—granddaddy of the mug shot file. Back then, Irving was known as a great character actor for villains. The Kevin Spacey of his day, he'd played Mephistopheles, Richard III, and Iago. The police obviously wanted him to take a stroll through a cache of real-life villains, and Stoker tagged along. But it was Stoker, not Irving, who was then creating one of the most well-known villains of all time.

Stoker worked on *Dracula* from 1890 to 1897, and his notes are detailed and meticulous. He was the manager, personal advisor, publicity agent, and assistant to Irving, even keeping Irving's schedule. Often, Stoker planned trips across Europe and North America for his boss. You can tell this was a guy obsessed with train schedules, with getting groups of people from one place to another on time, and with worrying about missing meetings and connections.

Here are the gripping, horror-filled opening lines of *Dracula*:

3 May. Bistritz. — Left Munich at 8.35 p.m. on 1st May, arriving at Vienna early next morning; should have arrived at 6.46, but train was an hour late.

It's from the diary of Jonathan Harker, the real estate agent who travels to Dracula's Castle only to find himself trapped there and fighting for his survival against creatures who wish to devour him. Stoker intends this to be shocking and horrifying, so maybe he never actually tried to buy a house. The rest of us wouldn't consider drinking the blood of Realtors a bad thing. But that's not the point. The book is the most famous and successful horror story in literature, and it opens with a half dozen pages of this guy griping about the fact that he's late, that he's tired, and that he's running around in a foreign country, sampling the food and seeing the local culture. It reads like some nineteenth-century version of *Condé Nast Traveler*. Critics have talked about the modern gadgets that litter this book—typewriters, train schedules, and gramophones— saying Stoker was trying to create a thoroughly up-to-date, modern world and chuck a medieval monster into it for effect. That's a good theory. But it overlooks how many of these items were office equipment. One of Stoker's first books was *The Duties of Clerks of Petty Sessions in Ireland*, a civil service office manual. He wrote a biography about his boss. He was devoted to Irving and devoted to his job.

Why are the notes so important? Because they list the books Stoker read. They show every aspect of the Vlad the Impaler story we know Stoker was acquainted with. And here it is:

There was a ruler named Dracula who fought against Turks.

That's about it. That's practically all he knew. Stoker read a paragraph or two about Vlad from a history guide. And as Elizabeth Miller points out in *A Dracula Handbook*, Stoker didn't know Vlad was an impaler. And he didn't even know Vlad was Vlad—the source doesn't give Dracula's first name. There's nothing to indicate he'd heard any of the grisly stories circulating about Vlad for hundreds of years.

One thing we do know is that Stoker liked the name "Dracula." He even wrote that it meant "devil" in the local language. Which is right—sort of. Actually, "Dracul" is the Romanian word for "dragon," not "devil," and although Christian symbolism often used the dragon as a symbol for Ol' Scratch, Vlad's father just assumed the name "Dracul" because he'd been inducted into the Order of the Dragon. Young Vlad, proud of the award himself, added the "a" at the end to indicate that he was Dracul's son, in the same way that Irish names sometimes begin with "O'" or English names sometimes end in "son." But Stoker didn't know about that, either. All Stoker knew was that here was a fierce guy from a weird foreign area with a name that suggested "devil." And he went with it.

One of the most telling documents is an outline in which Stoker sketched the plot in great detail. This outline has the original location of the vampire's lair—Styria, Austria (oddly, the birthplace of another movie icon: Arnold Schwarzenegger). And the original name for the villain who became Dracula? Count Wampyr. So Stoker had the whole novel sketched out and then tacked on this cool name that he had found.

Stoker finished his novel in 1897 and even had it performed as a play. But it would never become a clear-cut hit while Stoker was alive. When he died in 1912, his obituary in the *New York Times* was less than three hundred words long, and most of it was about his job as Irving's manager, his friendship with Irving, and his authorship of a noteworthy book: "His best-known publication is 'Personal Reminiscences of Henry Irving,' issued in 1908."

"If you were to tell someone living in London in 1897 that in a hundred years no one would know Henry Irving but everyone would remember Bram Stoker," says Mike Barsanti, "he would have thought you were crazy. Henry Irving was the biggest celebrity in London at the time. No one would have guessed Stoker would be the one we'd talk about."

So, after Saxons, Turks, and Hungarians ran a smear campaign against Vlad, a nineteenth-century writer took his last name and attached it to a bizarre vampire story that had nothing to do with him. If Vlad the Impaler hadn't been a murderous psychotic, you'd almost feel sorry for the guy. But that was just the beginning. During the 1950s and '60s, scholars and journalists were trying to find connections between Vlad and the literary Count—connections that didn't exist. Meanwhile, Stoker's notes sat in a bookseller's office in Philadelphia. And, in 1970, that bookseller sold them to the Rosenbach Museum, whose director at the time was a man named Clive E. Driver.

Even after they popped up in the Rosenbach, scholars wouldn't touch the notes for years. Meanwhile, in 1972, Raymond T. McNally and Radu Florescu published a book called *In Search of Dracula*, claiming that Stoker may have actually done extensive research on the life of Vlad the Impaler. His Count Dracula, they argued, was based on Vlad's cruelties. According to Miller, however, there is no evidence to support the claim. But other authors compounded the error by suggesting that Stoker had actually traveled to Transylvania ahead of his protagonist Jonathan Harker or that Vlad's favorite method of killing his victims, by impaling, became the staking that the heroes use to kill vampires. After the books came movies and TV shows, and the connection between Vlad and the Count froze solid.

This all started a frenzy of interest in the historical homeland of Stoker's Count, with Pan America World Airways selling a package vacation—a three-week tour of Transylvania for $900. People were showing up in Romania expecting to see the places where the real Dracula stalked the living. After *In Search of Dracula*, McNally and

Florescu wrote *Dracula: A Biography of Vlad the Impaler*, *Dracula: Prince of Many Faces*, and *The Essential Dracula*. Jumping on their own bandwagon for this whole find-the-real-character-in-the-fictional-book thing, they also cowrote *In Search of Dr. Jeckyll and Mr. Hyde*, and by himself McNally wrote *Dracula Was a Woman: In Search of the Blood Countess of Transylvania*. Florescu came out with *In Search of Frankenstein*, and just two years ago, he wrote *In Search of the Pied Piper*.

No word on when we can expect *In Search of Curious George*.

So when did scholars finally get around to reading Stoker's notes? And who was the first person to dig into them for answers?

"McNally was visiting the museum," according to Elizabeth Miller, "and the curator told him about this box of documents—these notes nobody knew had been preserved." It was three years after *In Search of Dracula* had come out, she adds, "so one can excuse them somewhat." But in the introduction to the revised version of *In Search of Dracula*, published in 1994, McNally and Florescu brag about discovering the notes and then write, "This proved that far from being a work of pure fiction, Stoker relied on extensive research both on the historical Vlad and on the vampire lore of Transylvania, giving his plot a definite geographical and historical framework." Big, hefty balls.

"They took the parallels even further, even though they *knew* the notes did not support their thesis," Miller adds. In fact, according to Miller, scholars have still not put enough weight on the notes while studying Stoker's novel. The legends persist. The facts get in the way of a good story, and by now that story has a powerful momentum.

The real Dracula and the literary Dracula became so mixed up that nothing could untangle them. In 1974, McNally and Florescu's book became a semi-documentary movie with the same name, starring Christopher Lee—the man who'd played Dracula in half a dozen movies with names like *Dracula Has Risen from the Grave, Scars of Dracula, Taste the Blood of Dracula*, and the little-known *Wax the Back of Dracula* (okay, maybe I invented that last one). For the film version of *In Search of Dracula*, he even played Vlad the Impaler in dramatic re-creations of the guy's life, right down to the weird hat and the cop mustache.

By 1976, just as America was having its bicentennial, the Romanian government was celebrating its 500th anniversary—but this was not a celebration of its independence, constitution, formation of its country, or even Vlad the Impaler's birth. In a desperate effort to raise public spirits at a time when the economy was beginning to slump, the government decided to have a nationwide festival celebrating the anniversary of Vlad's assassination. They issued commemorative stamps and everything.

Remembering your national hero by having a shindig to mark the year he was beheaded by thugs in the woods might sound morbid—we don't have fireworks over the Grassy Knoll every November or reenact the hijinks in Ford's Theater—but Romanians take what they can get.

By the 1980s, Clive Driver, the man who'd acquired the Stoker notes for the Rosenbach Museum, had retired from his post there and begun working as a consultant. Then in 1987, something odd happened. A curator from Sotheby's auction house called the Rosenbach Museum saying it had been offered a 1790 letter from John Adams—a letter belonging to the museum. Rosenbach officials called the prospective seller, who told them he'd gotten the letter from Driver.

And there were others. People at the Rosenbach uncovered that dozens of documents worth $250,000—letters from George Washington, Ben Franklin, Abraham Lincoln, Daniel Boone, Andrew Jackson, and Oliver Cromwell—had left their collection. Eventually, the number of missing documents climbed to more than one hundred, and the price tag was more than $500,000. The museum accused

Driver of stealing the documents and filed suit to stop him from dealing in the merchandise. They eventually settled the civil case with Driver and his buyer, getting most of the documents back. But federal prosecutors brought criminal charges against Driver, who eventually made what is called an Alford plea—in which a defendant can still claim to be innocent while admitting that the prosecutors have enough evidence to put him away. In 1991, a federal judge sentenced Clive Driver on one count of interstate transportation of stolen property and two counts of filing false tax returns. The judge slapped him with a $50,000 fine, three years' probation, and two thousand hours of community service.

Driver lived the remaining years of his life first in the small town of Truro, Massachusetts, and later in Provincetown, Massachusetts, writing a column of small, historical articles for the *Provincetown Banner*. When he died in 1999, the newspaper he'd worked for printed a loving obituary about his writing and even his old position at the Rosenbach. But it made no mention of the scandal that had destroyed his reputation in the book trade.

Fortunately, he'd been able to do one good thing: get Stoker's notes out into the open so that scholars would understand the real story—how the Irish author had created a work of fiction that had little to do with the fifteenth-century Wallachian prince. People would finally correct the mistakes of the 1970s, right?

"Stoker did . . . research on Dracula, reading a pamphlet published in 1491 that differs only slightly from the original *Dracole Waida*," according to a *Philadelphia City Paper* article. It continues, recounting atrocities that Vlad committed that Stoker "must have learned." This article was printed in 2005, and it was actually about the Stoker notes themselves.

The story of Dracula shows us that it's probably easier to smear a bad guy than a good one. It shows us that the celebrities of one generation become the nobodies of another, and vice versa. And finally, it shows us that people will lie to themselves, to others, and to anyone who'll listen if it makes for a good story. They will repeat the lie over and over, and if you tell them the truth, they will look at you blankly and go back happily to their bullshit.

There might have been a time when the legend of Dracula wasn't pure entertainment. But it's too late for that now. Stoker's Count and his eastern European counterpart became fused into one truly awful villain. He was so unbelievably bad, it was only a matter of time before someone made a theme park out of him. And it didn't take much time. As a matter of fact, back in 1976, while the Romanians were issuing their postage stamps, people were building the wildest, most bizarre theme park out of this mixed-up story—and it would take every historical and movie image of Dracula and clump it all together into one greasy, godawful stew.

When studying Vlad, you can never stay out of pulpy pop culture for long. We began this chapter tromping through a giant parade and then stopped for some highbrow document-hunting, but now we're going to head to the site of this theme park. I'm sorry if you feel cheap, but it has to be done. It's in Wildwood, New Jersey, a boardwalk carnival town where the rides are scary, the candy is plentiful, and if you don't like an attraction, wait five minutes, and someone will burn it down.

Funnel Cake and Arson

"To scare was our job, and we enjoyed it.
I would liken it to Dracula's craving for blood.
For us it was a craving for fear."

Funnel cake is never a good idea. But you don't remember that, and you fool yourself every time. You walk by the concession stand, and that smell hits you—the heavy, sweet smell of grease and dough and warm kitchens with something baking in the oven—and you don't even think about getting in line. You don't even think about fishing crumpled bills out of your wallet, and it comes out of the dark screened window hot on the plate, dusted like an early morning frost. And the first bite is crisp and rich and full of memories of every carnival you ever saw, knocking the milk bottles over on the first try and hefting that impossibly large stuffed panda out from behind the booth and giving it to your best girl. The first bite fills your belly and satisfies you in a way that nothing has in years. The

Queasy and confused on the Wildwood boardwalk.

first bite is everything you need. Funnel cake should come in pill form. You'd take a single bite every Monday morning to replenish your youth and wonder and to get you through your workweek.

But funnel cake doesn't come in pills. It comes in one size only: a hot greased chunk as big as your head. And while the first bite is wonderful, the second bite is where you realize you've just eaten a handful of Crisco and cake frosting. The second bite of funnel cake reminds you that the milk bottles were welded together, and even if you hit them directly, the ball would just bounce off. And you didn't have a best girl . . . just a carny giving you the eye—a carny with an odd number of fingers and prison tats on his paws. He pulled the lever to lock you into a Tilt-a-Whirl that looked like it was made out of scrap iron, and as it whipped around faster and faster, you saw the fat kid two seats over begin to make ominous, silent heaving motions, and you realized you had a second to close your eyes and mouth before the ride became a vomit atomizer. The first bite is Ronald and Bozo and Red Skelton. The second bite is the Joker and John Wayne Gacy. The second sinks into your gut like it will never, ever leave. And after that one, there are more. Your hands are greasy, your chin is covered with spit and sugar, and acid burns the back of your throat, but you can't stop, can you? You hunch over to keep the sugar from blowing away and indulge your filthy habit, and you know somehow you have to finish. So you do the only thing you can. You grab your friend, your relative. Someone close. Someone you love. And you betray that person.

"Here," you say, giving the person half, "help me." Like a family of junkies getting each other hooked, you huddle together feeling hateful and sick. And if you recover, you promise yourself you won't ever eat this crap again. Like any addict, you lie, and when you can't lie anymore, you make yourself forget.

Kennan and I buy the funnel cake at one of the few candy shops open on the boardwalk here in Wildwood, New Jersey. Two friendly middle-aged men from India sell it to us along with a small bag of Swedish fish. We tell them we're looking for the remains of Castle Dracula, the famous attraction that burned down in 2002.

"I don't believe in any of that," one of them replies. "When you're dead, you're dead." I have no idea what he means by this, but he keeps going. He launches into a long speech about this group of cannibals who live in the forests around his home back in India, cannibals who only come out once or twice a year to perform feats like eating fire in huge, scary festivals. They go naked and unkempt, feasting on human flesh and terrifying the locals. And when they decide to disappear into the wilderness, no one can find them.

"Maybe those people . . . have some ghosts," he says.

The friendly Indian guys are beginning to creep me out.

Kennan and I leave to find the castle. It's supposed to be next to a giant waterpark on one of the piers. We're hunting for it and working our way through the funnel cake, standing in a whirl of sugar and freezing rain. It is not a good day to be strolling on the boardwalk. The ocean and the sky are the same blank shade of gunmetal, and the shops—most of them shuttered—seem to focus the steady blast of cold, wet air like some sort of wind tunnel. Ahead of us is a lonely arcade with a handful of people stalking through the banks of tired video games and the slot machines that don't even dispense real money, just tokens for plastic crap you wouldn't accept for free.

We search through a nearby vacant lot and find a giant gaping hole and parts of an old wooden foundation—it's halfway filled with brackish water, and there's even some kind of Styrofoam snake-thing in the muck, almost as if someone originally made a dummy serpent to scare tourists. It looks like the real thing—the castle's remains.

"That's not it," a guy back at an arcade tells us later. He explains that the real Castle Dracula was right in the middle of the water park. We follow his directions and find ourselves at a clean, oddly neat sandy lot surrounded by a chain-link fence. It turns out that the other foundation was an old theater that burned down in a completely unrelated fire. How many fires did this place have? A lot, I eventually find out. And as many as I discover, I still don't think I ever got them all. But that's not the only mystery of this weird place.

Kennan is good with people, and though we live far away from each other, he's one of my best friends. I've brought him with me on many trips because he's sharp, funny, and he notices things other people miss. He's also a good photographer. We covered a barbeque contest together in 2004. And when we were young, we used to rubber-cement huge piles of fireworks together and light them all at once. It would make noise like an artillery shell going off and send us scurrying away like the hounds of hell were after us.

It's fitting we're visiting a tourist town in the off-season because it's the sort of place where we grew up. Both military brats, we spent our early years together in Virginia Beach, Virginia. During summer, the place was always choked with college kids, navy guys on shore leave, and paunchy French Canadian men wrapped in Speedos and back hair. During winter, it emptied out, and the strip got quiet and Dracula-spooky.

I pick Kennan up at a bus station in the narrow streets of Philly's Chinatown during a downpour. He's wearing a brown leather jacket, his overgrown hillbilly beard jutting out from under a dark rain hat that makes him look like a cross between a Hasidic rabbi and the bad guy from *I Know What You Did Last Summer.* He turns around and even in the rain, the smell hits me before the sight of it; he's wearing a full necklace of garlic bulbs.

"I thought we'd need this." By the time we leave town, the whole car smells like a delightful pesto.

A little more than an hour later, we reach Wildwood, and our first stop is the George F. Boyer Historical Museum—a tiny brick building made of narrow rooms clumped together, all of them piled high with books, photo albums, old portraits, posters, placards, statues, and even a couple ceremonial swords and daggers. Bob Bright, a local historian who is cranky and friendly, shows us around the place and points out the remnants of the Castle Dracula. It was a cult landmark for years, standing on the boardwalk at Nickels Midway Pier. But practically all that's left of the place are a few items here. For weeks after the fire, Bright says, visitors, some of them old employees, were constantly filing into the museum to pay their respects.

"Every Saturday the place was filled with them," he adds, "mourning the death of Castle Dracula." The most famous chunk of the place was a fiberglass coat of arms backed by two wooden boards.

"A fireman brought that in the day of the fire," Bright says, "and it was still smoking! He told me, 'Here, hang it quick before anyone claims it.' " The smoking thing stunk up the museum, but he kept it, and it became a regular attraction.

The coat of arms looks familiar to me: It's from the royal family of England, complete with harps, lions, a unicorn, and a crown. Probably sitting in the darkened castle, it looked medieval and impressive enough to pass. But once you realize what it is, you can never see anything else. I stare at it trying not to imagine Prince Charles and Camilla stalking around Buckingham dressed in matching *His* and *Hers* capes, biting the Beefeaters.

In the museum records—a pile of multicolored photo albums—I find mention of another fire that erupted on the same pier seven months after Castle Dracula burned down. And there are many others. In fact, when two teenage punks playing hookey wandered into the castle in 2002 (holding torches for illumination) and accidentally set the whole thing ablaze, they were continuing a long and proud tradition among the Jersey yoots of Wildwood: Torching shit up. A United States Fire Administration report on the boardwalk lists twenty more fires, about one every five years dating back to the turn of the century. And those are just the major ones.

"Fire is a constant enemy of a summer resort constructed entirely of wood," the report notes.

Fires in 1915 and 1919 took out a whole block and a whole pier. From the 1940s through the 1970s, more fires followed, leveling arcades, nightclubs, theaters, and sometimes entire sections of the boardwalk. Four fires hit the town in the early 1980s, including a 1983 conflagration that destroyed six stores and inflicted $1 million in losses. The very next year, another one followed, wiping out the

Fun Pier completely. And in 1992, an inferno ripped through the area where Castle Dracula was standing, but spared the attraction.

On August 29, 2000, there was a seven-alarm blaze that struck just before 2:00 a.m., destroying three stores on the boardwalk, costing $1 million in damage, and sending one volunteer firefighter to the hospital with a mild injury when a pipe struck him on the forehead. It took 120 firefighters about four hours to get it under control. Witnesses reported hearing explosions at the site just before it began. Investigators ruled that it had been arson after finding a suspicious ax hole in a floor, a V-shaped pattern where the fire began, and a detection dog sniffed out three spots where a residue of Acatone (a flammable, toxic chemical found in nail polish remover) was discovered. And then just a few months before our visit, in December 2005, there was another big one, a nine alarmer that took out a motel and a pizza parlor.

The boardwalk is connected to a good source of water, the report continues, but it only has four hydrants actually on the boardwalk with which to pump water into a fire. And since the wooden structure won't hold any vehicles heavier than pickup trucks, a department can't bring in the big equipment quickly. Plus, the whole damn area is made of old wood, the humid air coming off the ocean makes for thick, impassable smoke, and since most of the buildings are closed for months out of the year, the place is practically abandoned. Block after block of large, old, wooden, empty buildings—you could get a roaring blaze going, and nobody would even notice until it was too late.

The report explains why the fires do a lot of damage and why they're hard to stop. But it doesn't explain everything. It doesn't explain why they get started in the first place. The Wildwood boardwalk seems like it's always a windy day and a cigarette butt away from pulling a Richard Pryor. What's causing it?

Lightning?

Dragons?

Martian zap guns?

"Insurance companies," says Bright. And others agree with him.

"Arson has not been uncommon on the boardwalk," the report also says, and cites five cases of arson in 1993 and one in 1992 on the same pier where Castle Dracula stood—with a total price tag of more than $3 million. I haven't found evidence that the Castle Dracula fire was anything but an accident by some kids. The area just seems to flare up.

"In my early career here there was a lot of arson along the boardwalk," Walter Larcombe of the Wildwood Fire Department told reporters in 2000. "In the past few years there have been some [fires] that were questionable but never proven to be arson and a few that definitely were intentionally set."

The locals tell me that some merchants think the best way to do a little spring cleaning before the season opens is to burn your place down, collect the insurance, and build the thing up bigger and better. Insurance investigators might suspect, but unless they hang out on an icy boardwalk in the dead of winter, they're not going to prove a damn thing.

One town father, a state senator, was famous for it, according to Bright. Almost everything he owned burned down. But not everyone torches parts of the boardwalk for the insurance money. Some of them just do it for the hell of it. Some people are just stupid. The problem is separating the ambitious insurance crook from the ordinary hoodlum with a can of gas, a Bic lighter, and a Bon Jovi T-shirt.

Still, as Kennan and I wander through town, I'm half glad that the rain is so freezing—at least there's a good chance the whole place won't burst into flame while I'm here. And that's not all we have to fear in Wildwood, either: According to 2004 statistics, the city has a crime rate three times the national average, with about four times as many robberies, aggravated assaults, and murders and almost double the number of rapes of the rest of the nation. Its property crimes are also three times above the average. The only category of crime in which it doesn't beat the rest of the country is motor vehicle theft. These statistics might be misleading—the town has a population of 5,000, but it can swell to 200,000 in the summertime when tourists flood the place—so all that madness might just be the result of drunk college kids. Either way, I'm nervous.

Of course, it occurs to me that maybe we're the scariest thing here. Kennan still looks like waterlogged ZZ Top, and for some reason even I can't fathom, I'm wearing a T-shirt, shorts, and a raincoat. My bare legs poke out, and I look like I'm going to start exposing myself to people any minute.

Maybe it's always been this way. Perhaps this area has brought out the freak in people since the area was first spotted by Robert Juet, a crewman on Henry Hudson's ship, the *Half Moon*, which cruised past it in 1609.

"A very good land to fall in with—and a pleasant land to see," Juet wrote in his journal. He didn't stop, of course. Just gave it a nice compliment from a safe distance, sort of like when you take the Jersey Turnpike north and spot a clump of trees that look pretty. You're not going to slow down below seventy or anything. But it's good to notice.

A group of Algonquins lived in the area, but the first Europeans were a small band of fishermen who settled in the late nineteenth century. But even before that, farmers farther inland used to lead their horse and cattle to the area and let them graze before bringing them back. Some of the cattle got lost, and over the years became feral—up through the turn of the century the place had the buggers roaming all over.

Wildwood's tourism trade is wrapped around the boardwalk, but *that* came from nearby Atlantic City, where developers opened the first tourist boardwalk in 1870. A train conductor actually named

Alexander Boardman came up with the idea to keep sand off the trains shuttling vacationers to and from the beach.

In the early twentieth century, Wildwood was wildly, flagrantly corrupt. In 1934, taxpayers charged that the town was misusing more than $300,000 in funds for a construction project. The election of Republican State Senator William C. Hunt—a business tycoon who owned a chain of amusement attractions—was held up in 1936 on charges of voter fraud. Hunt ultimately resigned. During the 1930s, after the town elected New Jersey's first female mayor, Doris Bradway, she was investigated ten times while in office for stealing funds and even swiping gasoline from the city's stockpile for her own vehicles. Nonetheless the townsfolk loved her—reelecting her in a landslide. Known as the "Big Girl" because she clocked in at more than 250 pounds, she publicized her weight loss program and dropped more than 100 pounds. Plus, once during her term, while watching a wrestling match, she became mightily pissed at one wrestler's cheating, so she jumped into the ring and started whaling on the poor guy with a plank. So she was like Oprah, only with more graft and violence.

The place was like a younger, seedier brother of Atlantic City, the one who doesn't have a good job and calls home less often. Scandal, tackiness, and high weirdness have always clung to Wildwood like a koala to a tree. In 1938, a man named Joseph Dobish started an outlandish animal act on the boardwalk: His wife drove a motorcycle or racing car—accounts differ—around the walls of a high-banked bowl, astonishing spectators with her breakneck speed. And just for kicks, she had a 300-pound lion named Tuffy crammed into a sidecar.

Pretty soon, Tuffy got sick of being spun around inside of this oversized salad shooter, and during feeding time the big cat sprang loose, clambered up to the boardwalk, and took a swipe at the first person he saw—an auctioneer named Thomas Saito. Tuffy snapped

Saito's neck in one blow. Then the lion grabbed Saito's limp body and scampered down under the boards, where it proceeded to mangle him like my cat Pungo does with a little spit-covered mousey toy. Cops converged on Tuffy and shot him, but he ran off and hid in a nearby pier. Eventually, another cop crept up on him and shot him again, right between the eyes from five feet away. They put Dobish in jail on a charge of involuntary manslaughter. They probably made Tuffy into a dozen carnival prizes.

Things took a darker, smellier turn in 1988, when a pollution scandal hit the region. The authorities had briefly closed area beaches because they found high levels of fecal bacteria—which had most likely come from runoff from the sewage system. The beaches were reopened after only a couple days, but, later, five area businessmen were caught dumping fifty lbs. of chlorine pellets into the surf in an attempt to disinfect . . . uh, the Atlantic. The newspapers dubbed them the "Chlorine 5," and a court fined them $200 on charges of dumping hazardous materials. But the court suspended the fines, partly because the businessmen were authorized by a mayor of one of the boroughs and a head of public works.

Castle Dracula might be the most normal thing to ever hit this place, I think. The wind seems to pick up and the rain is colder than ever as Kennan and I wander around near a rickety carnival area with old wooden roller coasters and a giant Ferris wheel set against the dim sea. It's hard to describe how empty, lonely, and creepy the place is. The boardwalk stretches on for five miles—till visibility drops away and the shops disappear into the rain. You can walk for a mile and not see another person—just dim shapes moving in and out of the shadows in the distance. And the rain and wind muffles the sound, so you can barely hear yourself speak.

Some hotels and restaurants are open, but every lobby and every sitting room is cavernous and less than a quarter filled. It is like some kind of depression or disaster depleted a huge town, and the survivors are just going through the motions of running their businesses.

Wet, spooked, and freezing my ass off, I'm trying to imagine what it was like back in the mid-1970s when the Nickels family built the castle. The pictures and the scale model in the Boyer museum showed a building with imposing dark gray walls and tiny windows. According to press reports, the thing was modeled after the "real" Castle Dracula. But I'm skeptical since A) there is no real Castle Dracula, as I've already mentioned and B) I don't think Vlad the Impaler's fortress had an execution room with an electric chair. However, what's fascinating is that here was an early example of pop culture beginning to mix up the historical Vlad and the literary Count. The castle had dummies of people impaled on stakes—not found in Stoker's novel, but an element of the legends of Vlad himself. Before there was Elizabeth Kostova's *The Historian*, the carnival attraction in Wildwood, New Jersey, showed that even though Stoker may not have known much about Vlad, the legend of the Impaler and the pulp image of the literary and movie Count were ideally suited for each other. Perhaps through sheer serendipity, Bram Stoker picked the name of a historical figure who was so much like his villain that the two could be combined and recombined for centuries after. This carnival ride was a testament to that and also to the power of pop culture in America.

The castle had actors—sometimes young adults, sometimes schoolkids—dressed in costumes and makeup. They would crouch down in the boat tunnels and hide behind the 4-foot portrait of

Saito's neck in one blow. Then the lion grabbed Saito's limp body and scampered down under the boards, where it proceeded to mangle him like my cat Pungo does with a little spit-covered mousey toy. Cops converged on Tuffy and shot him, but he ran off and hid in a nearby pier. Eventually, another cop crept up on him and shot him again, right between the eyes from five feet away. They put Dobish in jail on a charge of involuntary manslaughter. They probably made Tuffy into a dozen carnival prizes.

Things took a darker, smellier turn in 1988, when a pollution scandal hit the region. The authorities had briefly closed area beaches because they found high levels of fecal bacteria—which had most likely come from runoff from the sewage system. The beaches were reopened after only a couple days, but, later, five area businessmen were caught dumping fifty lbs. of chlorine pellets into the surf in an attempt to disinfect . . . uh, the Atlantic. The newspapers dubbed them the "Chlorine 5," and a court fined them $200 on charges of dumping hazardous materials. But the court suspended the fines, partly because the businessmen were authorized by a mayor of one of the boroughs and a head of public works.

Castle Dracula might be the most normal thing to ever hit this place, I think. The wind seems to pick up and the rain is colder than ever as Kennan and I wander around near a rickety carnival area with old wooden roller coasters and a giant Ferris wheel set against the dim sea. It's hard to describe how empty, lonely, and creepy the place is. The boardwalk stretches on for five miles—till visibility drops away and the shops disappear into the rain. You can walk for a mile and not see another person—just dim shapes moving in and out of the shadows in the distance. And the rain and wind muffles the sound, so you can barely hear yourself speak.

Some hotels and restaurants are open, but every lobby and every sitting room is cavernous and less than a quarter filled. It is like some kind of depression or disaster depleted a huge town, and the survivors are just going through the motions of running their businesses.

Wet, spooked, and freezing my ass off, I'm trying to imagine what it was like back in the mid-1970s when the Nickels family built the castle. The pictures and the scale model in the Boyer museum showed a building with imposing dark gray walls and tiny windows. According to press reports, the thing was modeled after the "real" Castle Dracula. But I'm skeptical since A) there is no real Castle Dracula, as I've already mentioned and B) I don't think Vlad the Impaler's fortress had an execution room with an electric chair. However, what's fascinating is that here was an early example of pop culture beginning to mix up the historical Vlad and the literary Count. The castle had dummies of people impaled on stakes—not found in Stoker's novel, but an element of the legends of Vlad himself. Before there was Elizabeth Kostova's *The Historian*, the carnival attraction in Wildwood, New Jersey, showed that even though Stoker may not have known much about Vlad, the legend of the Impaler and the pulp image of the literary and movie Count were ideally suited for each other. Perhaps through sheer serendipity, Bram Stoker picked the name of a historical figure who was so much like his villain that the two could be combined and recombined for centuries after. This carnival ride was a testament to that and also to the power of pop culture in America.

The castle had actors—sometimes young adults, sometimes schoolkids—dressed in costumes and makeup. They would crouch down in the boat tunnels and hide behind the 4-foot portrait of

Dracula above the fire in the entrance room, waiting for the picture to slide open so they could spring out and announce in a terrifyingly loud voice:

> *How dare you enter my castle and disturb my rest? For this I should kill you all, rip the hearts from your chest and drink the blood from within as they beat . . . But I won't! Instead I'll leave you as mere playthings for the many monsters and demons that await you inside . . . Now get these pathetic mortals out of my sight. Their presence sickens me.*

Anyway, that's how Erik O'Brien remembers it from his time at the place five years ago. O'Brien is twenty-five now, and lives in Drogheda, Ireland, where he's studying psychology in college.

As they loaded people through the dark maze, they could tell who the "winner" was going to be, says Chris Klein, who worked there in the mid-1980s. The winner, the person so scared of everything that he or she could go into a conniption fit at the sight of Caspar, would be the target for the rest of the tour.

"The winner was someone we could get to pee themselves," says Klein. And they'd spot the winner after Drac jumped out onto the mantelpiece and made his speech.

"He'd stomp his foot as hard as he could," Klein adds. "It would reverberate and everybody would jump back. I mean, we would get *marines* in there that would jump back." And the winner would scramble for the exit door—which was locked by then. The other actors would disappear into their secret passages to jump ahead of the crowd. They'd describe their target to the people gathered in the far corners. And the monsters would prepare to pounce on some squealy teenage girl or wimpy office manager and make his or her life hell.

"Our big thing was trying to catch a name," Klein says. People hiding in the front room would hear a name mentioned and pass it back to people farther into the castle. The target would come into some room deep in the bowels of the place and a freak dressed up as a mad doctor or executioner would say a personal hello and scare the bejesus out of him or her."

Former ghoul Gary McQuitty remembers how staffers would dip a teddy bear in fake blood before presenting it to some sap in line.

"You would squeeze the bear and the blood would run out, at which point you could start screaming at the poor victim of the prank that they had hurt your bear and they would die for their crimes as soon as you got them inside.

"Very effective," he adds. "Even on adults."

"The castle job was one of the best jobs I've ever had," O'Brien enthuses. "I still think about it often. I'm still in contact with friends I made there."

But it was more than fun. Castle Dracula was an authentic piece of Americana—one of the last of the attractions built during the great era of darkrides, from the 1930s to the 1970s. Darkrides were carnival attractions that depended on slow-moving vehicles— boats, cars, or trains—to propel customers on a track through a series of pop-up monsters and other mechanical scenes. Thousands of them appeared in parks all over the country, according to Rick Davis, the director and cofounder of Darkride and Funhouse Enthusiasts, a historical organization on the Web at DAFE.org. But most of the last working rides are in Pennsylvania and New Jersey.

"A lot of the early ones were educational in nature, featuring simulated 'coal mines' and trips to exotic locations that people back then could only dream of visiting," Davis tells me. Over the years they dwindled down to around forty attractions, he adds, but they might be coming back in a new form. In a similar way to old wooden roller coasters having been transformed into the steel giants at parks across the country, we might soon see new-style darkrides.

"I think most of us still love the cheesy old darkrides though!" he adds.

Though part of the castle was a walk-through, it also had a darkride built under the structure—a half-boat, half-train that came out of an original tunnel of love ride that started out with an "Old Mill" theme in 1919. It was eventually changed to an Arabian Nights–style attraction in the '60s. Why would someone make a tunnel of love out of a trip through an old mill? How could grinding flour possibly be romantic to anyone who doesn't have a Pillsbury Doughboy fetish? Maybe people were easier to amuse back then.

Chris Klein found something special at the castle. He'd just gotten out of the army back in 1984—he'd been stationed in a field artillery group in Germany—and was wandering around Wildwood looking for work.

"I was in the army for two years," he says, "and I could not conform to military life. Castle Drac was the first job I had after the military . . . I was looking for a new start, and I figured I'd go to Wildwood." He was also in the middle of a spiritual crisis. He was searching for something to believe in, a quest that would ultimately lead him to becoming a Wiccan high priest.

"I was seeking like-minded people," he adds, "and where better than a haunted house to find freaks?" Klein says he made friends there whom he has kept in touch with ever since.

Klein quickly became one of the best employees at the castle— a regular who could eyeball the different customers coming through the line and spot how to get to them. One of the staff's favorite tricks was to hang upside down by their legs from the rafters and pop down out of nowhere like Spiderman. They'd play with hair, tickle ears—that's all it would take to set people screaming. Of course, Klein adds, legally you can't pull that anymore.

And when they weren't scaring customers, the staff was busy scaring one another. According to McQuitty, the old-timers at the castle would tell the new people a story about the tunnel of love the place was built on. Supposedly it contained a leftover room, called the Red Room, which could only be reached by a secret passage. And the dungeon boat ride itself had been the site of a freak accident when a girl got sucked into some pumping machinery. Her ghost supposedly haunted the Red Room. And down in the tunnels you could still hear her screaming.

Of course it was all bullshit.

"I think every new person must have spent days looking for the passage," McQuitty remembers. "I know I did." And the spot where the death allegedly happened was one of the most isolated in the castle. Any new staffers hanging out there would begin to get creeped out.

"When you worked that spot you were alone for hours at a time in almost total darkness . . . with the sound of wailing playing over and over," he says. "With tales of the Red Room floating in your head it was quite eerie."

Sometimes even the customers started acting creepy, according to former staffer Scott Forbes. Once, a customer somewhere in the building flipped out and sprayed a staffer in the face with a fire extinguisher. The exhaust tripped off the alarm, which rang through the halls, terrifying Forbes, who was alone down in the dungeon. But he wasn't thinking about the ghost of any dead girl.

"I thought I might die in that firetrap," he says. "I literally jumped into the fire door, and flew through."

There are other stories of customers scaring the staff. Klein collected a bowl of dead bugs—fried dragonflies and mosquitoes that had kamikaze'd on the floodlights—that he would offer to folks in line. One day, a customer grabbed a handful of the things and popped them into his mouth.

"It's the only time a customer ever freaked me out," Klein says.

"I told him, 'They're real.' He says, 'Yeah, I know they're real. You got any more?' "

But why do people like to play with fear? Why did people line up by the score to enter the castle, and why do so many ex-staffers still remember what a good time they had?

"It was the rush of the scare," Forbes explains. "Scaring another human being was strangely exciting. I could never quite understand the psychology of instilling fear. To scare was our job, and we enjoyed it. I would liken it to Dracula's craving for blood. For us it was a craving for fear."

"It was fun as shit," says Tom. Kennan and I find him at the VFW club—he's a retired navy man who served in the 1970s—and he tells me that when he was manager at the castle, alcohol made all the difference.

No one was drunk, he quickly adds—people just might have had a cocktail during the show to loosen themselves up. But since he's just some random guy we found at the VFW, I don't know what to believe.

"It was a great date place," offers the bartender. "Good spot to hook up with girls and grab a feel." Like submarine races or drive-in horror movies, the castle has joined a long list of attractions whose purpose was to allow teenagers to score.

Then Tom's friend speaks up.

"Y'know their grandfather is king of the gypsies," he says. Kennan asks him what he means, but all he knows is that the patriarch of the family who opened the castle is some kind of "king" of some kind of gypsy organization on the east coast. It seems a little unbelievable:

Stoker's novel had the gypsies working for Count Dracula. Now, this guy is telling me they'd turned his castle into a carnival attraction and plopped it down in twentieth-century New Jersey. Next he's going to tell me Frank McCourt brought his family over from the old country to create an Angela's Ashes Playland—complete with muck-soaked animatronic Irishmen singing "Danny Boy" and fighting one another with bottle glass. I'm dubious. But it turns out he's sorta right.

John Nickels, along with the rest of his family, are co-owners of Nickels' Midway Pier, where they built the castle attraction. His family is Roma, and John is also an activist for Roma causes—"Roma" or "Romani" are more politically correct terms than "gypsy" because that word comes from the fact that Europeans used to believe Roma tribes were actually Egyptians. In fact, in 2004, several groups petitioned an online site, dictionary.com, to replace the term "gypsy" with "Roma." Of course, two of those angry, offended organizations were *The National Association of Gypsy Women* and *The International All Gypsies Group.*

Nickels has worked for groups trying to get Roma compensated for their persecution during the Holocaust, and he even represented the International Romani Union in a 2000 tribunal to condemn Bill Clinton, General Wesley Clark, Madeleine Albright, and the heads of NATO states for war crimes during the action in the former Yugoslavia. According to Nickels, the reason he was part of the tribunal was that the local sides of this war all targeted Romanis.

"The Romanis suffered the highest casualty rates of anyone," he says. The lead prosecutor of this affair was former Attorney General Ramsey Clark, whose recent job was as Saddam Hussein's lawyer. I ask Nickels about Stoker's novel, which portrays the gypsies as servants of the Count.

"The Romani were slaves of Vlad the Impaler," he says. And some of the accounts of Vlad's cruelty do say he persecuted Nickels's people. But of course, Stoker said the gypsies were the villains . . . the creepy minions of the Count.

"Sometimes it's too difficult to change it, the image of Romanis," he says with a sigh. "Sometimes it's easier to let the picture go on instead of trying to explain that Romanis are people too."

After the 2002 fire that destroyed Dracula's Castle, the Nickels family's insurance company filed a massive $3.5 million suit against a tenant, a contractor, and families of the punk kids who torched the place. Some parties countersued, and the case turned into a legal feeding frenzy. Many of the individual suits were settled, but it doesn't look like Castle Dracula will rise again here anytime soon.

"I won't say 'never,' " Nickels tells me, "but you can't build it with 1976 dollars today."

Now it's night, and Kennan and I have come back for one more look at the boardwalk, which is even more abandoned—even the few shops that had been opened before were closed down.

"You know," I say to Kennan, "one of the guys we interviewed told me he wouldn't come here at night."

"What do you mean?"

"He told me he used to come here at night when he was a kid, but that he wouldn't be caught here at night now. The man actually said, 'I would never come here at night, and I know how to take care of myself.' "

"So," says Kennan after a pause, "why didn't you tell me this before?"

I don't know. I shrug.

There is one final shop, a clothing store, which has a door open while two clerks unpack what looks like next season's merchandise. They eye us, and we move on. The season begins the next day, and people will probably start coming. It will be too late for us—Kennan will be back in New York, and I will be home writing my notes up—but it's fun to think about. Off in the distance, silhouetted by some streetlamps and carnival lights, there are two or three figures moving. Then farther down the street, we see three more kids holding a vicious-looking pit bull by a chain. They could just be out for a walk, of course. Dogs gotta walk, even in the cold rain, and even late at night. But we've seen enough.

"Let's go," we both say, almost at the same time.

Drac or no Drac, the Wildwood boardwalk will soon open for the tourist season, and it will all be just as weird and tacky and cool as ever. The smell of salt and Coppertone will waft through the air, and the funnel cake will always be there to entice and sicken folks. Its remaining rides and attractions will fill up with young people.

We've tracked the Vlad of medieval lore and even visited the seaside theme park where he summers to see how his historical image and pulp image can stick together. It's clear that he seems to have slipped away from Transylvania and found a better home here in the land of carnival rides, arson, and fried food. America loves him and all his caped cronies. Now it's time to find the whole bunch on another American institution—the world of celluloid. And that means taking the perilous trek into the dark and foreboding depths of my living room.

Vamps on Film

"Some muthafuckas are always trying to ice-skate uphill."

can't believe you're doing this for work," Anne says, packing up to leave for the weekend. "I must be the most gullible wife in the world." And I have to agree, though I don't say anything. I help put the porta-crib into the back of the minivan. I strap our boy into his car seat and give him a kiss he squirms away from. I kiss Anne and go back inside. She backs the van out and the garage door rumbles shut as I walk from room to room drawing the blinds until the whole house is dark. It will stay that way for the next forty-eight hours.

I've spent years trying to explain the weird stuff I've had to do for work. Writing doesn't pay well, but it gives you the excuse to do things no respectable husband should get away with. The tour of Montreal

Back at home and digging into the Kit Kats.

strip clubs, shaving my legs to compare women's razors or wandering the house in my underwear—my wife has a suspicion that my job is just an elaborate ruse to justify never growing up. And what I'm going to do now will only convince her further.

We've seen how people have turned the historical Vlad into a pulp villain, and we've even visited his new incarnation as a former carnival attraction. But unless you're a folklorist or some kind of amusement park junkie, you've probably learned most of what you know about vampires from the movies. So how has Hollywood portrayed vampires over the years? What have moviemakers done to the image of the undead? There's only one way to find out. I am about to run a pop culture gauntlet . . . Well maybe "run" is not the right word for it since I plan to spend the next two days sitting on my ass watching every schlocky vamp movie I can.

I won't lie to you: I'm scared of what I might find. The most disappointing aspect of my long years chasing the vampire myth is all the terrible films I've seen. I still remember watching a 1994 black-and-white art house flick called *Nadja* that weakened me like a really bad bout of intestinal flu. I remember nearly passing out during Andy Warhol's *Dracula*, hovering at the edge of sleep, kept awake only by a cramped seat, the Jujyfruits lodged in my molars, and the fact that my feet had become epoxied to the floor with artificial popcorn butter.

Still, if these things are often horrid, they must be tested moneymakers. The Internet Movie Database (IMDB) lists more than three hundred entries with "vampire" in the title, and a keyword search turns up more than three thousand hits. *Interview with the Vampire* appeared in 1994 and grossed more than $221 million in theaters worldwide. Bloodsuckers make for successful movies. I'm going to see what they're all about. I'm going to see as many of these flicks as I can get my hands on—the good, the bad, and the ugly. Eventually, I hope my mind will snap and something will become clear to me.

It's a late Friday afternoon when I start the marathon. I pop in *Kindred: the Embraced*, a TV series by Aaron Spelling about warring clans of vampires who live in San Francisco and dress really sexy and talk and act like they live in some kind of *Melrose Place* of the undead. I have all eight episodes that were produced before the plug was pulled on the series. Watching it feels like finding one of those rare stamps printed upside down or stumbling over a photo of John Denver flipping the bird. It's fascinating because you sense that it shouldn't exist.

As night falls outside, I hunker down on the couch with only the flickering TV for illumination. Pungo, my black-and-white, morbidly obese cat squats contentedly on my ottoman, and my nervous hound Daisy curls up into an impossibly tight tortellini of dog nearby.

You can tell *Kindred* is a Spelling project because everyone is ridiculously pretty. The vampires are pretty and their victims are pretty and the cops chasing them are pretty, and even the random people on the street look like models. And oddly, it's not filled with bad vampire movie clichés. It's actually riddled with terrible cop show clichés.

It starts with two detectives running up the stairs to go to some mysterious meeting and talking in really stilted cop jargon about the "boss of bosses," who could have a cop's badge "shoved up your butt sideways" if he "called in favors" from his "friends downtown." Whoever wrote this was never a cop, didn't know any cops, and was probably absent the day that Officer Friendly came to school. But he or she definitely watched *Lethal Weapon* 135 times.

One of the detectives is C. Thomas Howell, the kid who got stalked by Rutger Hauer in *The Hitcher* and almost single-handedly brought back the minstrel show in *Soul Man*, playing a white guy pretending to be a black guy to get into college. He has some kind of nasally Bronx/Brooklyn/Dick Tracy villain cop accent that comes in and out like reception on a cheap radio.

"I thought he was so hot when I was twelve," my wife Anne told me before she left.

I watch four episodes until it's after midnight. Then I pass out. Pungo wakes me up at 5:00 a.m. yowling to be fed, and he stands on my head and starts biting my nose if I try to ignore him. Sometimes I'll get out of bed to fake like I'm going for the door, and when he darts out I close it so he can't come back. But by then I'm usually awake enough to give him what he wants, and I'm also afraid he'll take revenge by crapping on the floor just outside the door. I take my shower and accidentally squirt a hunk of shampoo directly into my left eye—it sears my cornea, and somehow this does not make watching the rest of *Kindred* any worse. I sit down on the couch with my coffee, and the plot thickens and thickens until it becomes a two-day-old chunk of oatmeal that requires power tools to handle. By the end, one guy is dead, a couple of people have turned into vampires, and the head vampire has confessed to his human girlfriend that he's a monster. Then, for her own protection, he uses his vampire voodoo to make her forget—exactly like the ending of *Superman II*. I'm feeling a lot of hate for the people who made this.

It's almost noon Saturday when I load *Dracula 3000*, a straight-to-video rip-off of the *Alien* movies—right down to the name of the spaceship, *Mother III*, and a tagline: "In Space, the Sun Never Rises." The first scene is the video log of the captain trying to cause his ship to self-destruct, and it counts down to blow up with a soft, pleasant female voice as he desperately fiddles with the controls. Why are all sci-fi self-destruct sequences counted down by a soft, pleasant female voice? It makes it sound like having your ship blow up is something that happens in a Summer's Eve commercial.

How bad is the movie? Coolio is the best actor in it.

As I watch it I realize something. Wasn't *Alien* a rip-off of *Dracula*? A good, inspired rip-off, mind you. But *Alien* is about a group of people who come in contact with a foreign culture—like Harker going to Transylvania—and come back contaminated with a monster that uses them to reproduce. And in the end, Mina Harker and Sigourney Weaver both play the same kind of liberated female badasses who help save the day. Mina, of course, learns train schedules and typewriters and other kinds of modern technology, whereas Signourney straps herself into a giant robotic exoskeleton equipped with flame-thrower arms and calls the creature a *bitch*. So there are differences, but still. The *Alien* movies take the best, creepiest parts of the *Dracula* story and update them for a sci-fi world. So taking that and turning it back into *Dracula* is not only deeply stupid, it advertises how unnecessary it is. But it does have a scantily clad ex-*Baywatch* actress. It doesn't matter which one.

At the end, I'm exhausted and Daisy is whimpering in a corner, confused because it's dark in the morning, and her whole schedule is screwed up. But I pop in *Dracula III: Legacy*, starring Jason Scott Lee as a priest who hunts vampires. This one has Rutger Hauer as Dracula, and I'm a sucker for all of Rutger's post–*Blade Runner* films. In dozens of movies and shows since the 1982 flick that made him famous, Hauer is all paunchy and squat, and the wardrobe folks wrapped him in dark clothes so he looked like a woodstove. But he was always trying to find work, dammit. He might be the Hitcher or Dracula or someday he could even play the lead character in the *Fred Rogers Story*, but he'll still be wisecracking, evil, doomed Rutger. He'll open your shopping mall or appear at your kid's bar mitzvah, and if you ask him, he'll put a nail through his hand like Jesus and let a dove fly away in the rain while talking some weird, pretentious bullshit about ships on fire off the shoulders of Orion. He's like the Ed McMahon of B-movies. He'll do whatever you tell him to.

By the time it ends, coffee cups and plates have somehow gathered on every surface in the kitchen and living room in that baffling way they do when my wife leaves me alone for the weekend. It's not that I don't pick up after myself or that I expect her to wait on me. It's just that my wife makes me more sensitive to disorder and squalor and filth than I'd be on my own. I'm like a lot of guys. And when Anne leaves, and the shades are drawn with the movies playing one right after the other, I don't notice the mess until I find myself sitting in heaps of it half-naked and using a picked chicken bone to scratch my shoulder blades.

I pop in *Bram Stoker's Dracula*, the film by Francis Ford Coppola. This movie is subtly bad. Watching it is like finding a piece of crap on your shoe an hour into a road trip. First there's this slightly off smell that you can't find, but you can't ignore it no matter how hard you try. You drive for a while and then stop, drive for a while and then stop, getting more and more convinced that something is very wrong. And by the time you discover the problem, it's too late.

Dracula starts out with great opening credits and wonderful special effects. Then comes the first scene with Gary Oldman promising to come back from his own death, and something about his girly locks and the blood spurting from the crosses strikes you as too much. But you're hooked by then. So you don't even notice that Winona's English accent wouldn't pass muster at a high school production of *Oliver.* And Keanu's known for emotionless acting, but he reaches new depths here. His eyes are just blank. He looks like a golden retriever who's just been hit on the nose with a rolled-up newspaper.

The movie keeps alternating wonderful special effects and lush scenes with truly horrible examples of acting and crappy, high-school-theater accents, and you thrill and wince, thrill and wince, like the worst S&M game ever, and eventually Keanu's hair turns gray because of living with the vampires for a month, only the gray hair doesn't even look real, and you realize Coppola must have run out of money halfway through, and you'd better get off this boat before it goes under. Plus Winona has a really stupid hat. I'm sure people back then wore them all the time, but this one seems particularly egregious.

And at the end, Dracula changes to a human and heavenly light bathes everything, and he says, "Give me peace," and when Winona stakes him, all is forgiven. Because we no longer have movies where the bad guys are just bad guys. Now every villain has to have a back-story and a childhood trauma and a need for redemption, like some washed-up heavy-metal rocker talking about his nightmare descent into booze and pills on a *Behind the Music* show.

Next I watch a hot-chick-vampire movie called *Blood Angels.* Hey, I'm not made of stone, here. By now I'm all alone in a dark and creaky house in a rural area, and my land happens to be sitting right on a (I'm not kidding) Civil War battlefield. Plus, I've been watching vampire films all day. How do I sleep that night? Like I've been chloroformed. Because none of these movies—not one—is scary. I'm depressed and I smell bad. But I'm not scared.

I start watching *Blade* early on Sunday morning. For any of you who have just been fished out of a block of ice along with a woolly mammoth and some primitive tools, *Blade* is a stylish action movie starring Wesley Snipes as a vampire hunter who uses guns and a wicked sword to mow through an army of the undead that mostly hang out in stylish nightclubs. Why are vampires always club kids? If I ever get sucked into the Living Darkness, I'll go night fishing or form a bowling league that plays at a twenty-four-hour place. I'll take a midnight-to-five shift as a security guard. Anything to get out of this whole vampire-club-kid rut. Do you really want eternal life wearing shiny, flimsy shirts in psychedelic patterns with a giant pacifier around your neck and listening to nothing but Oakenfold? I'd prefer the gentle embrace of the grave.

Donal Logue plays the loudmouthed Irish American vampire in this movie. This is a subtly similar role to the loudmouthed Irish American dad he plays in *Grounded for Life* or the loudmouthed Irish American militia fighter he played in *The Patriot*. He recently appeared in a movie based on the comic book *Ghost Rider*. I didn't see it, but I bet Ghost Rider wanders into a bar in South Boston, talks shit about the Bruins, and then a fight breaks out.

Blade features lots of blood splattering and shells rattling to the ground along with body parts. And when Wesley Snipes kills the head vampire, he says, "Some muthafuckas are always trying to ice-skate uphill." Which is such a cool line, I want to have a needlepoint of it that I can hang right next to my Samuel L. Jackson Bible quote from *Pulp Fiction*.

After *Blade* wows me with its huge budget and dazzling special effects, I'm ready to see a movie that looks like it was filmed in a single apartment complex with props that came entirely from Toys "R" Us. And that movie is *Vampiyaz*. It is filmed in one or two buildings, and there's a lot of tarp and paint cans lying around, so you figure they came in while people were making renovations. And when someone shoots an arrow, there's a half-second of footage from the arrow's point of view as it heads toward the wall, but you can tell that it's just someone running with an arrow and a camera, which anyone's mom will tell you is dangerous and won't look good on film.

This reminds me of the kind of movie my buddy Jason and I shot in his backyard when we were twelve, only ours had aliens, lasers, and a guy who melted to nothing. Well, actually that was just Jason's kid brother clutching his stomach followed by twenty seconds of jumpy footage of a lump of Play-Doh on the ground.

Next is *Vampires: Out for Blood*, which stars Kevin Dillon as exactly the same sort of tough, edgy cop that C. Thomas Howell tried to play. There's nothing to say about this movie other than that Kevin Dillon makes you realize that it's possible to look like a good-looking person without being good-looking yourself.

Matt Dillon is a handsome man. Kevin Dillon looks like Matt Dillon. Therefore Kevin Dillon should be good-looking. But he's not good-looking. He actually looks like someone tried to paint Matt blindfolded.

Anne comes home in time to watch *Vampires: The Turning*, which is a martial arts vampire movie.

"You could make anything into a vampire film," says my wife. "You could make *Driving Miss Daisy* into a vampire film."

"You could make *Mary Poppins* into a vampire film," she says while the movie starts. And she breaks into a cockney accent like Dick Van Dyke:

"It's a jolly holiday with vampires!"

I manage a grin, but I'm seriously tired and wrung out. And then comes *Underworld*, a big-budget film with armies of vampires and werewolves at war in a gritty, rainy city with a long, convoluted plot I can't remember because my eyes start glazing over within three minutes. As they kill one another, I find myself idly wondering, "Is this vamp/werewolf gang war something that Giuliani took care of back in the early '90s?" It seems like Rudy would have completely cleaned that up, and probably he'd get a snotty editorial from *New York Magazine* about how the werewolf gangs were part of the city's character, or some such. Anyway, the plot is more complicated than *A Bridge Too Far,* and that involved a real war.

And I don't care about vampire movies anymore. They're formulaic hack jobs full of plastic teeth and designer contact lenses and scripts that could have been written by Mad Libs. I am at the point of desperation when I pop in my last flick, *Vampyr,* a 1932 black-and-white film directed by Carl Dreyer. Dreyer used overexposed film and bad sound recording on purpose to make the film seem hazy and indistinct, I read. That's not promising.

But it's good. It's really good.

Opening a year after Universal's *Dracula,* with technology that predates the personal computer by decades, the movie features some of the creepiest, most unique shots I've seen. The director uses shadows that seem to detach themselves and characters who look ominous and terrifying. There is even a scene filmed from the point of view as if you are lying in a coffin with a little window in it. The gravedigger's face looms over as he screws the lid on tight, and one of the other characters puts a little candle on the windowpane above. Watching it, I get a crawly feeling between my shoulder blades that I've been missing for years, since I first saw the movie *Halloween.*

I realize something. Of all the vampire movies I've seen, not just this weekend, but throughout my life, the best were the four classic vampire films made in the 1920s and '30s—*Vampyr,* Universal's Spanish-language version of *Dracula,* the company's more famous English-language version with Bela Lugosi, and F. W. Murnau's *Nosferatu.* It's astounding these other more modern flicks suck compared to films produced seventy to eighty years ago. I have to study them.

Universal's *Dracula* starring Bela Lugosi was hugely successful when it opened. The *New York Times* film review notes that audiences got so tensed up that when Van Helsing turned away the vampire with a cross, many broke out into applause. It became Universal's biggest earner of 1931, doing so well that the company green-lighted other horror pictures, like *Frankenstein*, which opened later that year. In fact, some claim that this *Dracula* practically launched the horror film industry.

But it had weaknesses. Bela Lugosi himself gives a brilliant, eerie performance, but the direction is uninspired and the other actors stumble through their lines like they are on horse tranks. Also, the costume-makers wrap the women up in shapeless clothes like they're terrified of boobs.

And the whole time they were filming this movie, the cast and crew for the Spanish language version were using the same sets at the same time; they worked out a schedule with the Anglos so one group would film in the morning and the other in the evening.

The Spanish version is powerful and compelling. The actors have chemistry, and they put real emotion into their lines. The female leads are sexy and they're dressed in the provocative kinda way that will make you watch an entire soap opera on Univision, even if you don't know what's going on. The English-language Renfield gives a now-famous nasally laugh, but it's hard to think he's really insane. In the Spanish-language version, however, the guy really flips out. In short, if you want to watch the undead stalking the lifeless, go for the Anglos. But if you want chemistry, sex, drama, and full-bore crazy-guy-shouting, check out the Spanish *Dracula*.

I also think *Nosferatu*, praised by critics as one of the great horror films of the twentieth century, is better than the famous *Dracula*. Its pacing can be wooden, but its use of light and shadow makes each shot a work of art. And more importantly, the vampire, Count Orlock, scares the snot out of you. With bulging eyes and ratlike teeth, he looks like something truly monstrous. Bela's Count is urbane and witty, but Orlock is something that peers into your window at night. And

Vampyr, too, has wonderful, dreamlike images that seem to come right out of your subconscious. Watching the coffin scene, you get a queasy sense of what it must be like to die.

One factor in the weak-but-famous *Dracula*'s success is the same reason that scores of people swear by Mac computers, vinyl albums, and inner beauty, but we live in a world of PCs, MP3s, and Botox. Marketing beats quality. With wider distribution and clear trademark rights, *Dracula* became the most successful of the horror films of its time.

According to David Skal, whose book *Hollywood Gothic* chronicles the movie, this *"Dracula* achieved its cultural currency because it had a worldwide release by a major studio.

"It was simply seen by more people than any other vampire film," Skal adds, "and Universal later turned Dracula into a franchise of films and merchandise." He calls *Nosferatu* and *Vampyr* "art house oddities . . . not commercial or critical successes." And as for the Spanish film, Universal clearly sidelined it.

"Even the Spanish advertisements mostly used photos of Lugosi," he adds.

The company that produced *Nosferatu* was tiny and dirt-poor. And there was one problem they couldn't get around. They didn't have the rights to Stoker's story. So they changed the names of characters and the setting, turning Dracula into Count Orlock, and killing him off at the end—not with a blade through the chest, but with the rays of the morning sun. Stoker's widow Florence wasn't buying any of it. She sued them, won, and the court ordered all the copies of *Nosferatu* to be burned. Some survived nonetheless. Still, it wasn't until 1929 that it entered the United States.

Some film buffs have noted that *Dracula*'s cinematographer was Karl Freund, an associate of Murnau's. If Universal had somehow managed to bring the two of them into the Dracula project, they could have made an artistic masterpiece that also sold a hell of a lot of tickets. But by that time Murnau was filming a new movie, *Tabu*, in the South Seas.

Dracula hit theaters on Valentine's Day 1931, advertised as "The Strangest Love Story Man Has Ever Known." Murnau's *Tabu* was scheduled to open just a short month later. But days before the premiere, Murnau was driving his car down a highway near Santa Barbara, California, when it went off the road, dropped 30 feet down an embankment, and flipped over, pinning him. Murnau was rushed to a hospital with broken bones and internal injuries. He died the next day.

Dracula was not only a landmark film. It also played a pivotal role in the history of intellectual property law. It started a revolution in how companies own the rights to the movies they produce and how they share those rights with the actors. The importance of an actor's role in the success of a film became evident, because even though Universal had the copyright and even though it was their marketing that put it in theaters across the country, one of the only bright spots in the movie, the thing that made it work, was the performance of Bela himself.

"I think the success of the Universal Dracula is largely a tribute to Bela Lugosi," says Dr. Paul Cantor, literature professor at the University of Virginia. "Lugosi gave depth to the character, and above all gave Dracula the aristocratic sophistication that makes him stand out." He created a well-rounded version of Dracula, unlike the more animalistic portrayals that others had made.

"Lugosi humanized Dracula, and managed at times to convey his suffering," Cantor adds.

Born Bela Blaskó in 1882, he changed his name to Lugosi to commemorate his hometown of Lugos, Hungary. (Now it's part of Romania because the border changed.) And like Murnau, who was a German fighter pilot, Lugosi also fought for the Central Powers during World War I, spending three years in the trenches and eventually becoming a captain. In the chaos that followed, Lugosi fled to Germany as a political refugee, eventually settling in America by the early 1920s. His first roles were romantic leads—in his debut performance he played Romeo in a Hungarian production of *Romeo and Juliet*.

Later, he played the Count on stage, but he almost didn't get the part for the movie. The director wanted to cast Lon Chaney, the silent film actor who had starred in the *Phantom of the Opera*. But Chaney died of lung cancer in 1930.

Lugosi clearly used his romantic chops to make Dracula urbane and sexy. And he would later claim that he got more fan letters from women for *Dracula* than he ever did for his romantic parts.

Universal had the rights to *Dracula*, but it was clear that Lugosi had made the role his own. Lugosi continued to play any part and every part he could get, eventually starring in low-rent horror flicks. But after 1931, whenever millions of theatergoers would think of the Count, they would see Lugosi's face.

Universal Pictures began to use his iconic image as Dracula to sell all kinds of commercial products. His son, Bela G. Lugosi, saw advertisements with his dad's image on them and thought it was unfair. He brought suit against Universal Pictures when still a student at USC Law School.

The case launched his career, and now, forty years later, he is an intellectual property expert at a Los Angeles law firm. I interview him by phone to find out what happened. His photo on the firm website shows a smiling, confident middle-aged man in a suit . . . who looks eerily like something that should be stalking Abbott and Costello. And he has a laid-back, slightly Californian accent that is kinda disconcerting when you have *I vant to soock yur blood* ringing in the back of your mind.

Though his name on the firm site is listed as Bela G. Lugosi, he signs autographs "Bela Lugosi, Jr." for fans.

"The fans seem to like that," he says.

He chuckles as he describes launching a case as a young punk against one of the most powerful companies in the country at the time. At first, he scored a victory in the case, but the court overturned the decision in 1979. It recognized that celebrities have a "Right of Publicity"—that they can protect their names, pictures, and other aspects of their persona as a valuable commodity. But the court ruled that the right can't be passed on after death. In 1985, however, Lugosi helped get the "Celebrities Rights Act" passed in California, which changed all that. In fact, the *Lugosi v. Universal* case and the law that followed it became a key part of the history of an evolving notion of publicity rights.

The courts developed the rights in the mid-1980s when Johnny Carson sued a toilet company for using the phrase "Here's Johnny!" to market their line of portable crappers. The court ruled that even though the company didn't use Carson's whole name, they identified him through the famous catchphrase. In 1988, the rights expanded when Bette Midler sued Ford Motor Company because of an ad featuring a voice that imitated hers.

But it was the 1993 case of *White v. Samsung* that topped it all. The electronics company featured a futuristic episode of *Wheel of Fortune* in which a robot in a dress and a blond wig spun letters from the game show's board. Vanna White successfully argued something we all kinda suspected for years—that there was no real difference between the droid and her. What part of a celebrity's image is protected? A voice, a catchphrase, a costume, or blond hair? Anything. Everything.

In the late 1990s, George Wendt and John Ratzenberger, who played Norm and Cliff on *Cheers*, successfully sued a company to prevent them from installing an animatronic fat guy and mailman named "Hank" and "Bob" in their theme restaurants, even though the company had licensed the *Cheers* brand.

The problem is that with the right of publicity expanding to include anything that evokes a character, actors and copyright holders end up "fighting over the same bundle of intellectual property rights," Judge Alex Kozinski wrote in a dissenting opinion in this case. According to settled law, the copyright holder should have the right to create "derivative works"—say a spin-off of *Seinfeld*. But according to Judge Kozinski, with this growing right of publicity, if the actor playing Newman didn't want a part, he could sue to prevent them from hiring a fat replacement. So could any of the cast.

"A *Seinfeld* spin-off thus ends up in a bizarre world where a skinny Newman sits down to coffee with a svelte George," wrote Kozinski, "a stocky Kramer, a fat Jerry and a lanky blond Elaine. Not only is goodwill associated with the old show lost, the artistic freedom of the screenwriters and producers is severely cramped."

The *White* case had clearly changed the rules, he argued, and it was endangering copyright protection and even the First Amendment. With the *Cheers* case, the court should have set clearer limits.

"Instead," he added, "we again let the right of publicity snuff out creativity."

"We pass up yet another opportunity to root out this weed," he concluded. "Instead, we feed it Miracle-Gro."

"If these iconic images of celebrities can be private property eternally," says Dr. Kembrew McLeod, communication studies professor at the University of Iowa, "it freezes the images." Culture depends on the ability of artists to play around with this stuff, he adds. "Madonna appropriates classic Hollywood images like Monroe or Marlene Dietrich. Prince borrows elements from Jimi Hendrix, and Elvis Costello borrows part of his look from Buddy Holly. But this law allows stars to put a fence around that imagery."

I've known McLeod since high school, and he's been on this crusade for years. A sometime rock critic for *Rolling Stone*, he sold his soul on eBay several years ago in a publicity stunt that got picked up by newspapers and wire services across the country.

More recently, he trademarked the phrase "Freedom of Expression" to protest overzealous copyright law. What's at stake, he's argued, is the idea of the public domain—the writing and art that is out there to be borrowed and played with. This domain is shrinking as ideas and images become harder and harder to use and reuse. Right of publicity laws have appeared in sixteen states. In Indiana and Washington, they survive the death of the star for a century, and in Tennessee they last *forever*, provided that there is continuous commercial use. So as long as they keep cranking out those velvet Elvises, the King's legacy will live forever.

The specter of Universal Pictures exploiting the image of a dead Bela Lugosi without even contacting the family can't be right, can it? I'm not a lawyer, and I don't know what I think about all this. It's clear that if you go too far in one direction, you have a frozen celebrity culture in which Madonna can't dress up like classic stars for her concerts. But if you go too far the other way, you have large companies hawking snack foods with voice impersonators. And if you were kinda creeped out in the late 1990s when companies like Coors and Dirt Devil began using digitally enhanced images of dead celebrities like John Wayne and Fred Astaire to sell their products, imagine what would happen if no one ever had to go through the heirs to obtain permission for stuff like this. Does anyone doubt for a minute we'd soon live in a world where Gandhi sold Omaha Steaks and Jimmy Stewart tortured cops in *Reservoir Dogs*? What's the answer? What's the happy medium?

And also . . . what about Vlad the Impaler himself? Wasn't his name stolen by Bram Stoker, then by an entire media industry and shoehorned into some vampire myth? What if some descendant of the Impaler from a state with this law can prove that he meets the requirements? A Tennessean Dracula descendant who can prove continuous commercial use since 1476? Or what if the law expands someday? Could we see a class action suit by the Daughters of the Dracula Confederacy to get their cut of a multi billion-dollar industry? If Bela's heirs own a piece of the movie image of Dracula, don't Vlad's heirs deserve their own chunk?

"Good point," says McLeod. "That body of law is so confusing that I just don't have a straight answer for you, and I'm not sure a lawyer could either." Part of the problem, he adds, is that the law applies retroactively. He doesn't know how far back it reaches or what states and countries it covers.

"What if you're big in Japan," he asks, "but not your home state of California?"

My head is spinning. How would you get standing to sue in a U.S. court? How would you trace back a five-hundred-year-old lineage? It couldn't happen, right? Ridiculous cases don't pop up in court, do they? Oh, wait. Of course they do. Suing people for stupid reasons is more American than apple pie, cell phone freeway accidents, and testing your paternity on a talk show.

Keanu's emotionless face flashes into my mind. Isn't bland acting Keanu's trademark? Could he claim *that*? Because then . . . he might be able to get a cut out of almost every bad film made today. Every overpaid A-lister sleepwalking through an action blockbuster. Every porn star lying on her back and going through the motions. Every classically trained Shakespearean actor making a kid's film with a talking dog and a soundtrack crapped out by Elton John because the money was just too good to pass up. Keanu's winnings are potentially unlimited. He could take over. I shake the idea off. It's too horrible to contemplate.

I'm reeling from thinking about intellectual property law and in a deep funk about the complete lack of modern, decent vampire films when I watch *Van Helsing*, the 2004 action flick featuring the old Dutch guy who helps fight Dracula and gives everybody transfusions in Stoker's novel. Only in this version, Van Helsing wears an Indiana Jones hat and has wicked ninja stars and a machine-gun-style crossbow. This film brings it all together—the trademark wars between studios and actors and their inability to make a good, scary flick. This movie is not just bad. It actually gives you a unified field theory of Hollywood hackdom.

It was "originally planned in 1994 as a direct sequel to *Dracula* (1992) with Anthony Hopkins to reprise the title role," according to IMDB. "After it was pushed back, many story elements were changed." The result is an orgy of computer-generated effects, characters who are slightly flatter than figures in a video game, and an arsenal of other monsters—Frankenstein, the Wolfman, and Dracula—from Universal's classic monster movies.

The logic of it is clear. Universal stuffed a film with a roster of characters it already owned the rights to, as a way of leveraging its old content for a new generation of action figures, Halloween costumes, video games, and other kinds of junk. The look of the characters is different. Instead of a tuxedoed villain with a widow's peak, *Van Helsing*'s Dracula has an earring and a little ponytail like a guy who plays smooth jazz. Frankenstein and the Wolfman also look different from their famous, old-school styles. I wonder if this might be so that the studio won't have to pay the estates of the famous monster actors—a way of peeling off Universal's property from the rights and interests belonging to someone like Lugosi. I can't be sure about it though. I sent an e-mail to Bela the lawyer asking whether he has an interest in *Van Helsing*, but I have yet to receive a response. However, according to IMDB, the creators did change Van Helsing's first name from "Abraham" to "Gabriel." Why?

"So that the production company can hold certain rights to the character," the site says. Bingo.

The old vampire films had a mystery and a quirkiness that you couldn't pin down. They were *art*. Bela played Dracula as the suave European nobleman. Murnau's Nosferatu was a vermin-like villain hiding in creepy, inky-black shadows. And *Vampyr* was utter, acid-trip weirdness.

But with *Van Helsing*, Universal clearly wanted to create the next generation of rides at its theme park. It wanted to repackage its hoary monsters and ring them up at the cash register one more time. It wanted to *move product*. My question is why did it stop there? Why only throw every one of its classic monster villains into this crap-blender of a film? After all, Universal also produced *Erin Brockovich*, *The Breakfast Club*, and *Child's Play 2* . . . Why not feature Chucky as one of Dracula's minions and have him staked by a wise-cracking, big-hootered paralegal with a little help from Molly Ringwald? I'd want to see that. I'd want to see the Anthony Michael Hall action figure with swivel-arm battle grip and a tiny plastic bag of doobage hidden in his pants.

Then again, maybe I shouldn't be sarcastic. Maybe they're just saving something for the sequel. The commoditization of monster imagery makes movies like *Van Helsing* inevitable. They will pop up again and again, like, well . . . the undead. Because though Dracula has always been a figure of evil, it's *Van Helsing* that truly has no soul.

But I'm not going to lose hope about it. There are plenty of people who love to play with vampire imagery—to do deeply strange and wonderful things with it. And like the golden age of Hollywood cheesiness, what they lack in special effects, they make up for in raw enthusiasm. One group of these people are called LARPers. We will journey to a Louisville, Kentucky, hotel, hole up with them for a weekend, and try to get a little of their magic.

Games

All fanged up and ready to LARP.

"6'10"/One eye/Wears patch"
"Reeks of pot"

'm ringside at a heresy trial. A jumble of priests and cardinals in black and scarlet robes—a fashion show of ribbons, tassels, and Roman collars—clusters around a table. Behind them, dozens of spectators squeeze in tight, packed to the walls with barely enough space to move. Everyone is wearing weird, clunky Gothic crosses—I'm the only person who doesn't have one, and I feel a little out of place. I'm straining to hear the defendant, a quiet man with steel-rim glasses and a slightly round face, tell the throng that he's been hearing the voice of Longinus. Longinus, for those of you who've blocked out memories of Catholic school and the History Channel, was the Roman centurion who pierced the side of Jesus with a lance at the Crucifixion, which caused water and blood to flow from the wound. He then converted to Christianity and even became a martyr when some official got steamed at him and ordered his teeth and his tongue to be ripped out. Longinus, the legend goes, was still able to preach his faith after the horrific assault, astounding everyone around him. I think a better miracle would have been to grow new teeth, but that's just me. Anyway, the people in this room think of Longinus as some kind of founder, so they're taking the defendant's claim seriously. Seriously enough to get him in real trouble.

The guy on trial—I can't catch a name—claims he doesn't need to listen to the priests, bishops, or cardinals because Longinus made him a cardinal directly. He has two people sitting with him who appear to be his advocates or possibly codefendants. One of them could be a brother. They all look nervous.

The panel of clergy shift their weight and ask their questions, trying to get the guy to apologize—to acknowledge their power. Some look thoughtful, others bored, and the head judge, a man with an impressive robe, a shaved head, and wicked dark circles under his eyes, gives the defendant a piercing stare. The main judge's head has some smudge of red stuff on it, an Ash Wednesday mark of lipstick or blood. As he interrogates the poor guy, the crowd is grumbling, itching for something very bad to happen. I can sense they will soon be satisfied. The defendant keeps telling the panel they have no authority to judge him. He has direct orders from Longinus himself, and he won't budge. He goes on ranting about how he's a cardinal, insulting the counsel and telling them to go pound sand. The judges get angrier and angrier.

Finally, one of them—a pale, thin young fellow with red hair and dark eyes—hisses at the defendant and makes a strange gesture with his hand. Almost a magician's flourish. Jon Herrmann, my handler and guide, moves forward and talks to the man, then talks to the defendant, and they all agree that something has happened. What the hell has happened? The defendant supposedly can't talk anymore, and so he gets up and tries to just bolt out of the room. And that is a mistake because the entire crowd surges and attacks him as one. They clobber him with their fists and with weapons—they tear at him and punch him, and someone even fires a crossbow bolt in his direction. The melee is so confused that for a long while no one can figure out who hit him first or whether he's dead.

One thing is clear. He's definitely not going anywhere on his own steam. Soon we're in the hallway of the hotel with his body wrapped up in a sheet. A couple of people from the trial are talking with Herrmann, trying to carry him out of there without anyone seeing. The place is mobbed, and they don't want anyone to know. Suddenly this seems less like the punishment of a convict and more like an assassination. I stand by, not saying a word.

Okay, the guy isn't actually dead. In fact, they're not even really carrying him. They're miming the whole thing and discussing it with Jon Herrmann, who is a storyteller (a sort of referee who decides what you can and can't do), and the whole thing is a really, really strange game. Welcome to Eclipse 2006, the regional gathering of the Camarilla, or Cam, the official fan club for a series of live action role-playing games about vampires, werewolves, and all kinds of other monsters. This weekend, four hundred members are gathered in the Executive West Hotel in Louisville, Kentucky, to play the things that hide under your bed at night.

Herrmann is the East Central Regional storyteller with the Cam. He attends events like this one, where he gives people tips, makes on-the-spot judgments about which crossbow bolts hit and which miss, and decides whether the judge at the heresy trial was successful when he launched that spell against the defendant—a spell that makes its victim spout gibberish whenever he tries to talk. And the trial itself was held by a council of the Lancea Sanctum, a religious organization of vampires founded by the same Longinus who was whispering in the poor sucker's ear. Vampires in this game aren't terrified of crosses, which is why the Lancea are decked out in a whole Madonna video's worth of religious knickknacks.

The name Lancea Sanctum, or *Holy Lance*, refers to Longinus's spear. According to legend, Longinus's famous lance became the so-called Spear of Destiny, an object of power and awe every bit as groovy as the lost Ark of the Covenant or the Holy Grail. Whoever held it would have the power to conquer the world. A spear matching the description was reported in a shrine in Jerusalem in the sixth century, and several lances and parts of lances popped up around Europe throughout the Middle Ages. Charlemagne claimed to possess it, and after Hitler seized Austria in 1938, he raided a museum in Vienna to take its version and send it back to Nuremberg. So outside the game world, the story is strange enough.

But according to the Camarilla, the blood of Christ trickled down the spear and onto Longinus himself, and he was blessed with immortality by its power, but cursed by God for not believing in

Jesus' divinity. Longinus, Roman centurion, ancient saint, early martyr, and victim of the worst root canal ever, became a vampire. And
this group Longinus created, the Lancea, now has the job of showing
the terrible power of God and the horror that awaits those who cross
His Holy Bigness.

"I am God's holy monster, the drinker of mankind," Longinus
said—at least according to one of the rule books for this game, Vampire: The Requiem. "I am not some godless beast who stalks beneath
the dark grandeur of sanctity. I am the grandeur. I am sanctified."

The vampires are damned, to be sure, but they follow God's
laws nonetheless. Kinda like Yul Brynner doing the antismoking ad
toward the end of his life while half-eaten up by cancer, the vampires
of Lancea believe that they can scare people and other monsters
onto the right path and maybe ultimately get their souls back.

When you play Requiem, you can choose to join a covenant
like the Lancea. A covenant is a kind of vamp Masonic order, complete with ranks, privileges, secrets, and funny garb. There are the
Invictus, who see themselves as the royalty of vampire society and
want to dominate the rest of the world. The Circle of the Crone
believe in a mystical, pagan cosmos, and they and the Lancea go after
each other like nuns and Wiccans thrown into a burlap bag. And the
Ordo Dracul actually believe that they descended from Vlad Ţepeş
himself. A covenant of vampires is like a political party or a religion.
Some people actually pretend to join one covenant only to spy for
another.

"Some players are good at deep-cover, gathering information
and not exposing their identities at all," says Herrmann. "Others are a
little obvious and can be discovered and punished—cast out, sometimes killed. I've seen very good players go for years with an infiltra-
tion . . . I've seen bad ones discovered their first game."

In a tabletop role-playing game like Dungeons & Dragons, the
players sit around in someone's mom's basement with a bag of

Frito's and a six-pack of Mr. Pibb and pretend to be elves, wizards, and knights for one or six or fifteen hours. They talk about their actions and their plans—they draw maps and charts and roll dice—but they don't leave the room until it really begins to smell like feet. In a live-action role-playing game, or LARP, like the one played by the Camarilla, everybody dresses up like their character and they act out what their character does. The players use a complicated system of signals and hand gestures to tell other folks what they're doing as they wander the halls—a vampire who is using some kind of special seeing or hearing ability might point to his eye or his ear with his left index finger. While I follow Herrmann, I hold up my hand with my first two fingers crossed—the symbol for being out of the game, as well as the universal symbol for "I'm lying to you about not stealing your Pop-Tarts" on every schoolyard in America. A player might also cross a hand over his chest to indicate that he's invisible or make an *L* with her fingers to indicate that she's speaking a different language.

Just five miles from Churchill Downs, where the Kentucky Derby will be held in a couple weeks, and tucked behind the massive facilities of the Exposition Center and the roller coasters of Six Flags, the hotel here is the perfect place for creeping around like an evil creature of the night. Its walls and low ceilings are made of dark wood and the lights are dim. It has a rustic, western look like a Ponderosa-style theme park. A glass case in front is dominated by pictures of country music stars like Merle Haggard, but a few pop stars like the Beach Boys are thrown in for good measure. And one of the main hallways that leads to the back of the building is lined with portraits of famous Kentucky cattlemen—a sort of gallery of local founding fathers—and the politicians and breeders from centuries of state history. And they're creepy. Each one stares out at you as you walk down the hall, all of them ancient white guys in old-timey clothes. The most terrifying, an eighteenth-century landowner named Benjamin Tomkins the Elder, is listed as the breed founder of Hereford cattle. He's dressed in formal garb with some kind of felt top hat that makes him look like he spends his off-hours snatching urchins from their bedrooms and writing crazed letters to the police.

The Camarilla, either pronounced *Cam-a-RILL-a*, like some kind of Victorian-era whore, or *Cam-a-REE-ya*, like a special combo plate at Chi Chi's, is the club that plays these games. The games are produced by a company called White Wolf Publishing, based in Stone Mountain, Georgia. Since 1991, White Wolf has been one of the most successful role-playing companies in the world, distributing tabletop and live-action games and spin-off merchandise for vampire, werewolf, wizard, and other kinds of role-playing. The people pretending to be bloodsuckers are engaged in Requiem. But if you don't want to be a vampire, you could play Werewolf: The Forsaken, Mage: The Awakening (in which you can play a wizard), or Changeling: The Dreaming (in which you pretend to be some kind of fairy). There are even games in which you just play an ordinary human caught in this world of high weirdness.

Each of the different games gets a big block of time for every day of the long weekend. And during the Vampire game, each of the different covenants has activities in the different conference rooms. I missed the Lancea mass yesterday, but caught the heresy trial. And after we leave, the Ordo Dracul is scheduled to use the room for their shindig followed by the Carthians at 11:00 p.m. Just down the hall, Invictus is having their "Oaths" meeting followed by a "Trust" meeting—I have no idea what that is, but I don't think it involves that exercise in which one person closes his eyes and falls backward and the other guy has to catch him.

When they're not in their little meetings behind closed conference room doors holding counsel and having heresy trials, the covenants hang out in the hallways and great rooms of the hotel, eyeing one another from a distance like Crips and Bloods gathered together at some kind of GangstaCon '06. The different covenants are all vying for power in the game world, and part of the fun of playing is to hang out with your group and just enjoy your little place in the undead ecosystem.

In addition to a covenant, I have a clan—Nosferatu, the deformed, creepy guys with teeth like Bugs Bunny and ears like Spock. Covenants are like your club or your job. But your clan is like your family. From the moment you draw that drop of vampire blood into your own veins, you are reborn into a clan and you stay there for, uh, life. There are also the Daeva, who are almost the exact opposite of Nosferatus—they are those slinky, sexy vampires that Anne Rice wrote about before she found Jesus. The Ventrue have natural leadership abilities and a desire to run things. And Gangrel are bestial and hang out in the wilderness, turning into bats or wolves. The different clans are all the different literary and movie vampires out there. Dracula, Lestat, and the Lost Boys are all crammed together in the same game. The genius of Vampire: The Requiem is that it found a way for everybody to dress up and play together as they like. You can come as Count Orlock and I can show up as Blacula, and we'll both use the same rules. Looking at a group of people gathered together for one of these conferences is like watching Hollywood cough up one hundred years of movie history. There are some truly weird and godawful costumes—it's not all pretty—but it's fascinating to watch.

But it's bigger than that. The Camarilla is an organization of thousands of people across fourteen countries on every continent except Africa and Antarctica, and they act out a thousand plots in a kerjillion places. The werewolves, vamps, and other creatures hardly ever play at the same time, but they share the same game world. And the vast network of storytellers coordinate with one another through meetings, e-mails, and websites to make sure that if some group of wizards tries to turn the Statue of Liberty's torch into a soft-serve ice-cream cone—players actually tried this, according to storyteller Jessi Hixon—that the ice-cream cone exists in everyone else's world. The Cam is a club, a game, and an ongoing story with an army of editors, revising and rewriting it in conferences, living rooms, and a friend's mom's basement near you.

"In the Cam, most adversaries are other player characters, and smart players all over the world will challenge your plans for your character," says Herrmann. "That creates far better adversaries, to my mind."

Herrmann is patrolling the rooms where the vampires roam, and he's letting me tag along to watch him do his storytelling work. But Herrmann doesn't move very far. As a matter of fact, he can't move two steps without groups of people closing in on him, asking him to referee. One guy dressed in a floppy hat and shlumpy kind of suit like he's some kind of Philip Marlowe keeps coming up to us, asking about this research project he's working on—he's found a massive five-pointed star and he wants to figure out what it means.

People are constantly mobbing him, but Herrmann takes it in stride. Ruling on this and that, chatting with other storytellers, and greeting friends, he's friendly and talkative. He's so energetic that one of his friends once compared him to a Yorkshire terrier. And looking at him you can kind of see the resemblance. As he talks about rules and policy and rolls, he gets excited and subtly leans forward like he's about to start springing into the air.

The games take place in a conspiracy theory world where secret cabals run cities and every story has another story behind it. But what's strange, even creepy, is that the game takes place roughly in real time and in the real place where we are. The vampires are all pretending that they have come to a gathering in a hotel in Louisville just like the people playing them. The werewolves pretend to be in a field nearby. Whenever possible, people make the story close enough to the real time and place that it gets a little unsettling.

We move from room to room, and a white guy passes dressed in some kind of sumo getup with a sign pasted on his front that reads, "Appears Asian." Brian, the head of security, passes us a couple times, making his rounds. A no-nonsense guy with a beard and a shaved head, he's on duty, keeping people in line and checking in with hotel security to make sure that having dozens of people dressed up as monsters running through the hotel won't be a problem for the rest of the guests. The convention started yesterday, and he's had very little sleep. He nods and waves, and we walk past. The games close down around midnight, and people gradually file back to their rooms. But Herrmann and I head for a small chapel built into the hotel. It has high pointed ceilings and colored glass, but the dais has no lectern or cross. Instead, techs have a sound system set up. It seems that after playing vampires and werewolves all day, people like Jon Herrmann need to let off steam with a round of karaoke. Herrmann and two friends do a so-bad-it's-good rendition of "You've Lost That Lovin' Feelin'."

Herrmann is not going to win *American Idol* anytime soon, but watching him up on stage with his friends, I'm struck by how ballsy this guy is. These people have no shame—they run through a strange hotel dressed up like vampires and warlocks with scores of their closest friends, and they're not embarrassed a bit. And I don't know how I expected them to act, but they're not typical role-playing geeks. They seem friendly, outgoing, and comfortable with themselves. And women actually play this game. Couples often meet through this network, and folks get married. That's how Herrmann met his wife, who works with White Wolf.

"Live-action is far more social than tabletop," Herrmann says. "We spend most of our time talking, interacting socially, rather than fighting monsters and gaining treasure."

"But you have to keep in mind there are many kinds of social,"

Hixon adds. "Some women are there to meet other girls who game, some are there to meet men, and some are there just to meet people." She tells the story of a woman whom she knew whose only son had been involved in the Cam before he died. The woman became more involved in the Camarilla to meet his friends.

"She ended up joining the Cam," Hixon says. "She's served as an officer and generally being there for anyone who needed her with a warm smile, a hug, and if you were close enough to get there for it, dinner on the table."

Herrmann and Hixon also say that costumes play a big part of it.

"Girls like to have an excuse to look hot just as much as guys like to see the results," says Hixon. "In real life, you don't necessarily get a chance to dress up very often. Every little girl at some point wanted that Renaissance Cinderella dress."

Guys like to play war. Girls like to play dress-up. That may be oversimplified and a little bit sexist, but it's true. And the Cam brought both games together so people can meet at designated hotels and have a blast.

There are four things I'll be embarrassed about for the rest of my life, and here are three of them: losing an arm-wrestling contest to a girl when I was a kid, being sexually harassed by a female boss in my early twenties and not doing anything about it, and the time just after 9/11 when I actually gave $20 to the Republican party. But the fourth stings more than the rest. When I tell you that these people I've met at the conference aren't your typical role-playing geeks, I know what I'm talking about.

I've played role-playing games before.

As recently as last year.

In 1982, I was a military brat living in Portland, Maine. I was a sixth-grader at St. Joseph's Catholic school who was beaten up practically every Tuesday at gym class. At the annual roller-skating party, there was only one girl who said she would actually skate with me, and she kept putting it off until the thing was over, so that may have been an elaborate joke. Naturally, I turned to Middle Earth. I began to play Advanced Dungeons & Dragons with Philip, Steve, and Tom, three friends of mine. I believe I was a Neutral Good Thief, but my memory is hazy. I do know that within the next five years, I acquired games with names like Top Secret, Boot Hill, and Paranoia. I played them with friends on my street after we moved to Virginia Beach. My buddy Sean got the game Gamma World, in which you play mutants wandering around a post-apocalyptic wasteland, and my other buddy Marc got Twilight 2000, in which you play soldiers . . . wandering around a post-apocalyptic wasteland (it *was* the Reagan era). Most of the games took three hours just to prepare, so that by the time we were ready, we'd all have to go home for dinner. I played them almost continuously until I was a teenager, except for a short period in seventh grade when I got a *D* in English, and my dad confiscated them until I got *A*s and *B*s again.

In high school and college I hardly ever played at all—I was too busy. But that's like saying, "I hardly ever wrote erotic *Star Trek* fan fiction under the pseudonym KingKlingon" or "I hardly ever collected porcelain clown figurines."

My sad story continues around 1999, when I was in my late twenties and just married. I was hanging out with Kennan at a flea market in New York City. Kennan has always been a collector of old furniture, travel trunks, books, and even puppets—his place is filled with weird and crazy knickknacks. We were in a huge flea market on the lower west side near the piers—it was a football-field-sized space covered with dozens of tables and all kinds of arty, old-fashioned crap. Racks of clothes, pictures, and furniture were thrown all over the place.

The book was just sitting by itself on a box, uncatalogued, and I almost walked past it. But when it caught my eye, I instantly knew what it was: a near-mint condition 1979 *Dungeon Master's Guide*. It wasn't the very first printing—that one had a giant red demon statue on its cover that had been scaring the snot out of fundamentalists down in Virginia Beach for decades. But it was the first edition rules, written by Gary Gygax—the master, the Obi-Wan of D&D himself.

"Is Dungeon Mastering an art or a science? An interesting question!" the foreword began. "If you consider the pure creative aspect . . . that goes into preparing and running a unique campaign . . . then Dungeon Mastering may indeed be thought of as an art. If you consider . . . the attention to detail and the continuing search for new ideas and approaches, then Dungeon Mastering is perhaps more like a science. . . .

"Esoteric questions aside," it concluded, "one thing is for certain—Dungeon Mastering is, above all, a labor of love. . . ."

That was untrue, of course. It's none of those. It's an addiction. Looking down at that book in the vast flea market was like reaching into a coat pocket and discovering the single unfiltered Camel I'd forgotten to throw out when I quit smoking years ago.

"You have to get it," Kennan said, coming up behind me and spotting the thing, too. And I did—I'd made the decision to buy it almost immediately. Of course, I wouldn't actually play or anything. I mean, I was a twenty-nine-year-old married man. But after I got the *Dungeon Master's Guide*, it just made sense to go out and buy a copy of the *Player's Handbook*. Then came the *Monster Manual*. Then . . . madness.

Soon I was trolling eBay auctions to grab ancient copies of the *Fiend Folio* and hunting through shops with names like The Compleat Strategist and Campaign Headquarters for the *Book of Vile*

Darkness. I sought an original version of the *Deities and Demigods*, the one with the Cuthulu Mythos section that was cut in later versions after the estate of HP Lovecraft threatened to sue for . . . Okay, okay, I'll stop.

I know that for most of you, what I've just said is gibberish. It's like rattling off the chemicals I use to cook up the batch of crystal meth on the plastic tarp I keep in my storage shed. But some of you know what I'm talking about, and even now, you're thinking about getting a big ol' bag of dice and a couple dozen orc figurines out from that box in the attic. Yes, you are. Don't lie to me.

Anyway, before long Kennan and I gathered six or seven friends—some from high school—to hole up in Kennan's cramped, antique-riddled place on weekends with a pot of coffee, a box of Krispy Kremes, and enough graph paper to start our own architecture school. This would only happen about once a year. We kept the shades drawn and the lights down low. We were very discrete, and my wife and I have always had an understanding about this kind of thing. But for those weekends, I, Paul Bibeau, became a Dungeon Master. I rolled dice. I drew maps of castles and crypts populated with goblins and dragons. We all had long conversations involving Hit Points and Armor Class and other stuff you really don't want to know about.

Role-playing games go back a ways. In the late 1960s and early '70s, Gary Gygax and his partners developed medieval fighting rules for a group of geek war gamers called the Lake Geneva Tactical Studies Association. They eventually modified the rules to admit fantasy creatures, and by 1973, they'd launched a company called Tactical Studies Rules (TSR) to sell the thing. In 1974, TSR started printing its first copies of the rule book, which by then was called Dungeons & Dragons. It took off, and the market exploded in the 1980s. You could go down to your local hobby store and have your pick of a dozen new games in all kinds of settings.

White Wolf came late to the party, launching a live-action game called Vampire: The Masquerade in the 1990s and following it up with Werewolf: The Apocalypse and Mage: The Ascension. The creative force behind these games was a young developer named Mark Rein·Hagen from a small Scottish town. The weird dot in his name seems sort of like a buttoned-down accountant's version of the Prince symbol.

Soon White Wolf ended Vampire: The Masquerade and launched Vampire: The Requiem. Ditto for the Werewolf and Mage games—each one was replaced with a new title. According to people at the convention, the world of the old games actually ended in a massive apocalyptic war that was role-played out at different conventions around the country.

Which brings us to the present, as I wake up exhausted on Saturday morning after a strange night of game gibberish and funny costumes and role-player's karaoke. I'm up before most of the other players, and I find myself wandering the hotel at around 7:00 a.m. and checking in with security, who are bleary-eyed and barely coherent. The empty hallways and conference rooms look cavernous and only the stray chairs and the odd plastic cup give any indication that people were here the night before. I pass a few straggling role-players out of costume. There's nothing to do. There won't be anything happening for hours. Role-players are night owls—they live on Red Bull and Internet chat rooms and when they crash, they don't wake up early. I check the schedule for what's to come this morning. At 10:00 a.m., the werewolves are going to be converging on two of the main rooms, and the Changling people will be right next door. That will last until 3:00 p.m., when the Mage people will take over. Meanwhile, there will be a jail, where you can have the Camarilla security people lock folks up you don't like for a small gift to their charity, the Shriner's Orthopedic Hospital in Lexington, Kentucky.

A few hours later, I come back to one of the main conference rooms with the Changeling game already in progress. The whole place is blacked out, except for two small strings of white holiday lights that make a trail leading to the front of the room, and a projector that lights up the giant image of some kind of dragon thing on the wall. To one side of the lighted pathway, there are three or four large tables surrounded by people who are hunched over, talking amongst themselves quietly.

"They're up in the mountains," Herrmann tells me, when I ask him about it. They had to leave the confines of the hotel and do some serious climbing. It is dark up here and cold, and they're trying to find shelter. Evidently some dragons in West Virginia have been eating all the magical energy, and the players have to climb up to their lair to stop them. It's tough going, Herrmann says, because they can't teleport through this magic vacuum.

In the next room, the storytelling staff begins to straggle in to set up their game of Werewolf. They discuss the upcoming battle, which is supposed to be some kind of massive blowout that might kill huge numbers of players. The storytellers hang around, some sitting on the counter in front, some standing nearby, talking to one another about the battle and munching from a half-eaten bag of red licorice.

"At Eclipse 2006, the Forsaken will have a dark time ahead of them," the guidebook says. "Difficult decisions will be made—friends and companions will be found and lost, maybe in the unlikeliest of places. . . . Do the Forsaken dare ally with their foes to counter a larger threat?"

The werewolves all have to band together to fight off an army of enemy wolves, known as the Pure. Supposedly there was this ancient grudge between the Pure and the regular werewolves since the regular werewolves bumped off the ancestor of all wolves eons ago in some kind of Greek myth meets *The Howling* kinda deal. Now, they're all going to mix it up in a wolf brawl.

The players break into groups to talk about their strategy, and one guy starts setting up a rough layout of the battle in the middle of the room with an array of little plastic cups.

"I'm probably going to die," I hear someone say.

"I'm definitely going to die."

In fact, a lot of people are wandering around, talking about how they're going to die. And they don't even seem to mind it too much, either. Supposedly, someone explains to me, Saturday is death day for these conventions. As you're settling in on Thursday, they scare the hell out of you for what's going to happen Friday. Then Friday comes and you're shocked that you get to live, so on Saturday you relax. Then they nail you. Any betrayal, any assassination, any wolf getting trapped and whacked like a furry Sonny Corleone at the tollbooth will happen on Saturday.

As the werewolves mill about, I notice one with a note on his costume: "6'10" One eye/Wears patch." Another wears a note that reads, "Reeks of pot."

A hot redhead in a leather jacket passes by with a six-pointed star on her forehead, and there's someone in a cowl with a pattern that I can only describe as albino leopard. Another guy is wearing a T-shirt that reads, "I used to have super human powers but my therapists took them away."

But other than that, most of the players in this game seem less costumed out than the folks at last night's game. These might just be how their characters are dressed or they might just relax a bit with this event. And for an apocalypse, not much is happening. People are wandering around, planning this upcoming festival of blood and gore, but if you didn't know what they were doing, you'd think this was some kind of really casual sales convention. Everyone is talking about what's going to happen, but not much happens. The more exciting scenes, I notice, involve more rules and more actions, and they run slower in real time. The people involved are obsessed. But, to outsiders, it looks pretty tame.

I wander the halls. A small group of people pass in bathing suits, and I've been so immersed in this game that for a second I think they're in some kind of aquatic costume—maybe sea wolves. But then I realize that they're probably just a family out from a dip in the pool.

Farther away, in a room near the front entrance, the sounds of shouting startle me. It seems like some game has gone wild, and I almost barge in to get a look. But as I get closer, I see a sign indicating that it's an evangelical church service. A preacher in there is hollering, and he might be talking about fighting demons and magical powers, but it's different.

When I come back, the players crowd into the hall for the big fight, and Jim Fisher, the lead storyteller, stands on a counter and describes how it will unfold. The plan involves snipers, machine gunners, and even an "extraction triage unit." Fisher describes how the werewolves take down a massive enemy wolf named Bitter Fang with a hail of bullets and follow it up by charging the field with a group of armed cars, and I can't figure out whether these people are supposed to be in wolf form or human form or in that hairy-guy-with-the-underbite form from *Teen Wolf*. But either way, the wolfies have got solid tactics and a plan for evacuating their wounded out of the battle zone, and they're able to save almost everyone's life.

At the end, Fisher describes how they've managed to beat the Pure back and win the game. The storytellers give a round of applause as the players are congratulating one another. And then one of the storytellers speaks up and commends Fisher for running the whole show. Everybody claps for him, and he has a proud, humble moment and says nothing. For a bloody shape-shifting slayfest, there's a lot of love in the room.

The rest of the day passes, and soon it's time for the last session of Vampire, and this time I'm not just going to shadow Herrmann. I will actually play in the thing. I'm a little nervous. Herrmann has me paired with Chris Rhodes, who plays Cardinal Marcus Dirae of Boston, the guy with the shaved head who presided over the heresy trial last night.

All vampires have a Humanity rating, basically the residual conscience you still have from your human past that will be gradually worn down by doing the godawful crap you have to do as a vampire. Little by little, over the course of many games, your actions bleed away your Humanity, and you become more brutal and less refined and humane. And if your score ever reaches zero, you become a mindless fiend, fighting and feeding without any purpose beyond the next kill. I imagine it's a little like being Ryan Seacrest.

Rhodes's score is two, which means he would have to actually commit casual serial homicide in order to feel guilt. But in real life, he's a nice guy, and he seems like the type who would suffer pangs of guilt if he cut in front of you in line.

I'm supposed to be Rhodes's henchman. Since he's a powerful vamp (he's been Cardinal for decades and has a pile of other undead church titles—vicar of this and chair of that and first father of the other), he doesn't go anywhere without a swarm of hangers-on flanking him.

I didn't know what to wear, so I've dressed in a black long-sleeved shirt and a black pair of jeans. I was trying for some kind of subdued and classically scary look, but I really just look like a roadie for Johnny Cash. One of the others gives me a clunky cross to hang around my neck. And then I look like a roadie for Creed.

In the halls and conference rooms, Rhodes is constantly stopping to confer with other high-level vampires, and there are probably all kinds of fun, nifty schemes and plans that are unfolding, but they talk low and I'm in back of the crowd. Plus, I'm distracted because after a while my feet are hurting. This is the problem with being a henchman that they never tell you about—your legs and lower back really pain you by the end of a long day spent standing around the main villain. It must be hard being one of those Bond or Batman guys. I bet they use their health plan for a lot of lumbar trusses and Dr. Scholl's inserts. By the end, I almost get bored because nothing obviously cool is happening. And then we head for one of the hotel rooms so three of our party can plunge their faces into burning oil.

We pretend that we have gone to another hotel in the area to stay away from the rest of the vampires—the three people going through this ritual are supposed to get some kind of mystic vision from it, and we want to keep it secret. We act out taping over the fire alarm. There are no bowls, no oil, and (thank God) no fire involved—the three of the crew just stand side by side quietly while Chris narrates how it all goes down.

The three of them each mime holding their imaginary bowls filled with lantern oil. Chris takes a lighter, and one by one, sets them all aflame. Then each vampire plunges his or her face into a bowl. Rhodes describes the sickening sounds and smells of their flesh crisping and peeling off their skulls while the three of them look on impassively. One of them fails to hold still through the process, however, and doesn't get a vision. He collapses before the ritual is complete. And though this is a completely random game thing—they actually drew cards from a deck to see whether they receive one—I can't help looking at the guy like it's somehow his fault. *Chump*, I catch myself thinking. Since it's not just a game, since it's something you act out, you don't have a boundary between your character and who you are.

Then I catch myself thinking something else: I am standing in a hotel room with half a dozen strangers, and we're pretending to be undead religious fanatics burning our fucking faces off. This is *crazy*.

Why do people do this? Why dress up and pretend you're a member of an undead cult if you don't have to? What's the draw?

We wrap the three in towels, and cart them off to the elevator, but we take the towels off before the doors open because you want to limit how fucked up and bizarre you look when ordinary people get into the elevator with you. Everybody quiets down like we've all got a secret, and we make the bare minimum of polite eye contact when two normal, non-gamer guys enter. One of them gives Chris— still in his cardinal outfit—a look, but then they start asking us if we're going out drinking later. They're sort of chuckling to each other. They're tough-looking, friendly, and rednecky, and one of them keeps pressing home the fact that he is going to get absolutely hammered tonight and there's nothing any of us can do about it. The doors open, and we all split. They go off to the hotel bar, and we head back to the conference room.

"Man, I've got to get me one of those," one of the women with us says softly, sarcastically. It takes me a second before I realize she's making fun of *them*. As a geek in high school, college, and beyond, I've spent my whole life watching guys like the two on the elevator get the girl. This is a deeply unsettling turnaround. But not too bad.

Of course, by the end of the evening, I head for the bar myself, though it seems almost empty. Just a few businessmen are there pounding their drinks before last call. And the bartender, a kindly older woman, is telling me the place is haunted.

"Billy swears the cattlemen's eyes follow her," she says, talking about the spooky portraits in the hall. She adds that the TV sometimes just turns on by itself. The guy up on the stage here is belting out a series of bad classic rock songs. The businessmen probably don't know him and don't know one another—this is a hotel bar next to an expo center—and they hoot and clap and call out for one song after another. It is loud and cheery and deeply depressing in the way that only bus depots, airport clubs, and hotel bars can be.

"The Cam has a very special kind of social connection—one that's open to all kinds of people," says Jessi Hixon. People everywhere have a need to be social, she adds, and Cam folks stick together "because of how much we all identify with each other's potentially unmet need to feel accepted and included."

These vampires have a strange hobby. But they really seem to like one another, and they have a lot of fun. There are a million ways to kill a lonely Saturday night. The LARPers have found one of the better ones. And every forlorn businessman in this bar, I realize as the performer is winding down his show, could use a little Cam in his life. It might take some convincing to get the yuppies in the back booth to swap their rumpled suits for plastic fangs and Goth capes. But it would be worth it. I'm not the first person to notice how it's becoming harder and harder to connect to people. If you're like me, you live far away from your extended family and your friends, and you don't spend too much time with your neighbors. We're a busy, distracted nation of subdivisions and strip malls, brushing past one another in the commuter lots and chatting on our cells in the checkout line. Some of us sit next to the same stranger every day on the train while we text the friend from college we haven't seen in years. The Cam helps its members slow down and actually talk. And that gives it a powerful draw.

In the next few chapters, we'll get acquainted with other folks who have wrapped their subculture around the vampire. Some play around with the caped image for their art or for fun. Others actually believe they really need to drink human blood or absorb psychic energy. There are those who know their limits and those who clearly take it too far, and we will meet them all and try to be fair with each.

But as for me, when I get back home, I'm going to pencil in a date to see Kennan, break out the coffee and the graph paper, and let my inner geek run free.

Renfield Country

"I'm not going to make dentures for old people
when I can make fangs for hot chicks."

An airport hotel is the perfect place to do the unspeakable. Bed-and-breakfast inns are too cozy and friendly. Their owners smile and chat and helpfully suggest places to go while even the stuffed animals, the family portraits, and the glass-eyed Victorian dolls seem to follow your every move. If you come downstairs with wax burns and handcuff bruises, the lady at the front desk might not say anything. But she'll notice.

Give me big, anonymous Hiltons and Omnis with their long, blank Overlook hallways and their soundproofing. They thrill my heart in a secret, kinky way, and if you were honest, you'd admit they thrill yours. There are no friendly locals. There is no personal touch, no atmosphere. Just room service options in that thick, slightly sticky

Hanging out with some of the guys from Lugosi's Morphine.

vinyl booklet and blackout curtains and dial-up TV porn and drinks in tiny bottles and your receipt slid under your door to help you check out without talking to another human being. In an airport hotel room, you feel—just for those couple hours between the flight and the conference the next day—like some kind of business-class Caligula. You can do anything you want. That freedom makes an airport hotel ideal for what I'm doing right now.

Stripped to my boxers with CNN blaring and the tiny, individual coffeemaker gurgling a fresh pot, I sit at the artificial wood desk surrounded by complimentary pens and pads of paper and brush black polish onto my fingernails. Made by Manic Panic, the polish is called Claw Colors, and this particular color of claw is Raven. I make a mess of it, but I have plenty of Q-tips and nail polish remover.

On the bed sits a bottle of LA Looks styling gel and a mesh shirt that wraps me up like Right Said Fred in that "I'm Too Sexy" video. Next to them is another T-shirt that fits over it, made by Serious Clothing, a stretchy cotton thing with a skull and crossbones on the front. I also have a small, gray Gothic cross with a leather necklace and a pair of black, shiny, ball-hugging pants made of polyurethane. I find myself scanning the ingredients listed on the nail polish bottle and wondering whether it's made of the same stuff as my pants. They look exactly alike. I grease my hair up and put patches of black makeup on my face just below the eyes, so I look like the Crow's older brother, the one who doesn't get to the gym as often.

As I walk out of my room and head for the elevator, I get a rush of mild terror as I wonder how people are going to react to me. I find myself flashing back to that feeling I got when I was a teenager and my friends and I would trespass onto some abandoned park or construction site to hang out late at night—I was the one who was sure the cops were going to show up any second, put us all in jail, and mark up my permanent record card so that I'd never get into the college of my choice.

But the fear turns to excitement as I near the elevator and people actually sidle away from me. One guy even steps back and waits for the next elevator to come. And as I stumble out into the parking lot and a wedding party comes drifting in, all of them giving me looks and nudging one another, I remember racing through my suburban neighborhood with my friends and Becky, that vixen who always dressed in black. Doing age-inappropriate trick-or-treating that last Halloween I could get away with it and thinking that anything, absolutely anything, could happen tonight.

This is like the first day you come into the office after shaving your head and your supervisor gives you a look as if he's going to Taser you and barricade himself in the break room. I have been searching through Goth clubs and vampire groups to find out why otherwise normal people—friendly, helpful folks many of them, who are perfectly pleasant and intelligent—like to wear scary makeup and act like ghouls. I have gone from Virginia to New York City and talked to people by phone and e-mail from all over. But perhaps the best explanation is this rush I feel walking out of the anonymous hotel. I'm often overly polite and tip waiters far too much and get cut off in traffic and don't even do anything about it, but right now these strangers think I'm someone they shouldn't fuck with.

According to the ancient historian Jordanes, the first Goths did not come from the post-punk music scene in the United Kingdom, but actually appeared much earlier. They were a Germanic people who spilled out of Scandinavia, spreading out over Europe and eventually forming into groups like the Eastern Goths, or Ostrogoths, and the Western Goths, or Visigoths. They launched one of the first major assaults on the Romans in 267 C.E. By 410 C.E., the Visigoth ruler Alaric I sacked Rome itself.

Centuries later, with the Renaissance under way, the term *Gothic* was synonymous in art with everything barbarous and wild and Germanic. And even though people like Alaric had nothing to do with the creepy old cathedrals that dotted Europe, architects started using the word to describe them in a disparaging way. Kind of like when you clip your nails at the dinner table, and your mom says, "Were you raised by wolves?" She knows you weren't. But still . . . Go do that somewhere else, y'know?

So *Gothic* became a term for a style of art and architecture.

First it was used as an insult, but during revivals like the one that happened in the nineteenth century, people picked up the term, and they liked it. And with the Romantic poets starting to write about goblins and monsters, the term transferred over to a style of writing in which authors set their works in spooky old buildings filled with spooky old things. That's how the name of a barbaric hoarde became the word you use when everything in a book is dark, the women wear those fitted, low-cut costumes that could make Kate Moss look like a D-cup, and all the guys are in frilly shirts, but somehow it's okay. And from there it was a short step to Bauhaus, black eyeliner, and all your friends down at Hot Topic—even though the original Goths would have probably been much more into the Sex Pistols and would have handed Bauhaus a serious beat-down.

Goths use vampiric imagery, but they aren't the only ones. Some people actually think of themselves as vampires, often spelling the word "vampyre." And though they may dress like Goths, they don't necessarily think that being a vampire is a subculture at all, but rather a medical or spiritual condition. Vamps claim they can suck energy from others by using psychic powers or by physically drinking their blood, something Goths don't necessarily indulge in. It's confusing. I try to untangle what Goths and vamps mean for each other, and I feel out of my depth. But my simplistic definition of Gothic culture might be close to the original term that Renaissance architects borrowed to insult the creepy buildings.

Goth is everything weird and scary. It seems to come from an alien group of people who dress funny and talk funny and might just want to destroy civilization as I know it. When life is too slow and too boring, and you find yourself being pegged as someone limited, someone small, someone who is only one thing and can't be others, it's a temptation to become, or to pretend you've become, someone threatening. I've searched for this feeling everywhere. So have we all.

I must be the only one driving to the Goth club in a minivan, and it feels, well, *unwholesome.* The whole idea of being a happily married suburban guy with a son and another child on the way is that you spend your days at work or driving to the Costco to pick up vat quantities of Cheer and sample the bacon wrapped scallops at the little food stations. You worry about lawn care, and at night you might open a beer and watch the Jon Stewart rerun at 8:00 p.m., but by the time the new episode comes on at 11:00, you're asleep.

It's late at night, and I'm already tired when I park the van in some lot near Shockoe Slip, the hip part of Richmond, Virginia, down in the area that used to be a tobacco warehouse district. And as I wander the streets trying to find the bar where this club is happening, I realize I parked too far away, and I will have to hike it quite a distance. This isn't fun. I feel like some kind of nasty old guy trying to hang out with the kids.

Before coming, I e-mailed several clubs in the area. I asked them whether Goth and vamp cultures overlap—whether managers and promoters have seen the same kids pop up in their clubs.

"The folks who patronize our club lean more toward the Goth side of the spectrum than any other. I'm sure you'd find a few who have a fascination with vampires, but for the most part they're looking for a spot to dance," one guy replied.

"I don't know how well you can define our clients," said another, "but there are a few who are into the 'vampire' culture, as well as several who subscribe to both new Goth and older Goth cultures."

I wander into Mars Bar, a small, unpretentious joint. With a slogan "All '80s All the Time," this place has a counter out front where a couple of guys are chatting with the waitresses and watching the Mets play the Reds. And on the wall sits the largest collection of 1980s album covers I've ever seen gathered in one place and not soaked in gasoline by a torch-wielding mob.

Roger, a thin, friendly twenty-something guy, is glued to the set. He lived in New York briefly, he explains, and got hooked on the Mets. I'm kind of a Mets fan myself—the Yankees are like gravity, old age, and Madonna. They represent every bad and unstoppable force, and if you want to root for them, you might as well root for the eventual heat death of the universe.

The Mets lose, of course. Cincinnati comes from behind with a two-run single in the ninth for a 6–5 squeaker, and we mutter about how the team from Queens breaks our hearts. Meanwhile, a small trickle of dark-clad kids files in to the booths and the dance floor in back. There are still plenty of patrons in the bar area, but eventually the music begins and the Goth kids start milling around, talking, dancing, and ordering drinks. At no point do they really take over. In fact, for the next couple hours, the regular bar patrons and the club kids kind of mix around with one another like oil and vinegar in a salad shaker, never quite blending.

"Nerds," Roger calls them with good humor and a little malice. I ask him what he does for a living.

"I work at a comic book store."

Obviously, I should make fun of that. Comic book store guys and Goth kids aren't exactly far from each other's habitats in the nerd ecosystem. But I'm kind of a comic book geek myself. Roger and I get into a twenty-minute argument about Frank Miller's *Batman* series, before he uses his skills to tell me something about the style people are wearing here. Twenty years ago, if you were a Goth kid, you dressed in a frilly shirt with a cape. The people I see are decked out in lots of mesh, leather, and plastic. They seem to have a dark, space-age style.

"That's Tim Bradstreet," Roger tells me. He explains that Bradstreet, a comic book artist who illustrated some of the first vampire role-playing games as well as comics like *Batman* and *The Punisher*, had a style that was so unique it caught on. These people are essentially dressed like characters he created.

But as I mill around, chatting up folks, I realize there are no fangs and no mention of donors, the hunger, or any of the other stuff I'd expected. If there are vampires here, they're keeping it quiet. I'll have to continue my search for these "real" creatures of the night. Later, I visit Sacrosanct, a Goth night held at the Nanci Raygun club. Located on Grace Street amid a small group of shops near a residential district, it's a bigger spot than Mars and more of a music club. Mars Bar looks like the bar from *Cheers*, but the Raygun is laid out like CBGB—it's a deep, narrow space that funnels you in past the posters and signs and graffiti on the wall. In the back, there's a pool table where a small group is gathering. I plunk some quarters down, and pretty soon I'm shooting the world's worst game of pool with Josh, a big, affable guy with long fingernails. I sit down with him and his friends, and I tell them I'm looking for vamps. But they shake their heads.

"That's an old scar that won't ever heal," Josh says.

There was a time when vampire culture and Goth culture all mixed together with the role-playing kids, but that's passed. They are more wary of one another. Josh and his friends talk about how utterly wrong it would be if some guy came in wearing a cape.

"You'd shun him?" They don't quite go that far. Despite the post-apocalyptic clothing, they seem like a decent sort.

"But it would be . . . tacky."

"Bela Lugosi is our dad's Dracula," Josh adds. And today Goth isn't even Goth—the music style is split into all kinds of styles with names like Darkwave and Industrial. They try to explain what they mean.

"Darkwave is like music without a happy ending," one of them tells me. I don't understand. I need to hear more of it for myself.

Several weeks later, I'm at the Drop Dead Festival in New York City. Billed as the "Biggest International Horror Festival with Deathrock Psychobilly Horror Punk New Wave Goth, Dirge Gothabilly Postpunk and More," it started back in 2003 with a massive blowout in Philly, Boston, New Jersey, and New York, popularizing a type of music called "deathrock," a broad term for bands that love all things dark and wonderful.

They hold Drop Dead this year at the Knitting Factory, a tall narrow downtown Manhattan club. The place is packed with people over the next two days, watching more than a dozen bands each night on two stages with a dance club underneath. Down in the Tikki Room, I'm listening to Greg Phoenix, who wears a black cowboy shirt and sings songs he calls Americana Gothic. They sound like country music of the darkest sort, and Phoenix has this intense, slightly off-putting stare. He definitely belongs here among the black-clad urban crowd. But you could put him in any seedy beer joint back home in Virginia and he could win an open mic night.

Next are Psycho Charger, who cover themselves in some kind of white powder and jump around shirtless. They're local boys, and they play, well . . . I'll let them describe it, from their website:

N.Y.C.'s Bloodiest band and the Bastard Sons of
The King hisself, PSYCHO CHARGER, deliver an ultra-
Horrific death-march thru the rotting R'n'R graveyard
that's been described as "Horror Rawkillbilly"!!!

Their music sounds like being beaten with pool cues. And at the beginning of every song there is a loud, blaring clip from a horror movie. By the end of their set, I feel like I've pounded fifty-two cups of coffee and sat in Jersey Turnpike traffic for an hour. I could pick a fight with a hockey team and win. I think that's what they're going for.

Throughout the night, I'm hanging out with Lugosi's Morphine, a band from Scranton, Pennsylvania, who play "psycho surf horror punk," in the words of lead singer D. F. Lazarus, who is dressed in white face ghoul makeup with spiky hair and pointy ears. They have their own label, Creepy Rat Records, which they use to launch compilations of other bands.

I buy them a round and hang out with Slug, who plays lead guitar, and Marquis De Blood, who plays bass. Slug is wearing a leather jacket and jeans that look gray, but actually has a print with lots and lots of skulls on it. And his makeup makes his face look almost like a skull. We talk about the band and the music.

I take a couple of photos of D.F. and his wife Anastasia. They have an obvious chemistry—I get a couple shots of them cuddling in their creepy getups. They have plenty of fun with the image of death rockers, but the music is important, too. Their set has the intensity of punk from the late 1970s or early '80s. The crowd gets really into it. By the end of the evening, an energy has been building that explodes as the crowd actually starts slam dancing all over the place.

They definitely have surf music influences—the first track off their new album *With a Demoral Chaser* is a song called "Surf Scum," written by Slug, that opens with a clip from the classic *Dracula:* "Listen to them, children of the night. What music they make!"

The song then launches into an extended, dark, surf music riff that makes you want to dig up the body of Bela himself and head out to catch some breakers in a particularly polluted part of SoCal. Not all of *Demoral* is made of surf tunes—a lot of it has an edginess like skate punk. But the influence is definitely there.

What is it with surf music and Goth tunes? Vampire Beach Babes (VBB), a band from Toronto, has a very different style, but weaves together the same mix. However, VBB makes fun of itself more explicitly.

"Many Goths make light of their culture," says VBB frontvamp Baron Marcus in an e-mail interview. "It is the heritage of a subculture so rich in symbolism and history, that it has so many chinks in its black armor. Goth is endearingly hilarious—by its very nature. It is permission to be larger than life. A Goth can eat cheezies and it becomes an event. That is, for me, what makes Goth so completely fun and sexy."

And through it all the image of the vampire is powerful enough to seep through that, Marcus tells me, because it's a "mythical archetype," part of the "universal language of humanity." Play with it all you want, but it still retains its power.

As Lugosi's Morphine pounds out their tunes up there on the stage, I'm struck by the paradox of it all. On one level, we're supposed to know it's over the top and a bit of a joke. But it's still weird and powerful. It's fun to dress up to play at being dark, and part of why it's fun is because we know it's not real, and part of why it's fun is because we know it is.

I'm beginning to get drawn in by the craziness of this vampy stuff, and I want to see more. So I head back to Philly—to the Dracula's Ball. Patrick Rodgers, the founder and boss of Dancing Ferret Entertainment Group, which produces several Dracula's Balls every year, isn't sure he wants to give me an interview at first. According to Rodgers, people in the Goth scene are very leery of what media folks can do. He talks about a magazine that regularly makes fun of the scene and wanted quotes from him.

"I didn't want to say anything to them or work with them," he says, "because their coverage on anything related to the Goth scene in the last ten years has been a sort of snicker snicker . . ." He can't prevent the snickering, he adds, but says he'll "be damned if someone who spends seven dollars to go to that party every week" picks up their rag and sees a bad story in which he's quoted "as if I'm part of the nose thumbing." Goths are very wired, and they're sensitive to the criticism.

"A local newspaper does some sort of exposé on the dark and

evil Goth scene, and people in L.A. are commenting on it the next day," he says, adding that Goths have "a sense of mistrust" toward media types (like, well, me). I tell him I'm trying to be fair and open-minded, and he seems to warm up to that idea. And he's a nice, talkative guy who loves what he does.

The morning of the ball, I drive into the South Street section of Philadelphia in a rental car from downtown New York. I'm exhausted and hungover, with the vague smell of grease, sweat, and cigarette smoke clinging to me. I walk into a clothing store called Crash Bang Boom, formerly known as Zipperhead. A famous spot established in 1980, it was located at the center of the Philly punk scene, and it was even featured in the song "Punk Rock Girl" by the Dead Milkmen:

> *One Saturday I took a walk to Zipperhead*
> *I met a girl there and she almost knocked me dead*

South Street itself used to be called Cedar Street and was the southern border of William Penn's city. Later, during revolutionary war times, it was the site of "bawdy theaters." Today it's a small, arty place with modestly sized shops and restaurants. It's like New York's East Village, only a little smaller and less pretentious. It's Philly. No one's going to make an overhyped Broadway play about it.

"I need to go to a party tonight," I tell the guy at the counter, a serious-looking fellow with hair that comes up in two huge spikes like the spiny back of a dinosaur. He eyes me evenly. I am wearing a golf shirt and a pair of khaki shorts. My look can only be described as "barbecue on the patio."

"Let's see here," he says, leading me through a couple racks and handing me items. I try on the pants, which grip the flesh of my legs with all the clinginess of a girl with low self-esteem who sends you a twenty-eight-page breakup letter. I have to make a crucial underwear-

or-commando decision. Wearing underwear makes the tight pants even tighter. But I'm afraid going commando in this fabric will give my bad-touch-zone the kind of rash medical science will never be able to cure. I go for the underwear and tell the boys to move over.

The material feels strange and tight, and my breathing actually hitches a little. Plus, I've got some gut-hang issues to deal with. I walk out with my golf shirt on and the shiny, metal-death-pants on. Below the waist I'm Billy Idol. Above the waist I'm Billy Idol *today*.

"They're a little tight," I tell the guy feebly.

"They're supposed to fit like that." This worries me. Is the entire Goth scene wandering around with chafing problems and a lack of blood circulation? Next is the mesh shirt and the T-shirt over it. I come out of the booth walking funny and feeling like I've been wrapped up and put in the meat counter of Food Lion.

"What are you going to do with your hair?" I hadn't thought about it, but I tell him I'm going to slick it back, and he seems to approve. He holds up the nail polish.

"I'm . . . I'm not sure," I tell him.

He throws it in for free. And he also gives me his band's CD. Turns out the guy is Rob Windfelder, and he's the lead singer and one of the guitarists for *Live Not on Evil*. Their 2004 CD, *Next Time Nail It Shut*, has one of the creepiest cover photos you'll ever see. It's an out-of-focus shot of some apparition holding a baby doll that just seems to have crawled out of that place in my subconscious where I keep the image of Linda Blair climbing backward down the staircase in *The Exorcist*. The CD is exactly the kind of thing you want to blast while you're driving a rental car back to your hotel room so you can turn into a creature of the night.

"This collection of songs is dedicated to all those who inspired them," reads the liner notes. "Whether you are a reason to live or a reason to refuse to die . . . you are in here . . . somewhere." I like this Rob Windfelder guy. I like the way he thinks. And when I leave the hotel, I experience that fantastic, creeparrific sensation I described earlier, and finally I think I'm starting to understand.

The club Shampoo is located in an industrial-looking area. I drive around the place, looking for the entrance, but it's hard to find. The buildings are big and stark and anonymous. Eventually I notice a small, roped-off section in front of the door of a large, boxy structure. That's the place. I settle in—an hour early—with a small knot of people. A guy named Chris is one of the first. Dressed in a black tunic with earrings and a partially shaved head, he waits with his girlfriend. They've been planning this for some time. An expert on the Civil War, he also spends time as a reenactor, and he talks my ear off about his ancestor Robert E. Lee. The crowd is pumped and chatty. There's a separate line for people who haven't bought tickets yet, and in it I see a flash of something incongruous for this Goth group. There's a guy with a long beard and flowing robes who looks like . . . well, it can't be, but . . .

"There's Jesus," I hear a voice say. But then He is gone.

After a few more minutes they let us all in. When I run into Patrick Rodgers, I'm surprised by how he looks. He's very tall and has a neatly cut beard, long black hair, and high-quality fang implants. He's very striking and actually kind of scary looking. He doesn't seem like the laid-back guy I chatted with on the phone.

But as I watch him mingle, the old Patrick emerges—the guy seems to be buddies with absolutely everyone who comes to the club, and he introduces me around. The music is thumping, with live bands laying down a wall of sound upstairs. Downstairs there is more of a niche feel, with small groups of people lounging around. I spend the rest of the night wandering past club kids and sexy Goth women dressed in capes—and there's even a group of babes dressed like characters from *Alice in Wonderland* that trigger fetishes in me I didn't know I had. But I have to get an interview with Our Lord.

Patrick eventually grabs the Savior—a guy named Gil, actually—

who's happy to come talk to me. Turns out he has several things in common with the guy I remember from thousands of Sunday school classes. For one thing, he's an Israeli who speaks "modern Hebrew and snippets of ancient Hebrew and Aramaiic, as well as some Latin." Greek is one of the languages he plans to study, but he's currently immersing himself in Middle English. So he's Israeli Jesus and also Episcopalian Jesus.

And like the Hippy Carpenter, Gil has cheated death. A couple of years ago, this twenty-two-year-old found out he had a virus that caused his immune system to attack his own heart. Eventually, he found out he had idiopathic myocarditis, "which meant my heart was too big but they didn't know why," he explains. And soon he had to have open heart surgery to insert a Left Ventricular Assist Device (LVAD). And he also had to have a full heart transplant.

"I had to be plugged into the wall for most of the day and take many, many pills just to survive," he remembers. And when he could finally go back to Dracula's Ball, it was a real victory. He remembers it quite well, he explains, because he was able to get his doctors' permission just a few days before the ball. And his mom came with him.

"Part of the reason the ball is so important for me is that I feel a deep connection to the Philadelphia Goth scene," he explains, "and for the four months I was in the hospital, many people came and visited me." People from the club also sent two giant get well cards on which they had collected signatures.

He's loved this club for many years, experimenting with wild costumes like the one he rigged up out of dozens and dozens of those free AOL subscriber disks.

"For most people, this is one of the few chances they get to dress and express themselves in a way that is considered 'out there' and not be judged."

And maybe this is part of why Goths and vamps are leery of the media. They don't want the bad publicity because it kills the buzz in the same way that telling someone she looks fat or stupid in a new outfit is a letdown. We transform ourselves to feel different and cool, but it only works if we look that way to someone else. You need friends to validate your decisions. Different Goth and vampire groups understand one another best, but each of the many groups has its own rules and its own ways of being. And that tells you everything you need to know about why they sometimes love and sometimes hate one another—why they sometimes mingle and why they sometimes fight.

Go inside the back of a Halloween supply shop on Fourth Avenue in Manhattan, and you will find a one-of-a-kind business—the Transformatorium, which bills itself as the "world's only full-time fangsmith." For less than $300, they will take a mold of your teeth and give you a custom-fitted set of vampire choppers made of dental-grade acrylic. You can drink, talk, and sing with them on, and they look scary. This shop used to be the headquarters for Father Sebastiaan, who made his name as a major supplier of fangs to the club set before helping to create vampire culture as it is today and founding his own group of vamps, called Strigoi Vii. I go to the Transformatorium to see the man who runs it now, an old friend and colleague of Sebastiaan's who calls himself Lestat. Squeezed into a tiny booth, with a couple of chairs, a desk, and a moveable lamp, Lestat gives me his perspective on the sometimes fractious world of vamps.

"Vampire drama," he says with a sigh. "It should be a soap opera."

A stocky, imposing African American man who has a cool, slightly sinister goatee set off from a round, almost cherubic face,

Lestat is calm and methodical, coolly measuring his words with the same care he uses to fiddle with a small, shiny fang implant. Part of the reason people don't always get along with Sebastiaan, he says, is that Sebastiaan has influence. They love him and hate him because "the scene's always been around, but he's the one who figured out how to organize it."

People might resent this pull, Lestat adds, but "a lot of them buy his book and take what they want." Terms Sebastiaan developed to describe the vamp scene crop up all over. And vamps are independent. The vamp scene overlaps with the Goth and fetish scene, he says, and people have different definitions for what it is, and is not.

The image they project, with fangs and costumes, is a way of "self-filtering," of inducing folks who are curious to come further into the group and encouraging others to walk away.

"One main word at the clubs is 'respect,' " he says. People can do a lot of crazy stuff. Women dress scantily, and there is a "sexual vibe that goes with being a vampire." He talks about one party where people got freaky inside a coffin. The image of the vampire is a way of letting people know they're in for something different. And that means discretion.

"We make a pun on *Fight Club*," he says. Only they call it "Fang Club." And everybody knows the first rule is you don't talk about Fang Club.

"The NY vampyre scene is very elegant. It's mostly about dressing up in very old-fashioned and Victorian garb," according to a vamp named Asif, who I interview by e-mail. "The fetish scene also integrates itself in the vampyre community. But the basic principle is to be fashionable and be social." He says there is very little "blood fetish" in the scene. And Lestat tells me he's "an artistic vampire," and in his world, "blood doesn't really play into it."

Most of the New York vamp community are "lifestylers," according to Asif. And most of them are "very much like children at play.

"When we all congregate," he adds, "it is just to have a good time and chat away the night. Events that take place here do have a spiritual edge to them. A ceremony or ritual usually starts out the evening and poetry is read, Gothic bands perform. . . ." There might also be art shows; displays of paintings, comic books, and photography; and even magic shows. Everyone has his or her own way to express "vampyre aesthetics." And everybody has his or her own story.

The first time I interview Father Sebastiaan by phone, he tells me about his childhood, his first adventures in the vampire world, and his current group, the Strigoi Vii. His sentences all run together crazily, excitedly. He has an infectious energy and humor when he talks.

"I was into all sorts of dark stuff when I was a kid," he says. "I was always the dark Jedi. Before the whole Sith thing came out and everybody knew who Darth Vader really was." Sebastiaan would dress up like an evil Luke Skywalker—with a black costume and a red lightsaber.

"People would say, 'You're like Darth Vader's apprentice,' and I'd say, 'No, I'm Luke Skywalker gone bad.'" Growing up in the Redbank area of New Jersey, Sebastiaan's mom and dad split up, and his mom's new husband, an oil executive, brought him to Dubai at times. But back at home, he'd go out to the fields of western Pennsylvania and play live action role-playing games. However, it was missing something. Then in 1993, he went to one of the original vampire role-playing games in a nightclub in New York City. He brought his girlfriend, and they had a blast.

"Before, I'd go to a D&D game with some 400-pound guy in a T-shirt eating a cheeseburger. But here, 60 percent of the people were chicks," he says. "Plus it had intrigue." The basement had a lair where the vampires held court, he adds, but you could only get into the area by knowing a code word. And out on the dance floor the vamps mixed freely with the club kids.

"I thought, 'This is fucking awesome,'" he says. "It changed my life. I was not a dork anymore. I had a hot chick on my arm, and we were driving home at sunrise."

He started to plan. "I thought, 'I don't want to be a player. I want to make *this thing happen.*' " And he knew he could do it.

"I used to run parties for kids in high school," he adds. "I would make dress codes and force everybody to look good. I'd been a party organizer since I was twelve."

In the mid-1990s, he was working two part-time jobs that came together for him. One was as a shoe salesman at the Bridgewater Mall in central New Jersey. It was a place where a lot of club kids and strippers shopped. The other job was as a dental technician, helping to make dentures for old people. So when he went to a convention and saw his first set of real-life fangs, he knew what to do.

"I saw it and thought it was the coolest fucking thing I had ever seen in my life," he says. He and his girlfriend each got a pair for $50 each. Then Father Sebastiaan went through the dental catalogs he got from his work and started ordering his own equipment. And on Christmas Day 1994, his mother got what might be the strangest gift any mom ever got from a son: a pair of Dracula chompers. She thought it was cool and wanted to show her friends. And Sebastiaan knew he had the beginnings of a Goth empire.

"People started traveling from all over the eastern seaboard to my mom's farm in New Jersey to get my fangs," he says. "I made up a map to the place, got a site on the Internet, and went to conventions, a renaissance festival. I made everybody fangs." His new company, Sabretooth, was born. It was either that, he explains, or the Tooth Fairy—which probably wouldn't have seemed as menacing. And the fangs helped him score an in with the strippers who came into the shoe store where he worked. He could provide a service, and they could hook him up with all the right people. After all, he says, there was no way in hell he was going to launch a career as a dental tech.

"I'm not going to make dentures for old people when I can make fangs for hot chicks," he says. In addition to making fangs for everybody, Sebastiaan started running his own LARP games at nightclubs all over the city.

"I was making $2,000 a week," he says, turning out fangs from a Halloween store in the Village. He had his shop at the site where the Transformatorium now sits under new management. And more and more, he was deciding to run events without involving the LARP rules.

"I decided to run a vampire party," he says. "I thought, 'Fuck the rules. Let's have a bunch of hot strippers, cool bands—everybody wearing fangs and looking good.' " He threw the first New York Vampire Ball in January 1996, he says. Four hundred fifty people packed the place.

"It was unbelievable," he adds. "Very few of the LARPers showed up. And I was kind of weirded out by that." But LARPers would always give him trouble—they'd try to attach themselves to his parties whenever they saw the women Sebastiaan was bringing in.

"They wanted to be like the fourth generation king of the vampires, and use their powers in games to cop a feel on a girl," he says. He decided at some point to pull out of the LARP scene and just go straight vamp.

"My girlfriend at the time—she loved the fangs, loved to dress up, liked to play S&M, and I thought, 'Why are we wasting all our time making these character sheets?' " he remembers. "I wanted to hang out with cool artists and performers and innovative people, and I didn't want to go back to being a dork."

He says at that point he started fleshing out the idea of different households—groups of vamps—using terms and concepts from the Society for Creative Anachronism, a medieval recreation group, and even borrowing from the fetish scene.

"I basically got rid of the game," he says, "and my girlfriend was happy as a lark because she didn't have to go sit in a hotel all weekend with these nerds. She came from a really upscale neighborhood where all her girlfriends were making fun of her." Sebastiaan had started out dressing up like evil Luke Skywalker and having sword-fights in the hills of west Pennsylvania. But his party skills and his fangsmithing had gotten him a place in the world of strippers, rock stars, and club kids. There was no way he was going back.

The 1990s vamp scene and club scene had merged into almost the same thing, with different kinds of people hanging out at the same places. Father Sebastiaan moved through this world easily, he says, making friends and hanging out. Eventually, Sebastiaan says, he got big enough that people began to resent his success.

"Everybody hated my guts in New York," he says. "I was the corporation that had gotten successful." People in the vamp scene had even started calling him "Father Gates" derisively, like he'd become some kind of Microsoft of the undead. And after the terrorist attacks of September 11, he decided to leave. He went to Germany for six months and then headed to Amsterdam, where he lived for a long time in an office of the Church of Satan, studying in their massive occult library and having other kinds of amusements.

"I was having parties, orgies with hot Dutch girls, and going to England on weekends," he says. "One day I went to a music festival and did so many drugs I woke up in Sweden. Now I don't do any drugs, because I need to keep my head together. My body is not able to handle it anymore."

Father Sebastiaan is back in the Big Apple, and he's running parties at Avalon, the nightclub that used to be the infamous Limelight, which was closed down on drug charges in a famous case in the 1990s. He even organizes parties like Endless Night, where people from all over the vampire scene can come together. But these different groups in the vampire scene still have their feuds. One of them concerns a group down in D.C. and a friend of Sebastiaan's named Nico. I stumble into it and get an earful.

Father Sebastiaan might be angry with me. I sense it. I found a web-page that had posted IM discussions between Sebastiaan and Orthae Velve, one of the members of a D.C.-area vamp group called House Eclipse.

These discussions led to a huge flame-up. Now House Eclipse and Sebastiaan aren't talking to each other. The House's main reason is that Sebastiaan is close to a man named Nico Claux, the so-called "Vampire of Paris" who was sentenced to twelve years in a French prison for murder.

In the IM exchange, Sebastiaan asked House Eclipse to remove a mention of Claux's crime.

"I have met him and am counseling him now," Father Sebastiaan wrote. "He is doing some major steps toward recovery and restitution of the victims of his families. . . . We don't need any more setbacks."

The argument went on for some time, with Orthae Velve and Father Sebastiaan arguing over whether Nico was a vampire, and Father Sebastiaan saying that Nico is not affiliated with Sebastiaan's group, Strigoi Vii. And then it turned ugly, or at least really, really weird, when Sebastiaan threatened a "clan war."

"Clan war?" Orthae Velve (OV) wrote back, asking if it was a role-playing term.

"It is also a war between Scottish clans," Sebastiaan countered.

"I'm not Scottish," OV wrote.

I want to know Sebastiaan's side. Is his group affiliated with a murderer? Also, the IM exchange seemed to touch on other issues. When I ask him about them, the e-mail he shoots me back is terse and written in an all-cap font that makes it look official and scary:

PAUL,

LET ME MENTION THIS TO CLARIFY.

STRIGOI VII ARE NOT CRIMINALS. TRADITIONAL PSYCHIC VAMPIRES NOR CANNIBALISTIC BLOOD FETISH-ISTS. HOUSE ECLIPSE INCLUDES THE LATTER TWO.

He goes on like this, defending Nico Claux even while he underlines that the guy is not hooked up with his group:

NICO IS SOMEONE WHOM I COUNSELED AND INTER-VIEWED TO MAKE CLEAR HE IS NOT OF THE SAME FAMILY AS THE STRIGOI VII. AND IF SOMEONE COMMITS SUCH ACTS THEY ARE CLEARLY NOT STRIGOI VII . . .

THOUGH NICO HAS COMMITTED CRIMINAL ACTIVI-TIES, ACCORDING TO FRENCH LAW HE PAID HIS DUES AND IS NO LONGER A CRIMINAL. HE IS REFORMED AT THE POINT I GOT TO KNOW HIM.

THROUGH MY COUNSEL, NICO HAS ABSOLUTELY COME TO TERMS AND BEGAN TO REGRET WHAT HE HAS DONE FOR THE FIRST TIME. I TRULY ENJOY THE PERSON HE IS NOW. TO BE HONEST EVERYONE WHO HAS MET HIM REALIZED WHAT A GENUINE AND HONEST INDIVIDUAL HE IS NOW THAT [HE] HAS MOVED BEYOND DESTRUCTIVE ENERGIES.

And at the end he gets in a dig at his rivals:

HOUSE ECLIPSE HAS NOTHING TO DO WITH THE STRIGOI VII NOR THE SANGUINARIUM. THEIR ACTIONS HAVE SPOKEN SO.

EVEN REFORMED CRIMINALS CAN PROVIDE THE RESPECT THEY ARE UNABLE TO PROVIDE.

WE SIMPLY IGNORE THEM AND I CAN NO LONGER COMMENT ON THESE INDIVIDUALS.

And then he signs his e-mail, not "Sincerely" or "Truly" or "Hugs n' Kisses," but:

ETERNALLY,
SEBASTIAAN

Jesus. That's unsettling enough, but I ask him a small follow-up question about the spelling of his name, and he sends me a simple reply: "Please call me."

I can't get through to his number, and he eventually writes back that he'll call me at 11:00 p.m. And I find myself sitting at my desk with my computer and my phone and my cup of coffee—just waiting. I'm tired and a little out of sorts. And I suspect this is just when his day is getting started, not only because he's a vampire, but because he's also a party promoter. I'm also a little uneasy because this must be a flashpoint with him. In the IM discussion with House Eclipse, he wrote things that struck me as controversial, even strange and threatening.

When Orthae Velve told him that she considered herself and other vampires just "people like any others," Sebastiaan shot back, "I don't want to associate myself as a mere human.

"Vampyres should rule and not be ruled," he wrote, adding, "I am not equal to my food."

By now I realize that Father Sebastiaan is no stranger to controversy. People love him, and people hate him, and sometimes it seems like it's for the same reason—he's the vampire everyone knows about. If you watch a documentary or read a book about vampire subculture, the guy will probably pop up in it somewhere. In vampire circles, he has the megawatt profile. And it's easy to see why. He chats, brags, and makes outrageous claims about who and what he is, and then suddenly he seems like the nicest guy you'd ever want to meet. A normal, happy club kid from New Jersey and a recovering nerd, he claims to have a lock on one of the most exclusive vampire groups in the country. Like any promoter, his stock in trade is that heady mix of glamour and bluster, and he freely admits he likes to play around with the legendary nonsense behind the vampire. But he also says vampires are real and not what you think.

I mentally steel myself for an argument about his people-as-food comment—and, more importantly, for an argument about whether his group supports a killer. And I realize that more than the lateness or the potential for an argument, I'm mostly out of sorts because after finding myself immersed in the comments that vampires sling around—comments about their special powers and their off-human nature—I find myself . . . wondering if it's true.

It's not. It can't be.

But it's late, and I've been talking and e-mailing too many of these people, and their rhetoric has kind of seeped into the part of my brain where I'm not so rational or skeptical. It's the part that causes me to dislike taking a shower when I'm alone because that's how people get stabbed. That part only comes out at night. Father Sebastiaan is a friendly, chatty source, but he's also the guy who claims he can feed off psychic energy through some mystical process he won't share with me. He's a guy who claims you and I are pets—even food. He claims that he and his kind keep us in the dark and toy with our destinies. It seems sometimes that there are almost two Father Sebastiaans: the first is the chatty one I talk with about his own life, and the second is the serious and secretive one who guards the mysteries of his vampire group. The phone rings. I pick it up, wondering which of the Sebastiaans I'm going to get.

He is as polite and warm as ever, but he wants to know why I'm interested in House Eclipse. I ask him to explain some of the things he wrote in the e-mail and to tell me why his group and their group are no longer in touch.

"Oh, I was just fucking with her head," he says, laughing it off. "Those guys have annoyed me. They're a bunch of dorks from D.C. The Strigoi Vii down there don't even pay them any mind."

I ask him about his statements and support for Nico Claux. Shouldn't people reading this be afraid of his group?

"Strigoi Vii are not criminals," he says. "And we are not blood drinkers or psychic vampires." He tells me House Eclipse endorses psychic vampirism and blood drinking, which I'd already confirmed. We're getting into one of the main points of disagreement among different vampire groups. They all have different concepts of how they feed. Some believe they need to actually drink human blood, in which a person's psychic energy, sometimes called prana, is concentrated like potassium in a banana smoothie. Others believe they can suck psychic energy directly from their donors. From what he'll tell me about it, Sebastiaan's group believes they can kind of skim the ambient energy from a crowd, and that this does people no harm. He emphasizes that his group isn't a threat.

"We just like to party," he says. "But we don't even have any underaged sex or drinking. We're really strict on that." He also says that while Nico Claux is not in the group, members in France are very close with Claux, and Sebastiaan himself considers the man one of his "dearest friends."

"Nico is not a criminal according to French law," he says. He adds that Nico has served his time and "paid his debt to society" and that he's reformed and trying to make it up to his victim's family, though I don't know what he means by this.

"And he does not enter the United States," Sebastiaan says. "I only see him in Paris and Amsterdam." Claux has a full-time job, a beautiful apartment, and a steady girlfriend, Sebastiaan tells me.

"He regrets what he did," Sebastiaan says.

"Do you believe him?" I ask.

"He's direct and straightforward about what he did," says Sebastiaan. "Not gonna hide it. He's not going to run from his past, but he's going to say that my future's different." Sebastiaan continues, telling me that Nico was given a commendation by the warden as one of the most well-behaved inmates in his prison. Claux kept to himself, working out and learning to paint.

"And instead of doing destructive things," Sebastiaan says, "he does creative things." Nico now paints portraits of serial killers, which an American company has compiled and sold as a calendar.

"So painting is his way of channeling his curiosity about the primal nature of humanity," Sebastiaan adds. "I'll tell you something—a lot of people are very fearful of encountering someone like Nico." The first night he was hanging out with Claux, Sebastiaan found himself all alone with him in a dark alley, taking a back entrance into a building.

"And I turned around on him and I'm like, 'You're not going to kill me, are you?' " Nico gave him an incredulous look and laughed it off. Today, Sebastiaan tells me, Nico doesn't want to be interviewed anymore. He wants to live the quiet life.

"Nico's been closer to death than anybody we know," says Sebastiaan, "in regards to . . . he orchestrated it."

But is he truly sorry? The guy paints pictures of serial killers. How reformed could he be?

"He looked back on this as—he doesn't necessarily regret it as much as you might think," says Sebastiaan. "But he realizes what he did was . . . not cool."

He wouldn't do it again. Sebastiaan's confident about that.

"I've known him for three years now, and we hang out. We spend a lot of time together talking about the mechanics of death."

Nico is a friend, Sebastiaan tells me again. Not in the group, but a friend. I make a mental note to study more about this Nico Claux.

"Children grow up and criminals reform," he adds. "Or have the potential to reform. And you can't hold something against someone who paid his time." He can't come to America, he adds, because of "Interpol and the laws here." But Nico doesn't want to, Sebastiaan adds.

"He wants a quiet life with his girl, and to have kids."

We'll learn more about Nico later. But first we have to focus on someone much more famous, at least in America. And this person's story shows the constant struggle different vamp groups have in trying to set themselves apart from one another. One of the biggest reasons the different kind of vamps and Goths want to stay away from one another and from the rest of us is that they are afraid of being lumped in with people we've seen on the news. Some of them especially want to avoid any connection with a guy named Jonathon Sharkey.

"This site does not condone, support or endorse in any way the statements, beliefs, or opinions of 'Jonathon Sharkey,' " a notice on a vamp site called Drinkdeeplyanddream.com reads.

```
In fact, we find him disgusting, immoral and
absolutely insane. He does not speak for any pagan,
vampire, or witch group or organization, period.
His beliefs are psychotic and utterly in opposition
to common moral decency. His comments are NOT
indicative of anyone but himself and he does not
have any authority or recognition of any kind
within any group, website or subculture. He is, at
best, a fringe nutter and at worse, seriously men-
tally deranged.
```

In addition to highlighting how the groups don't want to be mixed up in one another's business, the Jonathon Sharkey phenomenon shows what happens when being a vampire becomes more than just something you do on nights and weekends—when it's not a game at all. But who is this guy?

Hunting Sharkey

"Jon is a moderate who leans left . . .
with the exception of the impalements."

J onathon "the Impaler" Sharkey entered the race for governor
of Minnesota in January 2006 for the "Vampyres, Witches
and Pagans Party." If elected, he promised to impale terrorists, rapists,
drug dealers, and child abusers in front of the state capitol. He was
ultimately arrested on outstanding criminal charges from Indiana, and
now his campaign is defunct. But Kat is who I'm after. Kat is supposedly his sister, a Wiccan priestess, an attorney, and Sharkey's lover. But
she might not really exist. She might only be Sharkey's alter ego or a
figment of his imagination. I hunt through the message boards, blogs,
and websites, looking for information. I meet some strange people.

Tray White talks shop with the Impaler.
(Photo courtesy of Tray White)

Help me find a publisher for my own book and I'll tell you what I know about Jonathon Sharkey and his "vampire" brood . . .

BellaDonnaDrakul (BDD) claims she knows Jonathon, or Jon, and Kat personally. But she has a price, and I don't know if I want to pay it. BDD signs her name "Bella," with a cute little picture of a cartoon vampire, like some Cathy comic gone to the dark side.

I'll give you simple answers to your questions if you help me find an agent first (this is not a bribe to get help from you—just a simple favor in return for my answers).

She seems to have honest-to-God proof Kat was real, and she claims Kat and Jonathon both threatened her, but that afterward she actually became friends with Kat. But over the next few e-mails, she reveals that she has only met Kat online. And she becomes more insistent that I help launch her career.

> **Can you contact your agent for me? Tell them my book is called "The Vampire Collection: Short Stories For The Vampire Enthusiast" and it is a first-person-based collection of vampire short stories unlike any on the market.**

Our interview starts to become a "I'll tell you something if you tell me something" exchange that reminds me of *Silence of the Lambs*. I have the feeling I'm the Jodie.

I want to know how Kat threatened her. But she shoots back:

> **As far as Kathleen goes—yes, we became close friends online and nothing more than that. I only wanted her for publishing contacts. BTW, why am I explaining myself to you? I know nothing about you! Basically, you'll get what you want when I get what I want first!**

Looking for answers, I register with her Yahoo! group. "Greetings, my children!" the front page reads.

> **I am Countess BellaDonnaDrakul and welcome to my vampiric/otherkin dream. This group is open to all enthusiasts who are vampires or otherkin (witches, werekin, etc.), enjoy talking about vampires or otherkin, enjoy vampires or otherkin in general, those who've lost the darkness within, and anyone who feels forgotten in the world.**

There's a photo on the front of a woman with jet black hair and Elvira makeup, and the picture has all kinds of gauzy things laid over it to make it creepy and ethereal. At the bottom of the webpage is a tiny plea: "Please no role-playing!"

Within a day, I start getting regular e-mails from everybody in the group. One of the first lays down the ground rules to keep the forum a "friendly and flame-free environment."

> **No generalizations, no assumptions. No fang jokes toward vampires, no doll jokes toward vodouists, no dog-collar jokes toward the werewolves, and for GOSH sakes, no dead baby jokes toward the witches and satanists! No calling humans or mundanes blood-bags, food, bone-bags. . . .**

After that, a horoscope arrives, and then occult and New Age news items. After that, birthday announcements. Soon I get jokes and urban legends. Then people are sending e-mail after e-mail about the new *Blade* series that appears on TV, and it dawns on me that I haven't joined a vampire's Internet coven. I've hooked up with the mother of all chain letter groups.

We have left the run-of-the-mill LARPers and club-hopping Goths and gone down the rabbit hole looking for people who take this vampire thing more seriously. So we should expect to find strange alternative cultures. But in a way, this isn't an alternative culture at all. This is a culture I know too well. I've lost old friends from high school, ditched college buddies, and shunned coworkers to get off this kind of thing. Now I've signed up for it.

Eventually, I get a message titled *Five Reasons Computers Must Be Male*. None of this answers my questions regarding Jonathon and Kat though.

The guy who gives me the best insight is Tray White, the documentary filmmaker who was with Jonathon Sharkey when he threw his hat into the ring. A down-to-earth, jovial, good ol' boy from Texas, White was at a somewhat low point in his career when he encountered the Impaler. He'd finished a feature film called *Caterpillar* that he hated and wouldn't sell. He was unsure of what to do next. He reached for the one thing that's always there for you in times of trouble: the remote.

"I'm kinda lazy, so I watch TV all the time," White confesses. "Pop culture is huge in my life, unfortunately." He'd been spending serious time in front of the tube watching cable news.

"I switch from CNN to Fox News to MSNBC," he says. And then one day Jonathon Sharkey appeared on Brit Hume's show *Grapevine*.

"They had a little segment on Jonathon with a picture of him wearing a cloak and sword," says White. "I just got a good laugh from it." White phoned Sharkey, researched him on the Internet, and was on a plane the next day. What was so riveting?

"Did you read his original campaign website? It was so unbelievable," says White. "It talks about his turn to Satanism. 'History tells of three famous incidents of good men turning to the dark side,' it says. 'One was Lucifer. The other was Judas. And the third was Annakin Skywalker. . . .' "

White knew he had something.

"I thought, 'I just gotta put the camera on this guy.' " He didn't completely know where this was going. He just knew he had to start shadowing Sharkey and get it all on tape. And soon he got blood feedings.

"I have five blood feedings on camera," he says. "The very first came out of the blue. I won't bore you with the background details, where he chomped down on his arm . . ." I tell him I don't mind knowing about the background details. In fact, when a guy chomps down on his own arm, I can't say I'm bored at all.

"I'm in Minnesota," he says. "I'm dying, it's so cold. I didn't bring a jacket or anything—so I'm just wearing a light sweater. I have bronchitis—fucking 104-degree fever. I am just struggling." Then White explains that Jonathon's partner Julie had just gotten a call from her mother, and they were arguing over a court case Julie was facing.

Julie Carpenter filed suit with the Equal Employment Opportunity Commission against her employers at a nearby school system, claiming that they fired her as a school bus driver because she's a pagan.

"So anyway the mom calls freaking out. They're screaming at each other," he adds. "And I'm literally leaning against the wall because I can barely stand—I'm so sick of holding the camera waist high. My eyes are closing." Jonathon and his wife were both upset and red-faced.

"So Jonathon starts staring at me, his eyes just popping out of his head and I start thinking, 'This motherfucker wants to bite me.' " But he didn't want to bite White. Instead, according to White, he rolled up his sleeves.

"He says, 'You recording?' and I say, 'Yeah, I'm recording . . .' And he just chomps down on his arm.

"He's staring at the camera biting as hard as he can, and he releases after four or five seconds. He's got this big pool of blood with little puncture wounds in his arm. Then he leans his arm over to Julie where she *erotically starts sucking on his arm* . . . like a bizarre porno.

"He looks kindly into the camera and says, 'I have to feed her because she has dentures.' "

Now, after his candidacy tanked when authorities arrested him on two outstanding Indiana warrants from 2005—one for stalking and one for escape on a $100,000 bond—Sharkey is making a different kind of spectacle.

"His last court appearance was on 6-6-06," says White, chuckling. And with his antics in the court, he adds, Jonathon made it harder on himself. "The judge was going to take it easy on him, but then he gets up there and during the oath, he says, 'I swear on Lucifer to tell the truth, the whole truth, and nothing but the truth . . .' "

White followed Jonathon through his short, strange campaign.

But could a candidate who wants to bring back impalements and considers Lucifer a chief booster ever be taken seriously?

"Obviously I did not expect anybody was going to take him as a legitimate candidate," White says. "They were running local news stories doing man on the street interviews, and people would initially have this look of shock on their face when the reporters would ask, 'What do you think about Jonathon Sharkey, the vampire Satanist running for governor?' " But Minnesotans are tolerant people.

"Then they'd stop and say, 'Well . . . it depends what his views were . . .' " he adds. And soon people actually began to give him a chance.

"His thirteen-point platform started resonating with people," White says. "People were like, 'Shit, I wouldn't mind seeing a child molester or a terrorist being impaled . . . that's okay with me. And he wants to help the farmers. He wants to improve the public schools.' " Plus, White adds, he was actually kind of a middle-of-the-road candidate.

"Jon is a moderate who leans left," White says, "with the exception of the impalements."

As he continued to run, the media couldn't help themselves.

"Phone call after phone call came from production assistants wanting to book him for radio shows. It started out as little local shows here and there," says White. "But before I knew it, Alan Colmes was giving him an hour on his show. He was talking to friggin' Danny Bonaduce for an hour segment. He was on *Fox and Friends*.

"He was getting written up in places like Russia, Poland, and whatnot," White adds. "He was doing BBC constantly and radio shows in Australia." The international crowd loved him, probably because he seemed to confirm every stereotype the cheese-eating bastards had of crazed, violent Americans.

As Jonathon Sharkey made the campaign rounds, it was obvious he didn't know the first thing about politics. And it was a real temptation for White to just mess with his head.

"At first I wanted to pull all these crazy-ass pranks on him," White says. "I wasted a couple of days just fucking with him, making up names and saying, 'So Sir Furrington of East Timor has threatened to nuke the state of Vermont. If you were president right now what would you do?' He'd start talking about how he was going to feed off the children of Sir Furrington." White threw in Thom Yorke, the name of the lead singer of his favorite band, Radiohead. He pretended Yorke was a political leader in Britain who had said he would invade the state of Minnesota.

"I have him on camera saying, 'I'm going to kill Thom Yorke.' "

But White gave up on pranking the guy.

"I realized I was being an asshole." Plus, there was something vulnerable, maybe even likeable, about the Impaler.

"He's the kindest, gentlest vampire you'll ever meet," says White. "When the cameras are on, he's obnoxious. You are completely zapped of all your energy when you are around him. But when the cameras are off he is a normal guy. If I saw him in a bar, I'd buy him a beer and have a conversation with him." White tried to play fair with Jonathon—to keep the cameras rolling and just do a straight documentary. But every once in a while, Jonathon Sharkey wanted advice. White says he rarely intervened. But once or twice he couldn't resist. Especially when angry on-camera Jonathon Sharkey would take over and start ranting about using his magical powers to kill folks he didn't like.

"While logging the tapes I tried to count how many death threats he made to high-ranking federal officials and I lost track somewhere around the thirty, forty range," White says. "He was constantly threatening to give people heart attacks." White says Sharkey claimed he could put spells on people, and that he had his own personal spellbook written in dragon's blood.

"He kept saying he was going to kill George Bush," says White. "I told him, 'Okay dude, you can't say that. You can say when you're elected, you're going to try George Bush, and once he's found guilty, then you're going to impale him . . ." He doesn't know how much good it did.

"I have no doubt we were watched by the Secret Service."

And then it got even stranger. A person named Kathleen Sharkey started contacting White.

"At first I started receiving e-mails from her," he says, " 'You better not make him look like a fool'—that kind of stuff." Someone with the same name identifies herself as Jonathon's wife on a Web bulletin board, challenging Pat Robertson to debate her husband. And in 2005 documents filed by Kathleen Sharkey in federal court, she claims she is Jonathon's sister as well as his attorney-in-fact. Jonathon Sharkey filed a document in federal court in Indiana giving Kathleen power of attorney, but a federal judge later ruled that it was invalid. It was clear, White says, that Kat acted as Jonathon's heavy.

"Anytime anyone gives him shit about anything, that's who he calls upon," White says. "He calls her his 'attack Kat.' " White says he began to receive a flurry of e-mails from Kat trying to put pressure on him to renegotiate the terms of his contract with Jonathon.

"I asked him about it. But he said, 'Oh, she's my lawyer, and she just wants to renegotiate. But that's between you guys—I don't want anything to do with it.' "

It didn't seem all that strange that with a campaign to run, Jonathon might delegate the contract haggling. But gradually, White says, he began to suspect Kat didn't exist. White interviewed friends and family of Jonathon, and he discovered that the photo of Kat wearing a cloak with her face obscured on a website he saw was in reality a daughter of Jonathon's. White says he met the daughter in Florida and confirmed it. White also says he's seen an actual death certificate of Jonathon Sharkey's sister, who died at birth. They listed her name as Kathleen Sharkey.

"I think Jonathon's using Kathleen to do any type of dirty

work. . . . If someone pisses him off, he's got someone on his side," says White. But he doesn't know whether this is a real example of a delusion. He thinks the creation of Kat might be part of an elaborate act that went too far.

"I think more than anything it's attention," White says. "He was just digging himself a hole and realized there was no way out." But there's even a weirder wrinkle. According to White, Jonathon claimed that he actually died, and when he did, friends of his began to receive calls from Kathleen telling them the details.

If Kat didn't exist, then who was calling?

"I don't know who the hell that could be."

In an attempt to prove or disprove the existence of Kat, I begin searching court documents to uncover the case that ultimately sent him to jail. What I find is bizarre. Jonathon Sharkey, using the name of Rocky Flash, Rocky Adonis-Flash, Rocky "Hurricane" Flash, and sometimes even Darth Hurricane, has spent years in a series of legal battles with judges, cops, state and federal officials, and an ex-girlfriend whom he accuses of being an alcoholic and a drug addict. Though her name is part of the public record, I'm going to call her Sharon Hill to protect her privacy in this strange matter. (And it's important to note that I have no idea whether the charges Flash makes against her— especially about drinking or drug use—are in any way true.)

Flash's "attorney-in-fact" Kat claimed that Flash committed suicide. And later in the complaint Kat claims that the actions of the state of Indiana turned Sharkey into a "demonic demon," adding "wait to [sic] you see what Lucifer has done to Flash." He claimed in another legal pleading that he possessed the "ability to rise from the dead." Sharkey also complained that his ex-girlfriend defamed him by saying he might be suffering from a mental disorder, and then later in the same document, he said that her actions caused him to enter a "Vampyre Slumber" for almost five months in 2004 and 2005.

According to documents Flash filed in federal court, on

October 22, 1999, he began dating Hill. Some of the pleadings describe the first night they met at a bar in New Jersey and go into great detail about the pinstripe suit, Italian tie, and boots he was wearing. They also describe how he cowed the other guys at the club who were interested in her, pouncing on her like "a lion," and scoring a first kiss. They fell "heavenly in love," he writes in one court document, and for additional evidence that the love was indeed heavenly, he adds an attachment to the pleading, a love poem titled "A Kind of Magic."

Though walls may fail, and seasons may change,
Heavenly "Magic," never ends.
For anyone who has ever read the Bible, knows,
Gifts from Heaven, never fade away . . .

Hill and Flash, the story continues, were serious about their relationship, but Hill wouldn't marry him unless he met one of his two professional goals: "make it as a Congressional candidate in the General Election for 2000" or get a license and a sponsorship deal to become a race car driver on the NASCAR/Busch series.

Rocky Flash claims he began to worry about Hill's drinking and drug use and even convinced her to go to a psychotherapist, who made Hill promise to give up drinking for thirty days. It allegedly didn't work and the relationship began to go south. Nonetheless, Flash launched a campaign for congress in Florida's eleventh district and a campaign for Senator from Indiana, and he even filed paperwork for a 2004 race for president.

"We have the power to make this the best generation of mankind in history or make it the last," the slogan on his letterhead said, using a slightly garbled John F. Kennedy quote that somehow manages to sound inspiring and apocalyptic at the same time. Flash made Hill his campaign treasurer, though there is some dispute about what she agreed to do. In fact, she filed suit with the Federal

Election Commission (FEC), claiming he falsely listed her as treasurer for his election committee. The case was dismissed in 2003 because of lack of importance.

By 2004, the campaign's year-end statement listed $18,000 in debt and had Rocky Flash marked down as "deceased" because, evidently, of the vampyric slumber. But during his quest for public office, Flash wrote a series of strangely personal notes to FEC bureaucrats about his troubles with Hill. In 1999, he wrote an official letter refusing to accept the resignation of Hill if she decided to file one. In January 2004, he fired her. Then in March 2004, he rescinded his firing letter and noted that he was "unprofessional and out of line." In April, he promoted Hill. Then in June, he fired her again, noting that he had "a sad and heavy heart."

Flash also began a campaign to scare Hill straight, trying to stop her from allegedly drinking or using drugs. According to his own court filings, he began to show up at bars she frequented, showing her picture to the locals, and asking that they not serve her. In one case, he got into an argument with a bartender who blew him off. According to Flash, the bartender told him he knew where he lived. Flash responded the same, and in his pleading says that since he is "from the streets of Elizabeth, NJ, and a former Army Green Beret, he takes it as a challenge by someone with a death wish." He also said he consulted with "a friend of his with the CIA" who told him not to worry.

Flash also attempted to get an antidrunk driving law passed that he wanted to name after his ex—in an attempt to shame her into a life of sobriety. After getting the jurisdiction of his cases moved to Florida, Flash e-mailed then-governor Jeb Bush. His letter took a chummy, familiar tone with Bush, asking the governor to help him get to the top.

"Jeb, I hope and pray all is well with you and the family," the note read in part, going on to describe Flash's ex's problems and asking for his office's help. The response was a little bit formal—not from Jeb himself, but from a bureaucrat in a state anti–drug abuse office. Flash then faxed a letter to Jeb Bush's brother, President George W. Bush. He got a note back from the special assistant to the president and director of presidential correspondence, who told him he was forwarding the letter to the Department of Health and Human Services.

Soon Flash was corresponding with bureaucrats from other agencies, who referred him to various antidrug programs. Reading the letters and e-mails, it's amazing how helpful the bureaucrats are. I don't really know if Flash was chummy with Jeb Bush or his brother. But it seems like someone writing heartfelt letters about a friend who is going through a terrible addiction would have to get a response like this from a PR-conscious government in a therapeutic age. Unfortunately, Flash also began to sue Hill in state courts and in federal courts, trying to slap her with punitive fines for emotional damages against him and force her to go into antidrug and antialcohol programs. And the helpful, respectful correspondence he received from these high-level staffers only fed the image he was creating of himself as someone with great political power who was marshalling scores of connections at his disposal to save the life of his love.

However, Sharon Hill was reporting him to the police, accusing him of stalking. And in the summer of 2003, according to Indiana prosecutors, Flash violated Hill's protective order against him by driving by her house, leaving notes on her car and in her driveway, and sending her thirteen more letters. During this period, he compounded his legal campaign against Hill by suing judges who'd ruled against him, cops who investigated him, and ultimately even the state of Indiana and the United States.

During these cases, while Kathleen Sharkey made her appearance as his attorney, she wrote e-mails to Hill and Hill's lawyer.

"I am going to replace you in Johnny's heart, whether you like it or not," she wrote to Hill. "Johnny took me out on our 'first date' last night, and freely slept in my bed with me. I will end his celibacy streak before it reaches four years."

To Hill's lawyer, she wrote, "The cards have revealed that Johnny is on one of his financial high waves, and after sleeping in bed with him last night I am staking a claim on him. . . . I want to sink my claws into him again."

The e-mail to the attorney concluded that once Sharkey had sex with Kat, he would never want to go back to Hill. Kat promised to sign a "magikal and legally binding agreement" in her own blood that would guarantee this. But if Hill broke it, Kat promised that Hill and her family would be "cursed for life." This is disturbing if Kat really is Jonathon's sister, attorney, priestess, and lover. If it's only Jonathon pretending to be Kat, it becomes so much more fucked up.

At some point, Jonathon Sharkey (acting as Jonathon Sharkey) also offered Hill an olive branch, a way out of these legal problems—if she would only agree to accompany him to a fertility clinic where staffers would impregnate her "with Hurricane's female chromosomes."

"And then nine months later (hopefully) Hurricane gets to be the daddy of a beautiful baby girl," he wrote in a notice to the court, adding that he always wanted a miniature version of his ex. She would be a little person whom he could raise right and keep from danger. In the notice, he also mentioned that he'd cast a curse on the entire state of Indiana, and he warned that "he would see this state destroyed and those responsible die a very painful and horrible death."

And in court documents Sharkey revealed a possible reason for his obsession with saving Sharon Hill's life. He claimed to have a previous girlfriend, a woman with the same kind of addictions Hill had, who was ultimately killed by alcohol and drug consumption.

By the time he'd moved to Minnesota and announced his candidacy for governor, he'd completely chucked the name Rocky Flash.

But within weeks, a sheriff's dispatcher connected Rocky Flash to the name Jonathon Sharkey, the guy who was on the air ranting about how he was going to become governor and impale people. He wasn't doing a good job hiding from the law on the cable news shows.

While in jail, Sharkey gave an interview to a local reporter who pressed him on his claims to have died and come back as well as the fact that he didn't reveal the unsavory aspects of his past to Minnesota voters.

"You did not put out your whole past there, did you?" the reporter asked.

"I didn't feel it was relevant," said Sharkey, who then denied that he lied.

"But you didn't tell the truth," the reporter said.

"I didn't lie," Sharkey insisted.

"You did not tell the entire truth, did you?" the reporter asked, later adding, "You chose to hide your past."

"I didn't bring it forward," Sharkey said, relenting. "If you want to call it hiding, we'll call it hiding."

"So you hid your past," the reporter said.

"Okay, I hid my past."

But Sharkey continued to insist that he did in fact die and rise from the dead on three different occasions. The reporter couldn't get him to budge from that story. Sharkey claimed that he downed two bottles of pills on one of the deaths and that he came back by the power of Lucifer. And his terms were slippery enough that maybe he wasn't lying—not really. Not in his world. In other interviews, he talked about how the drugs helped him lower his heart rate. If he were just lying about the death and rebirth, he would have gone further—he'd describe going into the dark tunnel down to hell and partying with Judas and Keith Moon. But what he seemed to be trying to do was describe something that really happened to him in terms that made it seem paranormal.

Finally, Sharkey gets out of jail and Tray tells me he wants to talk. I'm ready to jump at the chance to ask him about his life, his struggles with the authorities, and his campaigns—and whether Kathleen is real. Jonathon is supposedly living with a friend in Indiana. And Tray tells me Jonathon is trying to set up all kinds of media interviews to launch another campaign, but Tray is trying to convince him to lay low so they don't blow their publicity before the movie comes out. Meanwhile, Tray seems frazzled and worried that his vampire opus won't be everything he wanted it to be. I get the feeling the project has taken over his life. He asks me to mention his movie.

"Unless the movie sucks," he adds, in which case he wants me to "just stab [him] in the face." I'm pretty sure he's joking. I call Jonathon.

Sharkey is intelligent, articulate, and difficult to keep up with—talking at an auctioneer's clip about his life and career and trips to jail. He wants me to know that the "stalking charges were dismissed," though he seems to have still been found guilty of delivering a subpoena to his ex. This was a misdemeanor charge, he says, but many news accounts have called him a felon.

Sharkey still thinks he did nothing wrong. He admits that at times he's "locked horns" with the authorities. But he says his ex-fiance was in trouble—an alcoholic suffering from mental illness. Not only could she hurt herself, he says, but she could hurt an innocent.

"I wouldn't turn my back on her," he tells me. Sharkey also seems very serious about having paranormal powers.

"It's the advantage of also being a witch," he adds. "A lot of my power and strength comes from Hecate, like spells, curses, and hexes."

His family life was tumultuous, he says, and he tells me stories of his mom abusing him. But he remembers his great-uncle Louis as "the greatest man in the world" because he never gave up on his loved ones.

"When his wife had an emotional breakdown, instead of putting her in an institution . . . he took care of that woman for twenty years until she died," he says. "Cared for her every day, and she didn't even know who he was." It's clear he sees this as a pattern for how he's going to care for his ex—whether she wants him to or not—and also how he's going to care for his constituents if he ever reaches public office.

When running for governor, he says he promised he was "going to have the people of Minnesota as my children. . . ." And that's the same promise he makes for his next goal, the White House.

"That's how I'm going to be president," he says, "like a daddy with all other Americans as my children. We don't have that now." Of course, daddies have to punish people, too. He says that his ex will be one of the first people to be impaled. He won't kill her, he adds. But it will sting. After being inaugurated, he says, he will turn to his ex and say, "You've been the biggest pain in my ass. So guess where you're going to be impaled?"

Another policy shift in President Sharkey's administration will be on same-sex marriage, he tells me. Not only will it become legal, but Sharkey himself will marry same-sex couples in monthly or possibly bimonthly ceremonies on the White House lawn.

Can the president marry people? Is he like a ship captain or judge?

"I am an ordained Satanic Dark Priest," Sharkey says. "I can marry people." So a person might have a problem scheduling a performance of *Ave Maria* at the reception with Sharkey there, but still.

I ask him if Kathleen is a real, separate person, and he tells me she is. He has an e-mail address for her, but right now she's in Palermo. So I can't call her. He eventually sends me an e-mail address along with a picture of her. But it's not real proof. He does acknowledge that people in the past have doubted her existence, mentioning that he believes she appeared on C-SPAN once. But he doesn't have details. He does say that "if I have my way," when he announces his candidacy for the president, she will be on camera by his side.

I mention BellaDonnaDrakul.

"She's a whacko," he says. "She's trippin', man. I don't like talking bad about anybody who's in our community . . . but she's gotta get a life."

I'm not the first person to talk about how the Internet encourages role-playing. But it seems like the role-playing some vamps engage in is ideally suited for the Web. The virtual kingdom of the online vampire community ("OVC," it's called by some) encourages people to combine vampire role-playing with Internet role-playing. But it isn't just one piece of technology. It's an entire culture.

Even before he donned a cape and found his wife/sister/lawyer/alter ego, it's easy to see how Jonathon Sharkey invented and reinvented identities for himself through the legal system and the electoral system. He ran for office in three states. He formed a racing company. He took name after name, picking them up and dropping them the way most people change outfits. And it must have seemed easy. You find the e-mail of Jeb Bush's office, you send him a message, and suddenly you get a result. Soon after that, you're talking to people in different agencies—even the White House. You fill out paperwork and you're running for public office. You go online to find court clerks, and you're using the legal system to fight for the survival of your ex-girlfriend. The Web makes it all easy, just like it lets Bella and her group swap vampire gossip from their homes and offices. But even before the Internet, we've always encouraged people to be whomever they want. To trade-up jobs, towns, or spouses. Ours is one of the most mobile societies in human history, tied together by personal growth seminars and self-help groups. We want personal transformation to be cheap, easy, and available to all.

Maybe sometimes it gets out of hand.

Crime and Punishment

"We look at our human friends as we would pets."

According to a government report, a little less than forty seconds of surveillance footage confirms the last time prison guards saw Allan Menzies alive. It was Sunday, November 14, 2004, just before 5:00 p.m. in the segregation unit of Shotts Prison, a maximum security facility in Scotland. Menzies, a loner, had declined to come out for his exercise hour. It was raining, and guards thought nothing of it. At 4:58, three guards brought food on a little trolley—prison policy dictates that three of them must be present whenever they open a prisoner's door. When they reached cell five, the camera recorded Menzies accepting his meal. The door closed for the evening, and it was not opened again until the routine cell check around 8:00 a.m. the next morning—after Menzies had taken his final victim.

Vampire associate Steven Murphy shows the prosecution his lack
of fangs at Rod Ferrell's murder trial. (AP Images)

Guards found Allan Menzies's body hanging from a bedsheet tied to the top of a metal frame outside his window. He had five light, fresh cuts on his upper left arm. On a wall next to the window, he'd written a crude last testament: the single word "justice," scrawled in his own blood.

They searched the room and uncovered part of a safety razor. They assumed Menzies used it to cut himself as well as the sheets he used to commit suicide. The forensic pathologist couldn't determine the exact time of death, though she noted that it had been at least a few hours before the body was found. She also recorded that Menzies had older scars on his body, meaning that he probably had a history of cutting himself. But anyone who knew Menzies could have told her that.

Linda Menzies, the man's mother, told authorities that Allan had tried to kill himself many, many times. A "quiet, withdrawn" boy who almost never left his bedroom, he wasn't a drinker or drug user. Unlike most teenagers, he cleaned and dusted his room every day. But he'd overdosed on acetaminophen four or five times, sometimes having to go to the hospital. He'd threatened to overdose several more times. Convicted of assault charges for stabbing a boy in front of their classmates when he was fourteen, he'd tried to hang himself with his pajamas while in custody. And when he was about twenty, his mother saw him pick up a kitchen knife once and cut himself. Prior to his death, he'd attempted to kill himself yet again.

According to the report of his death, "He was a hard boy to understand and she [his mother] knew that there was something wrong with him."

At twenty-two years old, Menzies was imprisoned for murdering his friend by stabbing him forty-two times with a large knife and bludgeoning him repeatedly with a hammer. Menzies testified in court that he drank two cups of his victim's blood and ate part of his skull. He buried the body in a woods nearby, where it lay undiscovered for five weeks.

Menzies claimed that after watching the movie *Queen of the Damned* more than one hundred times, he actually began to hear the voice of the lead character, the vampire Akasha. She commanded him to kill and promised him immortality. He testified in court that his personality began to split into an alter ego called "Vamp," and it was Vamp who did the killing. The jury didn't buy it. After deliberating for only ninety minutes, they found him guilty of murder.

"Three psychiatrists recently diagnosed you as being a psychopath," said the judge as he sentenced Menzies to eighteen years. "In my judgment, you are an evil, violent and highly dangerous man, not fit to be at liberty."

Carrying a crowbar he'd pilfered from their garage, Rod Ferrell walked into the Eustis, Florida, home of Richard Wendorf and Naoma Ruth Queen, a middle-aged couple, one fall night in 1996. Just seventeen years old, he was the "sire," or leader, of a secretive group calling itself "the Vampire Clan." After ripping the phone from the wall, he and his accomplice, Scott Anderson, came upon Wendorf lying asleep on his couch. Ferrell beat Wendorf savagely with the weapon, leaving him dying on the floor with fractures in his skull and ribs and a number of chest wounds. Queen walked out of the bathroom to see Ferrell standing in the kitchen with blood splattered on his clothes. She fought hard—dousing the intruder with coffee—but he beat her down to the floor and cracked her skull.

Ferrell and Anderson, along with three other friends—including the victims' daughter Heather Wendorf—left Eustis in their car and the Wendorfs' truck, eventually switching license plates, dumping their own car, and taking the stolen car to Louisiana. They were caught in Baton Rouge on Thanksgiving Day 1996. During their trial, Ferrell's entire bizarre, sad life came out in the open.

Born in 1980 to a seventeen-year-old girl named Sondra Gibson who split up with Ferrell's father within weeks, he moved around constantly. He grew up as a wild kid. He stayed out all night, did drugs, and skipped class. He and his mother played *Vampire: The Masquerade* together. Ferrell began to go through some kind of transformation, telling people he was "Vesago," an ancient creature of the night.

Ferrell's group was long known by cops in the rural town of Murray, Kentucky, for their suspected rituals, sucking blood from small animals and even from one another in area graveyards.

According to friends, Ferrell was intent on helping the daughter of his victims run away from home. But he had other plans as well. According to one cult member, he wanted to open the gates of hell. And to do that he needed to kill.

What Marshall McLuhan said about our tools applies to our beliefs as well: We shape them and afterward they shape us. Some beliefs help us treat each other well. Some force us to engage in rituals that many people don't accept or understand. And some beliefs make us do terrible things. But when do beliefs become delusions, and when do delusions become dangerous? If we are all essentially living in our heads, how do we figure out who's crazy and who isn't?

"You get many people who are psychologically ill who believe they need to drink blood," says Bobbi Jo O'Neal, a forensic nurse who worked as deputy coroner for the county coroner's office before switching to the public defender's office in Charleston, South Carolina. "Probably there's an equal number who believe they are Jesus. So it can go either way. The disease process is the same. It's just how it manifests itself."

O'Neal has been compiling case studies of clinical vampires who have either committed assault or even murder or harmed or killed themselves by drinking their own blood. One case she came across involved a seventeen-year-old boy who was found crumpled in his room by his parents. Paramedics rushed him to a hospital, where he died. His diary described his transformation into a "Vampiresis." Autopsy reports show it was a Prozac and Zoloft overdose that killed him, but he'd filed his canines and ingested at least 16 ounces of blood.

"There are some conditions that are made in your mind, conditions that are psychological," O'Neal says. "But you perceive them to be an actual physical need." O'Neal has also reviewed studies of people who get a sexual buzz or feeling of power from drinking blood.

"They believe that by drinking blood they will have an increase in strength and immunity prolonging their life," she writes. She recounts a case in South Carolina of a twenty-eight-year-old man, aroused by the sight of his own blood, who had developed a grisly skill. "With practice he was able to direct blood spurts into his mouth," according to her report.

How do people get to this point?

"I think that's part of the mystery to it, because it depends why they started doing it in the first place," she tells me. "There is a whole continuum of those who are just playing around, and they can take it or leave it. You've got another group who are psychologically a little bit bent and truly think that they need it. And then you have those sociopaths who take it to a whole 'nother level."

A whole 'nother level. One such case is that of a woman who would repeatedly vomit large amounts of blood. Though she was hospitalized, staffers could not detect how she was drinking it—until an examination of her mouth showed bleeding wounds at the base of her tongue. The patient was sucking it out of her own tongue without anyone knowing.

"After her death," O'Neal notes in her report, "an autopsy revealed a stomach bloated with blood."

If investigators are going through cases that might be related to vampirism, O'Neal recommends they look for a "Book of Shadows," a composition book available at occult stores that can be used as a journal. She also recommends checking dental records to see whether a person has sharpened his teeth and checking blood samples found at any crime scene to see if animal blood appears. But if some kids who dabble in this stuff are just being, well, kids, what's the harm?

"Kids in their middle teenage years are searching," she says. "You get some who might dabble in the occult and move on—realizing it's not for them. You get others who, for whatever reason, go in a different direction." Plus, she says, even the ones who aren't ready to plan a Satanic killing spree might get caught up in the mayhem.

"You've also got another population who are not necessarily bad kids, but they're very naïve," she says. They're the followers.

Of course, people who commit crimes can be completely different from a variety of folks who—for whatever reason—really think that they need to drink human blood (or suck psychic energy from people). They're out there, and they don't hurt anybody. They do this stuff behind closed doors with willing donors. Should we be concerned?

"The problem with people who dabble in vampirism," O'Neal says, "is that as long as they're doing it by themselves, they don't ever get medical treatment. That's why you don't see it that much in medical literature."

It's hard to be a vampire. You have needs and beliefs that very few others can understand.

On the House Eclipse website, there is an article called "To the Parents of a Sanguinarian." It is filled with tips for a parent whose child has just come out of the closet as a vampire.

"Be supportive of them and chat about and meet any donors they have or any houses they join," it reads. "Help teach them safe blood drinking habits and help them find a vampire mentor that you approve of to teach your child more about themselves."

It has other "Vampirism 101" tidbits you can learn and tell your kid: "Always use sterile tools. Lancets are great for new vampires. Never cut near veins. The upper arm is a great place to get blood from a scalpel, and the fingertips are wonderful for lancets."

This makes me have a flash of my son growing up and having the Most Uncomfortable Conversation Ever with him.

Son: *I want you to know something about me.*

Dad: *I think I know what you're going to say, and I want you to know, it's all right. Your mother and I love you just as you are. There's nothing wrong with being gay.*

Son: *I'm a vampire.*

Dad: *(Pause) There's nothing wrong with being gay.*

Son: *I'm not gay, Dad. I'm straight. But I have a need for fresh human blood.*

Dad: *(Longer pause) You and your boyfriend are always welcome to come home, and I want you to know . . .*

Son: *I don't have a boyfriend. I have a girlfriend. She's a dental hygienist, and she's Type O positive. Dad, we're vampires, and we're happy together. We drink each other's blood. Vampires, Dad.*

Dad: *Couldn't you just try to be gay? For your mother?*

The people who just feel like they have a real, physical need for blood, for energy, however they describe it, often say they want nothing to do with the capes and fangs crowd. I snag an interview with a vamp from the area—Kendra, a young woman who has about ten members in her group. We meet at a suburban IHOP and she brings her boyfriend because she's always a little skittish about people she meets from the Web.

The IHOP is surrounded by strip malls and parking lots, and even though we both came from opposite directions, we're about equally late, each of us griping about the terrible traffic. We settle down to omelets and pancakes while she talks matter-of-factly about vampirism.

"We think it might be a medical condition," she says. Certain people need to absorb energy from others to keep from being sick. I ask her about blood drinkers, or sanguinarians.

"We have some people who don't think they can absorb energy any other way," she says. I'm skeptical that it's a medical condition, though. Vampire websites have talked about it like it is some kind of reverse Reiki—the Japanese art of focusing mental energy onto a person's injury and healing it mentally. It's the kooky thing that Mr. Miyagi did to Ralph Macchio's gimpy leg in the *Karate Kid* right before he went out and performed that whooping crane kick that won him the contest and got him a hug from the busty, slightly chubby, but definitely cute Elisabeth Shue back before she got hard-bodied and starred in movies like *Leaving Las Vegas, Hollow Man,* and *The Saint.* Not that I have an obsession or anything. But the point is that Reiki is a spiritual art that's respected by many people, but science it ain't.

"Reiki makes no sense. It would be easy to demonstrate that Reiki practitioners cannot detect another person's energy field," according to Dr. Stephen Barrett, a retired psychiatrist and vice president of the National Council Against Health Fraud.

Kendra says her group has asked neurologists to study to see whether a vampire absorbing energy from a donor experiences a change in brain wave function in the same way a person meditating does.

"I know they might find nothing," she tells me flatly. In the meantime, she and her group just think they need to absorb this energy. They don't believe that they can rise from the grave or that they can turn into bats.

"We don't let anyone into our group who says they're five hundred years old," she tells me. I explain to her about all the different freaks I've found on the Web.

"Welcome to my world," she says.

The Drinkdeeplyanddream (DDD) website also says that vampirism might well be a medical condition: "It is *very* much like a diabetic who requires insulin to remain healthy." The author of the site, a thirty-year-old computer expert and jewelry artist from Florida, writes that real vampires sometimes need blood and sometimes psychic energy. She completely discounts the need for any vampire to have a house or ranks.

"Say it with me now: THERE IS NO SUCH THING AS 'ROYALS' or 'PURE BLOODS' or any other lame ass titled 'Hierarchy' to vampires," she posts on her site. "It's as stupid as saying there are 'Royal' diabetics or 'Pure' multiple sclerosis sufferers." She seems to have similar beliefs as Kendra's.

A psychologist named Dr. Richard Noll proposes to call clinical vampirism Renfield's Syndrome, a mental illness in which the victim is fascinated with drinking blood. According to the vamps, though, that's not the same thing. Renfield's Syndrome is a sexual fetish, and "real vampirism," or their version of it, is not.

The DDD webpage also compiles a list of symptoms and abilities vampires have, like "extraordinary night vision" with intense eye strain in bright light, an ability to "tan more quickly," and "rudimentary telepathy." The site also claims increased speed, agility, and reflexes. The symptoms the site describes are either self-reported or they're so vague you can't really test them. And the site also offers different theories about what causes vampirism, from a genetic difference to something different in a vampire's soul or chakras.

Father Sebastiaan has his own beliefs about what makes a vamp, and they are influenced by a group he ran into long ago. During his first club years in the 1990s, Sebastiaan began to meet people from the Temple of the Vampire (TOV). This is a vampire religion based out of Washington State whose members are secretive and ultra-serious. Members gave him a book of their beliefs, but at first he didn't understand any of it.

"I read it, and it seemed totally fruit loops," he says. But eventually he'd come to agree with much of it.

If you want to join Sebastiaan's group, he explains, you have to order their first book from their website. If you agree with the first book, you fill out an application form and order the second. And so on.

"We have a series of books that go deeper and deeper into our tradition," he says. And at any point, if you find yourself disagreeing with them, you just bag out. They have no problem with it, he adds, and quite frankly, they don't want you.

"We don't proselytize," he says.

Many of the group's beliefs are secret, he says. But one thing is clear: Sebastiaan's group doesn't believe that vampires (or vampyres) can consume energy by drinking blood. In fact, he adds, blood drinkers are kicked out.

"I've never met a sanguinarian who actually gets any form of sustenance off drinking blood," he says. "When I was younger I played with it. It was a fetish, but I found it just limits me. . . . It has too many health risks. If people want to do what they want to do, fine. But my organization and I have nothing to do with blood drinking."

When in a large group like a concert or a festival, he says, a Strigoi Vii vampyre can consume the psychic energy given off by people without them even knowing. In fact, he adds, it's good for people to lose some of their energy and replenish it. It's like giving blood, which forces a donor to grow fresh new cells.

"We look at our human friends as we would pets," he says. "We want humans to be happy. If someone has a dog, they treat that dog well." Then he clarifies.

"We're physically identical to a human," he says. "The difference comes down to our soul. There's something different about our soul, which I can't really get into because it's a secret."

Out in Washington, the Temple of the Vampire is convinced that they're the only real vampires, and they don't want to be associated with anyone different.

"Thank you for your kind offer for an interview," this guy named Nemo who works as their Internet administrator writes to me when I ask to talk to members of the group. "However you should understand that there is no 'vampire culture.'

"It would seem that you have been speaking to ordinary human beings who are into costumed role-playing, sexual fetishes sometimes involving blood, and/or (probably) some people in deep need of more regularly taking their psychiatric meds.

"None of these are true Vampires.

"The Temple is and remains the only public outlet for true Vampires as defined in some detail at the Temple website www. vampiretemple.com. The Temple remains the only authentic religion of Vampirism in the world."

Obviously I have all kinds of problems with a group of people saying that they alone know that they're vampires and that others who call themselves vampires are just delusional freaks in capes. It's like me saying, "Those people who say they can read minds are crazy. I know because my telepathy works perfectly." It's also a bit like Protestants and Catholics in the Middle Ages fighting each other because neither wanted to admit that the other was a "real" Christian. Once you have a category that's spiritual or supernatural, or otherwise made up in your head, you can always say you know who meets the requirements and who doesn't. The only problem is so does everybody else.

"Since you are already writing about a 'culture' we view as both illusory and opposed to everything our religion stands for, I can see no value in being further associated in print via yet another book that includes such people," Nemo continues. He offers that the TOV might consider an interview if I'm willing to do an "exclusive documentary" and first submit an outline and a "contract for content control." He claims the BBC was willing to play ball. I want to ask if he gave them a tour of his fantastical submarine, but I don't.

"In the meantime, good luck on your book, but the Temple does not wish to be associated even passively with 'children' of the night," he closes. "We are the adults." Sebastiaan admits the TOV's belief structure is very similar to his own religion, only he doesn't call it a religion.

"We are not a religion," he says. "Religions are for humans in our opinion. We believe in nothing. We don't have any belief system. We have a system of theories that people can prove to themselves. If they agree with these theories then they can move to the next level.

"A vampire doesn't believe in anything," he adds. "Our whole philosophy is that belief is a tool. And we encourage humans to believe in things because it keeps them sedated. It's an opiate."

The TOV and Sebastiaan's group both practice skepticism— kinda. You don't accept the existence of paranormal stuff unless you can prove it to yourself, Sebastiaan says. But there's a catch.

"For the vast majority of people, they're not aware of it," he says. "It's like someone who has been blind since childhood and doesn't know what color is. Our subtle gene allows us to have that extra perception." So it's proof, but it's proof you can't prove to others. It's something you can feel. You can count on the results, but you won't be able to repeat them for the average person.

I was raised Catholic, so I've grown up practicing ritual cannibalism and blood drinking with a Jewish cult that just happened to have some very aggressive PR men. I believe in an undead hippy carpenter who died two thousand years ago, but who listens to me when I call him up to bitch about my career and occasionally say thanks for a bout of good weather and a nice vacation. So who am I to laugh at other people's crazy beliefs? But Sebastiaan says his "vampyre" group depends on something other than belief. Can he be right?

Well, whatever vampirism is, it's hard to classify it as a medical condition. One assertion I've found on vamp websites is that only you can say for sure if you are one of them. But the entire medical profession is set up so that you take your symptoms to other people who poke you, prod you, and drain your blood for centrifuges, and then tell you you've got all kinds of things wrong with you that you could not have guessed.

Patient: *Doctor, I feel lethargic and out of sorts. I think the cosmic energies that I usually draw into my being are tapped out. I need replenishment.*

Doctor: *Well, the tests say syphilis.*

The TOV church's website says that each adherent gradually proves the miracles of the faith to himself or herself as he or she climbs the ladder. And Sebastiaan echoes this. During one dead-raising ceremony, he adds, a friend of his who was deeply skeptical got so scared by the ghostly presence of a millennia-old Babylonian, he became a believer. But, Sebastiaan adds, you can't do the ceremony in front of outsiders. The gods won't come.

I call Joe Nickell to set me straight on this stuff. A former stage magician and private eye, he is now senior research fellow of the Committee for Skeptical Inquiry (CSI)—an international scientific organization that tries to study critically ESP, haunted houses, spontaneous combustion, UFO's, and anything else you might have heard from your weird college friend with those crystals and that patchouli oil stink. Joe Nickell has researched all kinds of mystical stuff. He likes to joke that he's "been in more haunted houses than Caspar." When I catch up to him, he has just come back from a project for *National Geographic* for which he tried to re-create the famous Nazca Spider, one of the giant shapes created by ancient peoples in Peru that are supposedly so intricate they prove that alien technology was involved. To see whether this claim was plausible, Nickell tried—and succeeded—in building a copy of the Spider himself.

"They were very happy with what I did," he adds, with a chuckle. "They filmed it from a high lift truck. I will be known henceforth as 'Spider Man.' "

I start to tell him about these people who claim that they need to drink blood or consume energy and that they can commune with thousand-year-old vamps, but he cuts me off.

"Hold it," he says. "The operative words are 'they claim.' Let's stop a minute and just explore that. Because I get this all the time. People call me and claim—I hear this daily. And the suggestion is that somehow I or some other skeptic is supposed to have some counter to that.

"Well, humbug," he says. "I wish this were taught in the seventh grade: The burden of proof of a claim is on the claimant. Never on someone else to prove a negative." He starts talking about how the undead might, just might, be creeping around Transylvania.

"We can't prove there are no vampires," he says. "Can't be done. We could search Transylvania and not find a vampire.

" 'Well, don't you know they come out only at night and are very elusive?' " he describes someone saying. And then he goes on, talking about how we could try to pin down a particular cemetery, grave marker, and time of day. And each time, someone making this claim about vampires could throw a roadblock in our way. It underlines how vague and how impossible to prove or disprove these claims about blood drinking or psy-sucking are.

Does it kill a vampire to avoid blood for one week? No, the blood is just required for you to "stay sane and healthy." What does that mean? How could you differentiate between someone who wasn't and someone who was? How would you set up a test to check for vampirism among your average group of hungry, tired, vaguely crazy people who fill every house, street, and office building in the country? Can't be done.

I tell Nickell about how some vampires say they can transfer energy from people, using it to feed on, and he dismisses this out of hand.

"This is the modern buzzword for almost all the paranormal claims," he says, adding that when physicists talk about it, they mean something very different.

"What these people mean by 'energy' is a mystical, magical force, unfindable by science." Why use the term "energy" at all? Why not say, uh, mystical, magical force?

"Because it's a familiar word. It makes it sound real and almost like a scientific fact. But it's not science." But why do people believe these things? I don't know and neither does Nickell. Once we can discount the idea that this is science, the easy explanations melt away.

I ask Nickell about my theory that vampire groups might just have a set of spiritual beliefs, no less valid than my lapsed-Catholic-Episcopalian-turncoat dogma.

"Catholicism has that whole blood fascination," he says. "I mean, Methodists don't do this. The bleeding wounds of Christ, the communion . . . so vampires are a perfect fit." And then he gets an idea.

"Let's suppose that all the claims of both Catholics and

vampires are true," he says. "So imagine a vampire has a thirst for blood. He converts to Catholicism and partakes of Holy Communion, which actually turns to blood when he drinks it.

"I guess we'll never be able to test this out," he says. "But it's an exciting thought. A possible remedy." So if you're reading this, and you're a vamp, maybe you should give the RC church a try. We've got blood. We've got wine. We've got babes in plaid skirts. What more could you want?

To make matters weirder, I begin to research different New Age groups and find a clique of people who have eerie similarities to vampires. They're called the Breatharians. These people claim that under the right conditions, they can live on almost nothing but prana, the energy that psychic vampires suck down.

There's evidence Breatharianism is flagrantly, dangerously stupid. For instance, a kindergarten teacher from Germany killed himself with the practice in 1997. Next, a lady from Melbourne died the year after. The year after that, a practitioner of Breatharianism named Verity Linn launched a twenty-one-day fast in Scotland. Police eventually found her emaciated corpse by the shore of a lake. However, vampires who just "snack" on energy concentrated in the blood or directly from the ether have created an untestable (and much safer) form of Breatharianism. I ask Selina, who's a friend of mine and a psychologist specializing in eating disorders. Hey, I figure that it might qualify. Actually, though she's never treated any vamps, she recognizes the behavior.

"People with eating disorders will swear by *all kinds* of absurd nutritive tenets," she writes in an e-mail interview. "They argue that certain types of foods are more likely to be converted to fat . . . Ingestion of such-and-such speeds metabolism . . . that kind of thing. And they *truly* believe it."

But her understanding of what makes a person delusional and

what makes a person a believer is even more perplexing. She says simply that head shrinkers don't have clear distinctions between delusions and religious beliefs.

"In diagnostic terms, we differentiate between 'bizarre' and 'nonbizarre' delusions. Nonbizarre delusions are things that *could* happen, although there might not be substantial 'proof' to hold the belief (for example, belief that one's spouse is cheating). To be considered a bizarre delusion, the belief has to be clearly impossible or implausible and not derived from ordinary life experiences.

"And here's where it gets tricky," she adds. "Cultural and religious context has to be considered in determining any kind of diagnostic-level delusion." In other words, religious people have a Get Out of Jail Free card. People in some cultures believe in talking to the dead. People in others believe in rain dances. I can essentially dodge the man with the butterfly net if I get enough people to go along with me. That can't be right, can it?

"There is a difference between believing in something you can't prove because the belief as defined is beyond observation and evidence (i.e., there is a God) versus believing in something that defies logic and our current knowledge of the natural world (i.e., I am a god)," according to Stuart Vyse, psychology professor at Connecticut College. "I believe a spiritual or religious belief is one that is not just unproven but untestable.

"Having said this, we are all deluded from time to time," he adds, "and I would not be quick to call those who accept odd beliefs mentally ill." And another expert is not so sure about why guys like me are the way we are.

"The surveys certainly show that the majority of people across all cultures have some kind of belief in the supernatural, in spite of the Enlightenment," says Terry Sandbek, a psychologist and president of the Sacramento Skeptics Society. "Many philosophers and psychologists are trying to understand this observation. Maybe it is

merely driven by culture or has had some type of evolutionary benefit in the history of human development. We just don't know the
answer yet." I think the nuns beat it into me. But I'm not ready to
publish.

As far as why people might actually feel like they needed to
take blood to alleviate physical symptoms, Vyse points to the so-
called placebo effect.

"There is much research suggesting that placebos are very powerful . . . in some cases outweighing the effects of the real drug," he
says. Convince someone that blood will treat his or her symptoms,
especially the kind of vague symptoms listed in the vampire websites
like lethargy and light sensitivity, and it might. It almost makes you
want to psych yourself into thinking you're a vamp and start draining
the cat every time you suffer that 3:00 p.m. sugar crash.

But what I really want to know is why some people have
beliefs that make them do good (or at least not do bad things) and
others start whacking folks after they hear the voices.

"I think it is quite tricky," Vyse tells me. "When people break
laws, then we get to step in and say that this is unacceptable. The
larger social group responds. And a belief may have encouraged that
action, but so what?" All kinds of beliefs might at one point or
another push people to do evil, he adds. And one more thing:

"Who gets to decide? Consider the happy alcoholic who both-
ers no one but just likes to drink all day. Manages to manage his
affairs, etc. Is drinking bad for his health? Undoubtedly. Is he short-
ening his life span? Perhaps. But who gets to say he should stop?" Put
another way, people in Kendra's group might think that drinking
blood will make their symptoms go away—maybe we can prove this
someday, and maybe we can't. But as long as it doesn't drive her to
violate my rights, I have to leave her alone. And I have to hope she
extends the same courtesy to me and to others.

But what about the case of the so-called "Vampire of Virginia

Beach"? In 1996, a twenty-six-year-old air-conditioning technician named Jon C. Bush was convicted of thirty sexual crimes against eight underaged girls, some as young as thirteen, during a vampire LARP game. The pattern of his attacks was similar in every case. According to authorities, Bush recruited his first victim, a fourteen-year-old girl, to play the game sometime in the summer of 1995, telling her she could become "embraced" as a vampire by "marking, blood, and sex." Marking, according to testimony by the victim, was a hickey, given just below the breast. The victim said that Bush sexually assaulted her within the next couple of months, giving her the vampire name of "Desiree" and recruiting others, sometimes through friends already in the group. Young girls learned from their friends that they should ask Bush about the game. He would explain the rules, then call and meet them later. Eventually he'd sexually assault them in a variety of ways, sometimes explaining the act as a way of "feeding" off them. According to the prosecutor, Bush used "scare tactics" to keep them in line.

"I would submit that not every single victim was terrified of him or intimidated by him, but that at least some of them were," the prosecutor said according to press accounts. And Don Rimer, the cop who helped put Bush away, says there were many more victims than the ones we know about—possibly as many as fifty.

"Those girls willing to testify," he tells me, "were the ones whose parents cooperated, the ones who were mentally healthy enough to cooperate. But there were dozens more whose parents grabbed up their kids and moved away. . . ." Rimer says the web of Bush's victims stretches through several cities in Virginia and even into North Carolina.

"The victimization went on and on and on because of him." And Rimer is convinced this was not just some consensual game.

"Initially they were invited to play a game," he says. "But when they would want to leave, he would threaten them with burning down their houses, killing their families, that kind of thing. Some of these young women were raped and sodomized dozens of times under threat of something happening to their families." One of the key witnesses for the prosecution in the case, Rimer is a veteran cop who was the Virginia Beach Police Department's expert on vampires, grave robbery, and the occult. Joining the force in 1971, he began to teach himself about these subjects in the mid-1980s, when his chief began to notice a disturbing pattern in the region. There was a case of someone ritually mutilating dogs and laying them out on an inverted cross near the Virginia Beach courthouse, he says. He talks about another group of dogs burnt near the Chesapeake Bay Bridge Tunnel, a couple grave robberies, and "just a whole smattering of things."

"The chief came to me and said, 'Don, nobody has got a handle on this. I need you to get on it, because this stuff is starting to show up too often.' "

During Bush's trial, a psychiatrist studied him and concluded that he was competent to stand trial. However, he did have "symptoms which are best diagnosed as meeting the criteria for the schizotypal personality disorder," the psychiatrist added in a letter to the court. Bush had "paranoid ideas of reference, odd beliefs and magical thinking" and "inappropriate and constricted affect and behavior and appearance that in general would be perceived as odd, eccentric and peculiar."

Sounds bad.

However, as the doctor noted, Bush was already having breakthroughs in jail.

"It appears to me in the interim since vampire-based activities ceased, he has come to recognize that a number of these behaviors were quite self-serving . . ." the psychiatrist wrote, adding that Bush saw how his crimes even allowed him to "gratify a number of rather primitive sexual and aggressive impulses."

So it wasn't just being a twisted, psychologically damaged creature of the night! Bush just wanted to have *sex with teenage girls*. How strange that he was able to repress his real motivations into his vampire game and only discover them after he was caught. Kind of like how I realized making fun of the fat kid in sixth grade was wrong after he threw me into a snowbank. Amazing what you can learn about yourself.

Since retiring in 2005, Don Rimer has been a consultant on occult crimes, traveling to police departments and conferences across the country to talk about the constantly changing world of ghoulish punks and the twisted stuff they do. Clearly, some of these crimes can get overhyped. Back in the 1980s, there was a rash of people disgorging repressed memories of Satanic ritual abuse—remember that?—and it turned out to be bogus. In the early 1990s, Kenneth Lanning, a special agent in the FBI's Behavioral Science Unit, investigated hundreds of these cases and couldn't find hard evidence in any of them.

It's easy to find examples of bands with hideously violent lyrics and stage shows. There are people who are cultists, Satanists, or devil-worshippers, and some of them do bad things. But is this "devil culture" causing mayhem or reflecting it? Was Allan Menzies a time-bomb before or after he popped that movie into his VCR?

Even though Rimer is always going to clubs and meeting people with all kinds of occult beliefs, he says he's still constantly learning about his subject. He calls himself a student and says the danger line is hard to find.

"My only concern is when they're underaged," he says. If you're an adult playing D&D or one of the Vampire games, you have the ability to distinguish between what's fake and what's real, he says. But kids don't have the defense mechanisms we take for granted. They believe easily, and they can get sucked in. Rimer says his Powerpoint lecture has several slides of a young kid who is constantly role-playing a character. He's in his role "twenty-four/seven," Rimer says, and he goes alone to clubs throughout D.C.

"He's a target."

Sometimes the danger is obvious. For all the ink spilled on a guy like Bush, in the end, he was a sexual predator. Not something new. He was the kind of guy the criminal justice system has been dealing with as long as people have had courts and cops. He wasn't really like Kendra or her group. Subcultures rise and fall, and technologies and pastimes change. But criminals don't change. Those around them do.

And all of this brings us back to Nico Claux, the "Vampire of Paris" and the guy whose case helped drive a wedge between Sebastiaan and House Eclipse. According to an article on Court TV's *Crime Library*, Claux was a morgue technician obsessed with death. He met a man in 1994 through an early version of the Web called Minitel, possibly with the ruse of having some kind of S&M experience. According to the article, Claux went to the man's apartment and, after being let in, shot his victim in the eye. While the man lay on the ground, Claux explored his apartment. A few minutes later, Claux noticed his victim gasping for breath and struggling to stay alive. Claux shot him several more times, but, bafflingly, the man hung on. So Claux found cookies in the victim's kitchen and sat down to munch them while he watched the man die.

He got tagged with the "Vampire" moniker because when cops raided Claux's apartment, they allegedly found body parts and bags of blood he'd been stealing from his job. He reportedly ate human flesh and drank blood. But according to the article, that part may have been a hoax. The documents in the case make no mention of Nico's cannibalism, and the French media merely reported him as a killer. The bizarre details came from Nico himself. They undoubtedly helped him launch his new career painting other killers.

More than a decade later, Claux has been interviewed many

times by magazines like *Bizarre*, by documentary filmmakers, and by kids with webzines. Because he's a freak. But he's the coolest freak of all. He has the best monster costume: the one with real blood on it.

However, looking at his MySpace page—yes, he has a MySpace page—it's obvious to me he has many friends and fans. MySpace is a petri dish of viral marketing, and having someone like Nico Claux link to your site can only help you sell your wares.

A "homicidal guitarist" from Clearwater, Florida, sends his "Infernal Blessings"—his page is so littered with goat's head pentagrams you can't read the text, and it makes your head hurt. Another linked to Nico is a tattoo artist from Michigan whose page reads, "Welcome to the Darkness, where art pulls you in and your mind will never leave!" A guy from Indiana posts, "i would like to say i'm a huge fan and not just of your artwork" (this guy's page is a giant collage of serial killers, a quote from Adolph Hitler, and photos of himself sitting in front of a giant Nazi flag).

Down at the bottom of Nico's page is a link to Mark "Chopper" Read, the infamous Australian criminal who spent almost thirty years in prison for everything from trying to kidnap a judge at gunpoint to stabbing a man with scissors to arson. He has a rap album out now.

There are links to an assortment of metalheads with hairstyles like Jesus' angry older brother and a sprinkling of guys with the shaved-head-and-goatee LaVey uniform. In fact, one of the links is to Stanton LaVey, the actual grandson of the founder of the Church of Satan himself. Stanton's website is littered with all kinds of devil symbols, and he actually looks like a younger, thinner, but somehow less-scary version of Granddad.

Many of these people seem about as threatening as Goths back in high school. And it might be the genius of MySpace that it's kind of a virtual high school, with its networks of people posting their artwork and favorite quotes, just like the kids scribbling lyrics on their notebooks to show what they believe in and who they are. The MySpace people play out these roles—they act like rebels, Satanists, Goths, and vamps.

Nowadays, people stretch their youth out well into their forties. Our parents woke up in their mud-smeared hemp tents and got jobs as they got older. Our grandparents packed off to go shoot Germans or North Koreans by the time they could drink. We might have houses and families, but we try to go to concerts, to keep current, to maintain our little shrines of pop culture just like the theater kid stockpiling clove cigarettes in his locker. MySpace encourages this. It allows you to act like you're avoiding adulthood while you go about the very adult activity of marketing your band or your business. Above all, it encourages you to create and re-create yourself.

In the permanent virtual high school world of MySpace, folks who believe strange things can meet other folks who believe strange things. Only now, through the magic of the Web, the number of those secret allies and friends is practically infinite.

And a guy like Nico Claux is cool in this world (despite the fact that his paintings are kind of wooden and artless) because he's the dangerous kid. He's the one you avoid. He's the one who might have brought a gun with him or stayed after to vandalize the gym. Every high school has a dangerous kid. But here again, the magic of the Web is at work: MySpace has a virtually infinite number of dangerous types to work with, so this dangerous person is not just the scariest dude in your town, he's one of the scariest in the *world*. MySpace provides a safe brush with a scary man—like the thrill of a movie monster jumping out at you. But how safe is it?

Looking at the photos of the people in Nico's world, with their shocking statements, pentagrams, made-up rules, and make-believe powers, I'm not only thoroughly unafraid of them, I'm actually worried for them a little. A guy like Nico crossed a line they can read about and sing about and watch movies about, but it's a line they'll never really know. Hopefully.

Once you cross that line, it disappears. You do the terrible thing, and the heavens don't open up. No one comes down to smite you and make things right. We might live in our heads with our own private mythologies, but the world we share is made of nothing but airplanes and computers. Of killers, victims, and the quiet gods who let it all happen.

Faith or no faith, you have to recognize that here on earth only humans police the line between good and evil. All our history has been trying to keep people from crossing it. People want to fly off into their dark fantasies. That's what we all do. And there's a whole world of people in strange costumes playing scary roles who are genuinely good and kind.

But some do cross the line. Some go so far that when they come back, home will look strange to them. And they might always do it again. Because crossing the line is stupidly easy. The people who write to killers, who send them pictures, and try to make friends . . . Do they know how easy it is?

Nine

Dr. Maggot and the Ruby Slippers

*"There was nobody at the seminary
I could talk about vampires with."*

Glittering from a shelf on Jeanne Youngson's bookcase, the ruby slippers look bright arterial red and gaudy as costume jewelry. Just like I remember them, stuck on a pair of striped dead legs sticking out from under that house newly whisked away from Kansas and plopped down in the Technicolor Land of Oz.

But they're not *those* ruby slippers. They're close. These shoes are also-rans. They are the footwear equivalent of any poor sap unlucky enough to enter *American Idol* alongside Kelly Clarkson. The studio, Youngson explains, had a hell of a time finding shoes that fit Judy Garland's feet. They made countless pairs of them, she adds. Whether it's because Judy had one of those tricky between sizes or

Jeanne Youngson with her memories. Up and to the left are the
Oscars and the ruby slippers.

whether it's because she was insane—or possibly an entertaining
combo of the two—Youngson doesn't say. But she grabbed herself a
pair, and here they sit just above two other pieces of Hollywood
memorabilia: the Oscar statues won by her late husband Robert—
one in 1952 for directing the short film *World of Kids* and the second
in 1955 for *This Mechanical Age*. He had an illustrious career even
after that, going on to direct famous documentaries such as *When
Comedy Was King*. But it was *This Mechanical Age* that first grabbed
young Jeanne's attention.

"I fell in love with the movie before I ever met Robert Youngson," she says. She was working as a receptionist for the studio MCA,
catching glimpses of movie stars in the hall, when she ran into her
future husband. She remembers how he asked her out for coffee, and

she turned him down at first. But he persisted, asking her out again and again until finally she relented. They were married in 1960. He died in 1974.

We're in Youngson's penthouse apartment on the west side of Washington Square Park in New York City. The windows and deck look out over the jumble of buildings in lower Manhattan. It has high ceilings, a doorman, and an impressive view—the kind of place you'd rob banks and bribe supers to get. Its rooms are absolutely stuffed with books, pictures, and strange items. Raggedy Ann dolls and toy rats peek out everywhere.

"I call this one Mortimer," she says, putting a big, rubbery, remote-controlled rat on the ground and making it zoom around. She explains how Mortimer is the name a guy named Walt Disney wanted for his cartoon mouse before he thought up a better moniker. She has a million stories like this.

Jeanne Youngson, who founded the first Dracula Fan Club in the world, now runs the Vampire Empire, and her office is a publishing headquarters for the newsletter on all things vamp. Once every quarter, a half dozen people gather in the place to put the thing out.

Youngson started her Dracula Museum—a huge collection of horror mementoes—back in 1990. It sat on Fifth Avenue (as six thousand fans visited over the next nine years) until it was moved to Vienna. They had a party to celebrate the new location, and Youngson almost had another brush with greatness. A letter arrived at her place inviting her to the festivities, where she would be honored up on stage with luminaries like Roman Polanski. But she missed the chance. She opened the letter three days after the ceremony, when she'd just come back from a horrible trip to the South Pole.

"If you go to Antarctica, go by helicopter," she says. "*Don't* take the Drake Passage." She says she was on a ship crossing the body of water below the tip of South America, bored out of her mind, surrounded by people throwing up on deck, while she could have been hobnobbing with Polanski and crew in Vienna.

Chatty and adventurous, Jeanne Youngson seems to know practically everyone in the network of Dracula scholars and fans that reaches across North America and Europe. She has traveled with many of the scholars to conferences around the world and has been to Romania more times than she can remember. She met—and developed a little bit of a schoolgirl crush on—Bela Lugosi Jr.

"He was glorious!" she says. "Much taller than his dad."

She's feuded with other scholars, including a self-styled "real" vampire hunter from England whom she says has actually accused her of being a spy for the CIA. Youngson is one of the luminaries in the world of undead fandom. And her Vampire Empire is one of the major international organizations for scholars and aficionados of Dracula. One other is the Transylvanian Society of Dracula, with its headquarters in Bucharest and chapters in Canada, the United States, Germany, Britain, Spain, and Italy. Scholars who study Dracula and vampires come from fields as diverse as literature, film studies, religious studies, and forensic entomology.

Ironically perhaps, it's books like McNally and Florescu's *In Search of Dracula*—whatever their mistakes—that put Dracula scholarship on the map. Because of them, J. Gordon Melton says, courses on the subject popped up in universities across the country. Because of them, the vampires have an empire.

Melton is a colleague of Youngson's. The two and their friend Elizabeth Miller met at a pub in Ireland while taking in a conference on Bram Stoker and planned "Dracula 97," the conference, convention, and massive blowout—even Elvira was there—in Los Angeles to honor the one hundredth anniversary of the publication of *Dracula*. But Melton is not just an expert on vampires. He's also a Methodist minister.

A graduate of Garrett-Evangelical Theological Seminary with a Ph.D. in the history and literature of religion from Northwestern University, Melton is famous as the creator of the *Encyclopedia of American Religions.* With a list of more than two thousand different faiths, it's one of the most influential and detailed books about religions in this country. Melton also wrote a book on Scientology and cowrote books on Catholicism, Islam, and Native American beliefs. He's just as proud of *The Vampire Book: The Encyclopedia of the Undead.*

"I hope the books on vampires are just as scholarly as the others," he says.

He was under contract to the publishing company Gale Research, he says, and they asked him to prepare a list of projects he might like to do. A book on vampires was just one of the items he threw in. But the publisher was excited by the project, and they "jumped on it immediately." The same editor who worked on his religious encyclopedia helped bring *The Vampire Book* to life.

The reason Melton wanted to write it, he says, is that people were constantly publishing vampire books with misinformation, and as a scholar, it made him concerned.

"They'd just write anything, and it could get published," he marvels.

His twin interests, in religions and vampires, have always developed side by side, and both began back when he was a young man. He got started watching vamp flicks growing up in Birmingham, Alabama. And in high school, he got the "call to the ministry." He went to Birmingham Southern College, a Methodist school just across town from where he grew up. He majored in geology and prepared for a career as a teaching minister. Then he went on to seminary in the Chicago area.

But during all that time, Melton was a collector of sorts. Even before he knew what he was doing, he loved to catalog the different kinds of religions that existed in his region.

"Once I got a car and had free time to move about, I could go visit them." Throughout high school and college, Melton visited church services and revivals like other kids might follow a band on tour.

In a 1995 interview with *Time* magazine, Melton said that America "now has a greater diversity of religious groups than any country in recorded history."

Many of these were New Age religions, he tells me, but part of the growth is related to more traditional churches—Lutheran, Presbyterian, and Methodist—that merged or split. These churches emerged as "mainline the day they were formed," he says. And they were part of the incredible variety and scope of religious organizations that had always been part of American history. This country is a huge producer of religions for two reasons, he explains. The first reason is that we've had the freedom to do it longer than anyone. And the other reason, he says, is that massive numbers of immigrant groups have brought their religions over here, and they have changed and sometimes mingled those religions.

"We have invited people from all over the world to come here," he says, "and they have come and brought their homegrown religions, and then those have splintered and diversified.

"I tell people," he says, "that Los Angeles is the only place in the world where you can find viable worshipping communities of every form of Buddhism. You can't do that in Asia."

Melton was determined to catalog as many of these groups as possible. A serious student, he found himself paring down all his leisure activities in that way grad school kids do as they enter crunch time.

But one thing he kept was vampires. And soon this budding religious scholar found some friends.

"I got connected with the vampire community in Chicago during my seminary days," he says. Groups of fifty of them would gather to watch movies, and Melton had a blast. It was a way to get away from school and unwind with people who were completely unlike his classmates. They weren't grad school nerds.

"They were people who went straight into a work career out of high school," he says. He and one of them, Marty, became fast friends.

"Marty had started the very first vampire interest group in the west," Melton says. "He's an interesting guy—he worked for many years as a hypnotist, and he was putting together some of the Chicago psychic fairs.

"There was nobody at the seminary I could talk about vampires with," he says with a chuckle. Many of them were straightlaced. And the ones who weren't did not exactly share his interests—the seminary had its share of "wild children," just busting loose from religious families for the first time in their lives and hitting the booze and hooking up with everything in sight. Melton wanted to hang out with his nice, tame group of vamp fans. He made ties he kept for the rest of his life, including his current wife.

In the late 1980s and early '90s, he began to read more nonfiction books about the phenomenon of Dracula. By 1992, he says he was very comfortable working on encyclopedias, and it made sense for him to work on one about vampires. But during the writing of it, Melton found himself practically paralyzed after a major heart operation. An admitted workaholic, he spent six months unable to do anything. The only way he got through it, he says, was asking his wife to bring him a constant series of vampire films. That way, he reasoned, he could watch movies, and tell himself he was doing research.

"I probably watched one hundred fifty to two hundred vampire movies that year," he says. At the end of the summer, he was better and actually took a trip to Romania, where he celebrated by hiking up the 1,500 steps of Poenari Castle.

"When I got down I pronounced myself well," he says. "I did it very slowly, but I did the whole thing. I've done it two times since. I don't plan to do it again." He brought back a little chip that had fallen from the castle wall to remind himself.

Vampires had always been a kind of alternative to his collection of religions. But at some point, the worlds began to collide. The current edition of his religious encyclopedia contains vampire religions like the Temple of the Vampire in Lacey, Washington. And he's still trying to decide whether the sanguinarians, people who believe they need to ingest human blood, meet the criteria to be a religion.

"The sanguinarians were just coming on the scene when the last edition of my encyclopedia was being done," he says.

His interests have also given this Methodist minister an insight into the Church of Satan (CoS) and related groups. He calls the CoS a "Satanist group that didn't believe in Satan" because their members are often atheists who use Satan as a kind of symbol for the freedom that they say Christianity forbids.

But members of the Temple of Set—"a schism of the Church of Satan," founded in 1975—believe that Satan is a real guy, and that his real identity comes from the Egyptian god Set. Where the Satanists use their guy as a symbol, the Setians are trying to reclaim him. But can you take definitions and just change them around to suit yourself?

"That's one of the great ways you revise theology," he says. And vampire groups have also been constantly shifting and changing, just like religions. Psychic vampire groups he's cataloged have mutated into sanguinarian groups.

Melton is also attempting to build a vampire library. He was inspired to do this after meeting Robert Bisang, a book collector and member of the Canadian chapter of the Transylvanian Society of Dracula in British Columbia. The first time Melton met Bisang, he went to his house and was astounded by the massive number of books he'd collected.

Over the years, he's become determined to rival it. Every time he has visited the area, he says, he has dropped in on Bisang and made lists of books he needs to get. But Bisang is still ahead of him. Melton is a collector of many things, but in this one case, he seems to have met his match.

"Rob's is still the best," he says. "He has got a hundred books that nobody else has." These are books from the nineteenth and early twentieth centuries, Melton explains, and some of these books are the only known surviving copies.

Bisang did the tough work of tracking down titles that didn't even sound like they were related to vampires and putting them into his collection. Melton mentions that Bisang is working on new, mysterious projects with Stoker's manuscript of *Dracula*, a manuscript that had dropped out of sight for almost a century before it surfaced in 1980 and later hit the auction block at Christie's. But Melton won't go into detail about it. He doesn't want to cause trouble.

"There are certain people within the vampire scholarly world who'd steal anything," he tells me. Bisang himself won't tell me much more. I ask him about the location, the buyer, and any details about where he's looked at it and when. Nada.

"PAUL," he e-mails me in all caps, "I CAN'T ANSWER ANY PART OF THIS QUESTION WITHOUT COMPROMISING SECURITY." But he will say that the manuscript is "full of surprises" for the scholarly world.

"It hints that Dracula resembles Bram Stoker's employer, Henry Irving, and compares the three vampire women in his castle to the witches in *Macbeth*," he tells me. And he adds that the manuscript solves once and for all a question that Dracula scholars have been fighting over for years—the question of whether Stoker's short story, "Dracula's Guest," was actually part of the novel. For years, scholars have been debating whether this was true. According to Bisang, the manuscript "leaves no doubt" that it was.

Bisang describes how he first learned about the *Dracula* manuscript just after it slipped through his fingers. A bookseller told him he'd just sold the thing to another collector. But after the Christie's auction—at which it failed to meet the minimum price to be sold—he was able to see it again.

"I've seen it twice since then."

Clocking in at more than five hundred pages, it is the only surviving full-length manuscript of Stoker's story. And it has Stoker's original title, "The Un-Dead," along with an aborted ending, in which Dracula's Castle is destroyed by a volcanic explosion. (Explosion? Was Stoker's editor working for some ancestor of Jerry Bruckheimer?)

Bisang writes that he first read *Dracula* when he was eleven years old, and he fell in love with the heroine, Mina, "who was both intelligent and adventurous." But it's not just the subject matter he loves. He's a fiend for collecting itself. He says that book-collecting "evokes our primitive memories as hunter-gatherers.

"No matter what you collect, it is the hunt that's fascinating," he adds. "In my case, the books are like trophies. As I look around my library, I can recall finding certain books and the thrill that went with it. The fact that I specialize in vampire books allowed me to become an expert on a fascinating subject." In fact, when I ask him whether he has any major holes in his collection—items he's desperately trying to acquire—he tells me, "Sadly, no."

The item in his collection that gives him the most pride is a Hutchinson's Colonial edition of *Dracula*.

"When it was offered for sale on eBay a few years ago, I thought that it might be the true first edition—i.e., an edition that preceded the well-known Constable publication of 1897," he writes. "Research bore this out. Although half of a dozen copies of this book have shown up since then, I had the privilege of making the discovery and announcing it to the world."

He and Melton are working on various bibliographies of different kinds of vampire literature—including comics, *Dracula*-related work, nonfiction, and different periods of literature.

"At some point, I would like to do an annotated edition of Dracula as well as a book on Dracula and Jack the Ripper," Bisang tells me, adding, "I've already published a paper which shows that *Dracula* was based on the Jack the Ripper murders." It's an exciting time for Bisang. He's worked on many of these projects for twenty years or so and they're finally coming together. But he has no doubt that we will never solve all the mysteries around Stoker's novel.

"There is no doubt that many questions about how and why Stoker wrote *Dracula* will never be answered," he tells me. "How did a second-rate writer create the world's best-selling novel? Or how could Stoker have been oblivious to the fact that he had written an erotic novel?"

According to Melton, more is to come: "There's some other exciting stuff in Stoker studies coming out that is going to blow some people's minds."

Working with Bisang on at least one of these projects is Elizabeth Miller, a retired Canadian professor of English. Middle-aged, friendly, and momish, this woman has made it her life's work to kill your buzz. Reading her website, particularly the section on twenty common misconceptions about Dracula, you will learn that the story was *not* inspired by a meal of bad crab that Stoker had, that Stoker did *not* die of syphilis, and that he was *not* secretly in love with his boss, Henry Irving.

And in her books like *A Dracula Handbook* and *Dracula: Sense and Nonsense*, you will learn that most of the connections between the historical and literary Dracula are bunk. You can chat with her and in five minutes, she will tell you how almost every intriguing, fascinating story you've heard about Stoker and his novel is wrong. One of the foremost experts on the subject, she's spent more than twenty years on a mission to dispel lies about Dracula in literature and history. Though she's pleasant and loves to gab about the lore, as she talks about the horribly false things people have been saying about her Vlad all these years, she gets a bit of an edge in her voice. She's a woman on a crusade. She remembers when she first started looking at the books about the subject and realized they seemed "fishy."

"There were some things I was suspicious of," she says, adding that she sees a scholar as a kind of detective and that she decided to open the Dracula file.

"Once I scratched the surface, I saw a lot of material was flawed," she says. "It had no basis in fact—especially a lot of the stuff on Vlad the Impaler."

She's head of the Canadian chapter of the Transylvanian Society of Dracula and editor of the *Journal of Dracula Studies*. But she's most well known for first dispelling the myth, popularized by McNally and Florescu, that Stoker had in-depth knowledge of Vlad the Impaler himself.

Countless magazines, newspapers, and TV shows have interviewed her—and she tries and tries to dispel the hype about her hero. Miller has become the Shelby Foote of the Undead. The definitive chronicler of the Impaler, the Count, and everything in between. But she can't always keep people from making their mistakes.

A native of Newfoundland, she got a Ph.D. in English literature studying Lord Byron, and though she's read *Dracula* as a child, it did not leave much of an impression on her.

"I had no interest in it whatsoever," she says, "and I had no interest in horror films. My interest was in political novels like *1984* and *Darkness at Noon. . . .*"

But that changed "right out of the blue" in 1990 when she was looking for new material to teach in her courses. She read Stoker's book for the first time as an adult and was blown away. It had everything—it was the kind of fun, teachable book she could use, and it had interesting sci-fi elements, almost like a modern thriller. Plus, Stoker had embedded all kinds of quotes from Shakespeare and other worthwhile references into his story.

"There were all these little threads," she says. "So many little trails. No end to little paths I could go down." And once she started realizing how much misinformation was out there, she'd found her calling.

In her book *Sense and Nonsense*, she is passionate about rooting out Dracula falsehood. She reviews claim after claim that people have made in books, documentaries, and radio shows and then shoots them down mercilessly:

> **"Bram Stoker was an English writer." (*The New Webster's International Encyclopedia*, 1996, 324)**
> **Balderdash! Stoker was Irish.**

Here is another example:

> **"Previous to his classic study of Count Dracula, [Stoker had] been the author of only one earlier volume" (Manuela Dunn Mascetti, *Vampire: the Complete Guide to the World of the Undead*, 177)**
> **What a crock!**

And so on. Each entry goes into much more detail and shows the kind of encyclopedic knowledge that comes from a lifetime of fighting back baloney. And even though she's friends with many scholars in this field, she's fearless about criticizing them.

"It's a decision I made fairly early," she says. She warned colleagues, and even her own publisher, Clive Leatherdale, that she would spare no one. She says it was important "to set the record straight wherever I see it." Even in her own work.

"I said to Clive, 'If I do this, even you're on the microscope. Because people depend on the scholarship.' "

"Few are spared," Leatherdale writes in his introduction to *Sense and Nonsense:* "not Elizabeth Miller herself . . . and certainly not me, whom she hauls over the coals—rightly so—too often for comfort." Miller says she found out "there was some bad feeling" when her book came out. But she won't elaborate.

"There were people who told me that the first thing they did when they got the book was look at the index and see if their name was in it," she says.

Is this job a blessing or a curse?

"Melton has accused me in a lighthearted way of taking the fun out of Dracula studies," she says with a chuckle. But she says she's "thoroughly enjoying it."

"It does annoy me," she admits. "Just this week in the *Sunday Times* there was an article about Prince Charles buying land in Transylvania," which was called "home of the origins of Dracula.

"I want to write him," she says about the reporter. "It has frustrating moments, but I don't regret a minute of it."

Like Miller, Dr. Mark Benecke is a person who is determined to hunt down the truth, no matter where it leads. His work, which he calls his "bride," gives him an odd lift and sense of inspiration.

"It is about truth," he tells me. "Truth is not depressing if you dare to look at it, I guess." And his truth might seem grim to the rest of us. Benecke is a forensic entomologist. He is an expert on the ecosystem of insect larvae and other kinds of critters that bloom from a decaying human corpse.

Called "Dr. Maggot" by scholars and media reports, he has a

Ph.D. in molecular biology from the University of Cologne. He's also an expert in DNA typing and invertebrate zoology.

Benecke believes we have a tendency to believe in fantasies—a tendency that can explain spontaneous human combustion as well as vampire legends.

"The brain evolved in a way that you have to believe things, e.g., 'the other person in the subway there will not kill me. He looks normal,' " he writes in an e-mail interview. "This is why when a story comes up that explains things nicely, people have a tendency to believe it."

In 2000, during the Second World Dracula Congress held by the Transylvanian Society of Dracula (TSD) in Romania, Benecke gave a speech about the vampire subculture in New York City. A member of the TSD, he also hosted a National Geographic TV special called "Dracula Unearthed" in 2002.

He worked for the New York Medical Examiner's office in the 1990s, and during this time wrote a report on extreme body modification—including self-cannibalism and tongue splicing—among people in the East Village. He lived right in the area during this time, near St. Mark's Place.

"I spent my *complete* income on the rent—not kidding," he tells me. "Apart from that, I ate falafel and burritos."

And for another National Geographic TV special, he visited Moscow to examine the teeth and the skull of Adolph Hitler. Kept separately—the teeth in the KGB archives and the skull (in a plastic floppy disk box) in the state archives—they proved that the Russians held the remains of the führer. Though Hitler's henchmen had tried to burn Hitler's body, they didn't have enough gas to do the job. His charred corpse was hidden by the East Germans until the Soviets torched it completely in 1970, according to Benecke. But Hitler's dental work gave him away.

"Hitler's teeth were so bad—and uniquely bad—that his teeth

alone made it possible to identify his corpse" Benecke wrote in an article. "The state of his teeth might also explain why everybody complained about Hitler's oral malodor."

Benecke goes picking at bodies all over the world. And in 2006, his book *Vampires Among Us*, an account of vampires in New York City, along with an interview with a real female vampire, was published by the TSD.

But one of the most exciting documents to come out of the vampire scholarship scene is on the net. This is *Dracula Blogged*, a project by Bryan Alexander. Alexander has a quiet intensity to his voice as he talks about the funny and surprising things about him—like his wife who developed a fascination with the *Alien* movie series when she was pregnant. A professor who teaches at Middlebury College and is currently editing a new version of *Dracula*, he came up with a stroke of genius. He realized that the journal entries and letters of *Dracula*, unfolding over the course of a year, perfectly matched the text of a blog. His creation became one of those instant communities that appear on the Web.

"I'm doing this partly to explore the novel, which I teach and write about, as well as to continue my research into blogs," he says.

He first got interested in Dracula when he was working on his Ph.D. in English at the University of Michigan—he was studying Romantic and Gothic writers like Blake, Shelley, and Radcliffe.

"I ended up reading *Dracula* for the first time as an adult in a reading group," he says, "and I was blown away by what an extraordinary novel it was—how *odd* and *slippery* and disturbing it is.

"It's not a great novel," he adds. It's better than Stoker's other stuff, which is "awful," and it also compares well to other vampire books of the time, "hysterically bad" novels like *Varney the Vampire*, which was a mass-produced penny dreadful that appeared across England in 1845. Still, compared to the great Victorian novels, *Dracula* is deeply mediocre writing. But there's something undeniable about it.

"Still, it's got this appeal to mess with our heads and then when we look back we think, this must have really warped Victorians, but they don't respond in that way," he says. "It's a subtler, sneakier novel than the readers then gave it credit for." I ask him whether there is a parallel to the movie *Psycho*, a movie first released in June 1960, with all its stuff about bathrooms and obsessing about your mom and women with bras like missile cones. He agrees. The other thing *Dracula* does is cross a couple of genres—not only is it horror, but with its modern technology like typewriters, sound recording, and blood transfusions, it's science writing. *Psycho*, which mixes a crime story with a serial killer movie, does the same thing.

"I taught *Dracula* in the first literature class I got to teach and the students ate it up," he says, "and ever since I've always taught it whenever I could. The most advanced English major types can find everything they want in it and people who aren't really good at reading novels, they dig into it right away." Meanwhile, Alexander had been blogging and teaching courses about blogs for years. And one day he was talking about *Dracula* with his wife.

"And we were talking about the weird structure of *Dracula*, the scrapbook style," he says, when his wife noticed how the structure could fit perfectly in the blog format. Alexander had the entire text on his hard drive—he was working on a new edition—and he decided to upload it date by date.

He opened it and "deliberately spent no time designing it." With a "minimalist setup," the blog had no pictures or gadgety features. Alexander gave it no publicity—just e-mailed a couple friends—and before long he was getting write-ups about it in the British *Guardian*, the MSNBC site, and the German magazine *Der Spiegel*.

"What is especially important for me is it's altering how people look at the book," he says. Reading it as a serial, he and his readers have begun to notice the gaps between different entries that build suspense.

"And when entries pile up on the same day, the text becomes exciting," he says.

"It's a very different creature."

The "documentary novel," Alexander adds, is a product of society's fascination with progress in the late nineteenth century. The idea would be that all the different artifacts would build the case for believing in something weird or uncanny—the dates and bylines giving it the aura of a newspaper account or scientific document. It's reminiscent of the *X Files*, he says, in which every scene begins with a dateline appearing across the bottom left of the screen, identifying the time and location. And reading these novels stuffed full of letters and journal entries, it should seem eerily contemporary to someone who hits the Web and reads entries, commentaries, and hyperlinks—all set on the same page.

Reading *Dracula* online for the first time makes you realize that we're using very different technology to organize our thoughts, but our thoughts themselves are not all that different. The Brits of a hundred years ago had that same feeling of too much information and of accounts and stories and different testimony fighting each other side by side on the page. Perhaps it's a way of thinking that's as old as language itself.

And the creepiest part of the novel, he says, has nothing to do with vampires. For Alexander's money, it's the accounts of Seward's notes, which were dictated onto old wax cylinders in his asylum. It's "wacky and hi-tech," he says, but also deeply disturbing, because it happens in a lunatic asylum.

"You've got to imagine the sounds that are behind his voice," he says of the recording. What sounds? The screaming in the background, of course. The best elements of *Dracula* don't pop out at you like a guy with a cape. They're things you have to ponder for a while. And showing *Dracula* in a new way—playing around with the text—does this.

This wide-ranging group of scholars and enthusiasts are a fun bunch. Fascinated with the image of the Count and the history of the real Vlad, they come up with interesting ideas and sometimes they can even produce some truly weird and marvelous things. They meet at conferences around the world. They all seem to know one another, almost as if they're part of some huge extended family. And of course, every family has its black sheep. Like Kurt Treptow, one of the most respected and accomplished Dracula scholars—who spent time in a Romanian jail on charges of pedophilia.

Treptow allegedly used his prestigious think tank as the center for some kind of child porn ring. And another *Dracula* expert, a reporter based in Romania, has published articles accusing the U.S. embassy of covering up for him. But that's not even the really interesting part of the story . . .

Treptow lived in Romania off and on since the 1980s. Selected as a member of the Romanian Fulbright Commission by former ambassador Michael Guest, he founded the well-regarded Center for Romanian Studies in a city called Iaşi, located in the east of the country. And he is author of *Vlad III Dracula*, considered to be one of the best biographies of the Impaler. But in 2002, Romanian authorities raided Treptow's office and uncovered "videotapes and photographs of underage children."

Treptow was briefly detained on September 11, 2002. Over the next few months, authorities accused him of inviting two girls, aged ten and thirteen, to his house for some sort of sexual activity. He was eventually convicted of "sexual perversion and sexual abuse of minors." He received a seven-year prison sentence, the maximum, and was ordered to pay $35,000 to his victims. The Associated Press quoted Treptow's lawyer admitting he had had sex with the thirteen-year-old, but he had not known she was underage. The attorney said he would appeal the verdict.

And he didn't fare well in jail. A human rights report describing violence in the Romanian penal system notes an incident in which he was "brutalized" by roommates in November 2002 at the Iaşi Penitentiary. "There was no tragic ending," the report adds, because guards intervened and "discouraged any action from inmates with 'righteous,' but totally illegitimate impulses."

It was the most sordid story imaginable. And one local newspaper, *Bucharest Business Week*, made more damning allegations in a series of articles describing a "trail of corruption by top U.S. officials." It speculated that Treptow was hiding on the embassy grounds, and it quoted an anonymous diplomat who accused the embassy of "sheltering of a pedophile." It accused U.S. embassy officials of attempting to shield Treptow from prosecution and even insinuates that people in the American diplomatic community forged documents to protect him.

The articles related conversations between diplomats and referred to documents *Bucharest Business Week* had obtained. The paper obviously had some kind of inside source in the U.S. diplomatic community, perhaps even on the Fulbright committee. But as we shall see, *Bucharest Business Week* was hiding something.

I try to get in touch with the reporter of *Bucharest Business Week*'s articles, Corina Mica, but she doesn't reply. But as I start making calls and sending out e-mails to people all over the U.S. diplomatic and business community, another name pops up: *Bucharest Business Week* editor Sean Hillen. People from the diplomatic and business community, on and off the record, tell me that Hillen is almost universally reviled, infamous for alleged cases of blackmail. Also, he supposedly used the Treptow scandal to tar the reputation of former U.S. ambassador Michael Guest.

Like Treptow, Hillen's a Dracula maven himself. I find a book he wrote ten years ago, *Digging for Dracula*, from a small publishing outfit called the Dracula Transylvanian Club. The picture on the back of the book shows a bluff, hearty Irishman who looks like Martin Sheen, as one associate pointed out to me.

John Sean Hillen was an Irish-born reporter who'd worked for the *Kansas City Star* before coming to Romania with a flood of people back in the early years after the fall of Ceauşescu. And at first, according to a newspaper profile in the *Kansas City Business Journal*, he worked at several nongovernmental organizations.

"Sean did amazing things," remembers a former friend Ken Norcross, a businessman who now works as the executive vice president of a company that develops wastewater treatment technology. "He was helping out orphans and doing fund-raisers for an AIDS clinic. He put a lot of energy into it."

Hillen covered many different subjects, but because he was in Romania, Dracula and vampires came up again and again in his job—articles with names like "Stoker Suffers a Bite" and "Romanians See Red Over Bram Stoker's *Dracula*" and "Hollywood Dracula Pierces Romanian Hearts." Over and over, major newspapers would need some guy to tie a story in to Dracula. And because he was on the spot, Hillen was that guy.

In 1997, he and Norcross published an English-language newspaper about business matters. Back then, says Norcross, Hillen had high standards. He remembers watching him lecture his young reporters.

"He said you must report all the facts," says Norcross. "They fought all the time against the Romanian corruption. And especially back then the system was so raw. They were just constantly having to defend themselves, and maybe that took a toll. . . ." Norcross withdrew his support, he says, primarily because it took time away from his family and his other business interests. However, he also says he and Hillen had a sharp disagreement over whether the paper would go after people with aggressive investigative reporting. Norcross didn't find fault with his ethics, but he didn't believe the coverage belonged in the paper.

"If you've started a business newspaper, then you report on business," Norcross says. "You don't go after people." It led to a falling out.

"He and I were great friends until we got into business together over there," he says. "We sort of agreed to not talk anymore."

By 2002, Hillen was clearly cutting corners. He wrote a profile in the *Daily Telegraph*, for example, about the British ambassador Richard Ralph attending an event sponsored by *Bucharest Business Week*. But he neglected to mention that *Bucharest Business Week* was his newspaper, something that the English audience would not have known. It was an obvious conflict of interest.

According to several sources, Hillen had a friendly relationship with the previous U.S. ambassador, but he was on cooler terms with Michael Guest. The new ambassador was "uncomfortable around journalists," says a U.S. government official who wants to remain anonymous. The official adds that Guest wasn't about to give Hillen the kind of "special treatment" he was used to.

Guest was controversial for other reasons, the source continues. He was outspoken in his opposition to corruption in Romania. In addition, Guest was only the second openly gay ambassador from America. The previous openly gay man to hold an ambassador's post, says my government source, was a "political appointment." Guest was the first professional and brought his partner with him to the swearing in ceremony with Secretary Colin Powell. And because of this, he made an easier target.

Meanwhile, according to several sources, including State Department staffer Kiki Munshi, Hillen was on the Fulbright board when an opening for the position of director appeared.

"He wasn't chosen and Hillen took his ire out on ambassador Guest, the embassy, and anyone within spitting distance," Munshi remembers. When the Treptow scandal hit, Hillen's newspaper went after Guest and the embassy. Several times in its articles on Treptow, *Bucharest Business Week* quotes conversations in meetings and refers to documents that the paper somehow obtained. It's obvious that Hillen was the most likely source of information on the inner workings of the committee. But if he acted as both editor and secret inside source of articles about his committee, he did not disclose his connection.

Hillen's paper allegedly crossed another line, taking an action that was reminiscent of the bad old days of communism in eastern Europe. According to an account confirmed by a half dozen diplomatic and business officials, Hillen had a falling out with a businessman named Ron Barden, and his paper actually airbrushed Barden out of a group photo.

"Sean claimed that it had been done without his explicit approval," Barden tells me, but adds, "Sean had a reputation of being very aggressive in securing advertising for his paper (some would call it blackmail) and was known to write negative articles if companies refused to advertise."

Hillen, Barden adds, botched the job, and produced a photo that made it seem as if a fellow board member had more than two legs. The guy with the extra legs was Obie Moore. And about a month after the photo, according to an open letter Michael Guest had printed in a local paper, Guest made a joke to an American Chamber of Commerce crowd: "Obie Moore is not here tonight. In fact he is having surgery to remove a third leg. . . ."

Philip Stephenson, a top exec at a local oil company who says he fended off an overt blackmail attempt by Hillen, organized several people from the business community and published an open letter in a local publication, laying out their complaints against Hillen. The newspaper *Nine O'Clock* got into the act, writing a profile of Hillen in 2004 in which it stated that he "has turned to blackmail for financial gains."

I e-mail Hillen at his office asking for his opinion on these matters and whether he can confirm or deny the allegations of his feud with the Fulbright. Within a few days he writes back, oddly asking what my favorite Irish whiskey is. At first I don't understand what he means by this, but it occurs to me that I wrote about my preference for Irish whiskey on a personal webpage. So he's Googled me. Good, I think. Then I catch myself wondering if he is trying to say something like, "You might research me, but I can research you." I have stories of commie-style airbrushed photos, blackmail attempts, and smear campaigns running through my head. Is this guy threatening me?

He doesn't answer my questions about the feud. I e-mail him several days later, asking about the rest of the allegations. I mention most of what I know and ask him for comment. I follow up with a third e-mail, days later. Hillen never replies.

It's possible he made some enemies, writing about corruption and influence peddling throughout the American diplomatic and business community. And many of the people I've talked to seem to know one another and come from a small, tightly knit group. So the possibility that they're just throwing countercharges is there. But the facts that are most damning come from *Bucharest Business Week* itself: Its wild, thinly sourced accusations, its omission of conflicts of interest, and its outright spin are obvious.

We often refer to places like Romania as the "Wild East." And clearly, part of the fun of visiting it—part of the reason scholars, scientists, and journalists are drawn to Vlad and his homeland—is this "impression," as Jonathan Harker describes in his journal, that we are "leaving the West and entering the East." And as we journey into it, the ordinary rules no longer apply. But as we explore how we've turned Vlad into our own commercial icon in this next chapter—before trying to track him down in the land of his birth—maybe we should remember that this isn't the fault of the Romanians. After all, it's people like Sean Hillen who come to this place and perhaps no longer think they have to obey the rules of good journalism. And it's folks like Kurt Treptow who use their influence to get away with breaking rules on a whole different level. Maybe these folks bring the wildness with them.

But these fans and scholars are an interesting mix of contrasts. A guy cutting corners like Hillen is almost a negative doppelgänger of someone as obsessed about accuracy as Elizabeth Miller. If you want horror, look no further than the sordid and unbelievably depressing story of Treptow's crimes. If you want wonder, consider Bryan Alexander's remarkable invention. The stories of these Dracula people sometimes seem to eclipse Drac himself.

Ten

Wal-Mart Halloween

"Smell the latex? Now I can't smell it anymore."

Leering at me from across the canyon of merchandise at the Wal-Mart Supercenter is a giant inflatable lawn statue of Mickey Mouse dressed in a tuxedo and velvet cape with a widow's peak and tiny, somehow cute fangs poking out of his mouth. He doesn't look like Bela Lugosi. He doesn't look like Stoker's character. He doesn't look like a vampire from eastern European lore. And he sure doesn't look like one of the rodents I'm trying to kill in my garage before they find a way into my kitchen. What is he? He's a testament to America. He is symbol piled on top of symbol and trademark on top of trademark until he's everything and nothing at the same time. He's supposed to remind you of all the scary vampire movies you saw when you were a kid, somehow made cute and unthreatening. Technically an undead mouse, he doesn't look like

Sitting down to dine with the Count.

something that wrenched its crushed little skull out of the trap and clawed its way into your bedroom to feast on your blood. And above all, he's what people all over your subdivision will plunk down $50 to buy.

I've come to my local Wal-Mart Supercenter to buy a pair of fangs. My county is a rural spot of Virginia, but it's one of the fastest growing in the nation. Stores like that Supercenter are popping up all over. And with Halloween coming, vampires are capering throughout them.

But wait, as Ron Popeil would say . . . there's more.

Looking for "Dracula" on the U.S. Patent and Trademark Office databases, I find eighty-five trademarks and seventy-three patents. "Vampire" and "Vampyre" turn up about 350 trademarks and patents combined. I find entries for wine, vodka, soft drinks, video games, a restaurant named "Dracula's Stakehouse," a "novelty urn" with the "simulated remains of Dracula" (I'm guessing it's just dust), and even the "Dracula Pipette"—a device for injecting embryos used by a biomedical company called GeneSearch, Inc. A guy in California has registered the trademark of Kungfuvampire, for some kind of "live and recorded music" business, and someone in Olney, Maryland, registered the name "Tuxxer" as a fictional vampire character for "entertainment purposes." (That trademark is now dead—abandoned in 2005. So whoever Tuxxer was supposed to entertain might not have liked the show.)

A company called "Tish & Snooky's" in Long Island City, New York, has the name "Vampyre's Veil" locked in for a line of "cosmetics, namely, sunblock." And a Vegas company has reserved the name "Vampire Strippers" for its budding empire of TV, cable, and pay-per-view entertainment featuring "exotic lifestyles and beautiful women."

I also discover "a convertible figure doll," vampire-shaped pasta, Halloween-themed board games, and fangs made of digestible materials in case you accidentally swallow the damned things.

But for some reason, Patent No. 3,818,100 chills me. Filed back in 1972, it's not a real vampire-related piece of merchandise at all. It's a system for controlling (killing off) vampire bat populations by "application of a slow-acting toxicant to the bodies of the individuals, and subsequent release of the treated bats." Using mist nets to capture them at night, the cattle farmer is supposed to use a spatula to smear the critters with a mixture of petroleum jelly and some chemical with a name that's a string of zenes, lenes, zyls, and hydroxys. The bats fly back home filthy and confused like they just woke up on the floor of a strip club in Reno. Then, one by one, their little cohorts die.

I know they spread rabies. I know they kill cattle.

But I can't help thinking this is exactly like the first *Alien* movie, only the bad guys are *us*. I can just see two of them roosting together in a dark, quiet spot of the cave, where they can talk without causing a panic.

Maury (a bat): *Hank's gone. Died in the night.*

Robert (another bat): *That's five of us.*

Maury: *Since last week. Since Steve came back.*

Robert: *Don't talk like that.*

Maury: *I'm serious!*

Robert: *So am I. We can't afford to scare the others. Stay calm.*

Maury: *But did you see him? The terror in his eyes? That glop in his fur? He came back* changed, *man.*

Robert: *I know. We'll do something about him. Meet me at the Labrador carcass tonight. Bring a rope, a bag, and something heavy.*

Maury: *I don't have any of that. I'm a bat.*

Robert: *Right. Sorry. I guess we'll just have to tear his throat out with our claws then.*

Maury: *God help us all.*

Along with vintage comics and John Wayne collectible plates, eBay has more than 2,600 listings for "Dracula," including auctions for about four hundred books, seven hundred movies, and scores of trading cards, pinball machines, photographic images, a sexy Vampirella decal, and even thirty-eight "knives, swords, & blades." As I write this, "vampire" and "vampyre" have almost eight thousand current auctions, including a *Buffy Smile Time Vampire Angel Puppet Replica* and a set of stakes with ornamental stand.

A few years ago, eBay listed a "vampire killing kit" for $4,500. And another kit went for sale at Sotheby's in 2003, where it netted $12,000. But the kits are probably bogus, according to some.

"Caveat emptor," writes urban legend expert David Emery on his website. "There seem to be quite a few of these kits about these days, each purportedly assembled in the 1800s by a 'Professor Ernst Blomberg' (of whose existence I've been able to find no evidence whatsoever . . .)." And during the Sotheby's auction, an official for the agency told reporters she believed the kit "was assembled in the early twentieth century and sold to travelers as a souvenir."

Who makes all this stuff? Who invented these kits—or Count Chocula? What kind of financial empire has the vampire created? I have to find out. I want to delve into the kingdom of the mass-market vamp—the products and services made in his image and likeness. Come with me. We have some serious research to do. Let's start in New York, a city that knows something about making a buck. Our first stop is one of the most successful costume shops in the country.

"Smell the latex?" Erin Winters asks. She used to hate it, she says. "Now I can't smell it anymore." And it's everywhere. Masks of Satan and Uncle Sam, toy rats and rubber cobras—the staff has packed costumes and accessories into every nook of the cavernous Halloween Adventure on Fourth Avenue in the middle of Manhattan.

"Founded in 1981 by Bruce, Darron and Maureen Goldman, Halloween Adventure today has grown to become one of the Nation's largest, most respected and most successful Costume and Masquerade retailers," its website reads. According to Winters, it has 32,000 square feet of space. The store is a city landmark. I interview her right before Labor Day weekend, the very beginning of the season. And though it's a Friday morning, customers are already filling up the place. Business will double and double again every week until Halloween.

"There were two-hour lines every day," she says, describing the last two weeks before her last Halloween. She talks about fighting through a packed crowd just to get to the offices. The staff generally triples in the run-up to the thirty-first, with people working long hours to accommodate the rush as the company squeezes more than half its yearly business into this one intense season. They monitor new products at three trade shows a year and begin taking on extra inventory back in July as the place readies itself. The owner keeps a lucky rubber chicken out in front to ensure that the retail gods will smile on them.

Some of the store's merchandise changes from year to year. Costume and party stores follow cultural trends—politicians and scandals and movies. It's less than two months after *Pirates of the Caribbean: Dead Man's Chest* opened. (In its first weekend, the film grossed more than $135 million and was shown on more than four thousand screens nationwide.) As a result, pirates are everywhere. Big black hats, eyepatches, and plastic swords surround you, with the Jolly Roger poking out at you all over the shop, like a guy you owe money. And from sea to shining sea, swashbuckling insurance executives and desperate, sword-swinging schoolteachers will descend on countless office get-togethers and condo costume parties.

Piracy will run rampant this Halloween. But unless another big movie pushes the look next year, trendy costumers will search for something else. Meanwhile, the vampire will remain. And though a few vampire costumes in the store are alternative or modern, you can always find the old standbys—the cape and tux look that Bela made famous.

Everyone can remember the odd inventive costume from Halloweens past. I still recall riding in a subway car next to someone wearing a giant cardboard platform covered with sand, plastic bags, and a couple syringes—he was going to a party dressed as the Jersey shore. But vampires are classics. And Halloween Adventure will always stock up on the classics.

"We're always going to sell rubber vomit," Winters says.

This is only Erin Winters's second trip through the madness of the Halloween rush. Last August, she left her home in Utah and came to New York City for the first time. Landing a job in the store about a month after arriving, pretty soon she was deep into the season. She remembers being rattled and excited by the incredible scene, beginning each day with an extra-large coffee and donuts and sometimes taking the edge off with a 40-ounce malt liquor. And on Halloween night, after the last customer has made off with the final rubber rat, the staff will close up, clean up, and head for their blowout party. Last year, she says, it was at a nearby club. This year, she's in charge of the festivities. And after the dust clears, she will spend November thinking about what to do when the witching season comes back.

Vampires don't just move costumes. They can help you meet strange, new people and have filthy encounters with them at a club near you. That's the idea behind *Midnight Seduction*, an erotic roleplaying game.

"This is the first version of the game which we've produced and have run at adult retreats," says the creator, a guy who goes by the name ANoN. "We have actually played with up to eighty people taking part in one game at a time."

The rules are simple. Each player picks a role with a sexual identity—or kink, to you laypeople. You can be a Dominator, a Hedonist, an Exhibitionist, or a Submissive. You get cards with instructions. And you try to meet other people and get involved in some swinging, consensual, strictly adult action.

"Everybody has cards to initiate a scene," ANoN tells me. "You go up to someone and talk to them in character. Then you give them a card and say, 'I'm seducing you.' If they accept the card you can go someplace private. Everything in your scene is negotiated. You can sit down and talk about the weather or you can make out . . . or you can go a lot further.

"We've had some pretty wonderful stories," he adds with a chuckle. "Some pretty interesting stuff . . ."

Needless to say, no one comes to this game with a calculator and a plan to run the board by grabbing up the utilities and railroads. It's more about having fun. In fact, he adds, the last time they played with a big group, many people never made it through the whole game.

"They ended up hooking up with somebody during the course of the scene."

ANoN started out in the Goth world, and he's played other kinds of role-playing games. But at some point, he and his fiancée decided to do some exploring.

"And one of the things we took an interest in was the local fetish community in the D.C. area," he says. "And we went in not knowing what the hell to expect. What we found was a wonderful crowd—some really great people who were very honest and very true to who they were." He realized he could put together a game and invite these people to play it.

"I found it really works well with swinger groups," he says. "They're not necessarily Gothy at all. But the role-playing aspect appeals to them and makes it easy for them to meet and to mix.

"In the fetish scene," he adds, "they actually do scenes and have specific terminology. There are safe words which allow you to stop and control the progress of the scene. You can slow it down; you can stop it entirely."

So the different characters mix, occasionally wandering off into dark corners for some nookie. But somewhere in the group is a vampire who can turn others into a creature of the night.

"During the event they will slowly enthrall the mortals in their undead spell," the website reads. "Before the end of the night everyone will have the choice to experience the enticing freedom of a Vampyre Seduction." ANoN has high hopes for his game. And it's already given him an unexpected thrill.

"I learned my own personal fetish is role-playing," he says.

When people come home from a long night of leading each other around on dog leashes, they might kick back in a house decorated with kinky paintings made by a guy like Colin Bradley. A confessed art school dropout from Austin, Texas, who moved up to Pennsylvania, he's made money doing Gothic airbrush works—some of it featuring movie icons like Dracula and Frankenstein.

He started out with an interest in "spooky stuff" and landed a job at a haunted house, which pushed him on his way.

He told the manager he knew how to use an airbrush, but he didn't.

"So I went home and learned real fast," he adds. He got paid "pretty handsomely" for the job, and he then got a gig "painting crazy tattoo art at a tattoo parlor." Now Bradley makes T-shirts. He used to research his art in magazines like *Fangoria*. But these days, finding inspiration is easy.

"Google 'vampire' and, *goddamn*, you can spend all day looking at images."

It's hard to make a living, though, because for the amount of time he puts into his T-shirts, they're still, well, T-shirts. But it's not just something he does for money. He loves it.

"Ever since I was a kid . . . I can remember painting monsters and ghouls and all kinds of crazy shit," he says. "I had kind of a damaged childhood."

But suppose you didn't just want to make T-shirts. Suppose you ran one of the largest food companies in the country? Suppose you were rolling out a pair of kids' breakfast cereals and you wanted a duo of cartoon characters to front them? You'd ask someone like Laura Levine for help.

A native of Brooklyn, New York, who had worked as a reporter at a small-town newspaper in northern Virginia, Levine was a young writer working at an ad firm that had the job of coming up with the new spokestoons for General Mills. It was one of the first assignments she received.

"They had a chocolate cereal and a strawberry cereal with the marshmallows in it, and they wanted character names," she says. "My boss, a hip kind of guy, wanted it to be funny, or reasonably amusing . . ." She came up with a laundry list of possible pairs, but she remembers only one combo—because you can still find them in supermarkets all over the country thirty years later.

"There was no agenda in my creative little head saying, 'Oh man, I gotta do Count Chocula and Frankenberry. I gotta immortalize the vampire.' " But immortalize him is what she did.

Levine is a writer, not an artist, so she didn't develop the actual look of the creatures. And her memory of these things is hazy. But she seems to remember the corporate bosses having a fuss about Chocula's dental work.

"The client was always concerned about every little detail, and one of the details they were concerned about was whether the Count should have fangs or not," she says. "The debate raged on for months."

Obviously, you don't want a child's cereal icon to look like *Jaws*. The Count they rolled out looked less dangerous than most undead bloodsuckers. If you look carefully at one of the earlier Choculas, he seems to have buck teeth that make him look slightly like an emaciated beaver. And as the years passed, everything else about him—his cape, his ears, and his hair—became rounded and, well, cuddlier. He doesn't look like he could gum you, even.

"I remember working on the initial batch of commercials," she says. Probably a sixty-second spot and a thirty-second one. Each script was only a couple pages long. But they would go through round after round of revision. It was two years before she saw the ad appear on TV.

Though she invented the characters, she didn't stay to work on them throughout their career. And she didn't have anything to do with the spots rolling out their new buddy, the ghastly blue specter. Instead, Levine says, she continued her career in Los Angeles, eventually getting freelance gigs like writing two episodes for *Laverne and Shirley*. She still has a vivid memory of getting that writing assignment—and of the day soon after when she found herself driving through town with the sunroof open and singing the theme song that had just come on the radio.

Today she's a successful mystery writer, with a half dozen novels under her belt. She's quick to say she's not someone who goes to parties dressed all in black. But she loves her vamp character and delights whenever she sees it surface.

"I do get a kick out of it," she tells me, adding that it's funny how it's one of her more famous creations.

"I'll be reading a book by somebody I actually like," she adds, "and I'll see the words 'Count Chocula' and say, 'Holy Mackerel!' "

Recognizable the world over, the vampire is a reliable commercial icon. You can count on him to make the sale or to wow an audience. No one knows this better than Vlad. No, not *that* Vlad. I'm talking about a stage magician who works in Salem, Massachusetts, and uses the image of the vampire to create a persona for his show, a creepy act in which he tries to crawl into your brain. Specializing in what he calls Gothic magic, Vlad performs locally and around the country, trying to give more chills than the average magician. How does he jolt an audience?

"If you invade their personal bubble they are much easier to manage than if you stand away from them," he says. "They have to retreat a little bit. You're making them uneasy." Vlad also introduces his tricks with dark imagery.

"Why do people care about card tricks?" he asks. "Pick a card, lose a card—why do I care what my card is? So I came up with a routine called the death card. The whole premise of it is you die during your sleep, and now I'm offering you a chance—we can either walk beyond the veil right now or I will gamble with you to be able to return to life.

"So now you have a personal stake," he adds, "because you probably don't want to walk through the veil right yet. If I'm gambling for your life, you're going to pay attention."

Starting out as an actor at a haunted house in upstate New

York, he soon realized that he had a taste for it. He began as a creature wearing a mask and a costume, he explains, because it was easier. But eventually he allowed himself to try bolder roles. And he put them together in the form of his vampire persona. Being a stage magician, he reasoned, was a way for an eternal creature to handle the mundane details of making a living.

"If you've existed for a long time in this age of modern information, you're sort of going to have to justify where all your money came from," he says. Plus, "a vampire would find amusement in the fact that he could do something that was second nature, but everyone would take it as a feat of mysticism."

Throughout his act, Vlad makes little jokes and asides that suggest, without saying it, that he might be the historical Vlad Ţepeş as well as the Dracula of novel and legend. He'll mention his "misguided cousin" Elizabeth Bathory. In this way, he's mixing the historical and literary Draculas just like Elizabeth Kostova does in her novel *The Historian* and just like they did in the Wildwood, New Jersey, park.

While he is an actor playing at being a literary vampire, Vlad actually is a sanguinarian and psychic vamp himself. But then again, he explains, that's just another way of saying that he's a performer.

"And whether they want to acknowledge it or not, I don't think any true performer can say they're not a psychic vampire," he says. Actors and comedians describe being pumped up after a good show and drained after a bad one, he says, as if they are really transferring energy or food one way or the other.

His is not the only vampire-related venture in Salem. I also discover that there is a fangmaking business called vampfangs.com based in town. There is even a Vampires' Masquerade Ball, which is held yearly. And Spellbound Tours stages what they call a "Vampire and Ghost Hunt" in the city.

This is Salem, I think. Salem. Founded in 1626, the town became an important port and thrived. The famous witch trials of

1692 sent nineteen people to the gallows and . . . oh hell, you know the rest.

I wrack my brain for everything I know about it: the guys in buckled hats, the women in their oversized Dixie cups, the teenage girls swooning over hallucinations of the devil like he was some kind of infernal Justin Timberlake, the slave woman who told them all about the voodoo, the show trial, the fact that everybody was hanged unfairly, and the use of the words *witch hunt* for the next three hundred years to describe everything from McCarthyism to what happens when someone starts stealing lunches from the office fridge. I can't think of a vampire among 'em.

So what is it about this place that's attracting the vamp market? I decide I must drive up there and see it for myself. As I approach the place, it seems like a fairly normal, even cute, New England town. I've visited the region many times, so a hilly, cold burg with a Dunkin' Donuts every 5 feet is something I'm used to. But as I roll up on the downtown area and turn the corner on Essex Street, I'm stunned. I figure that the fame of the witch trials would have brought a couple paranormal industries and maybe a gift shop or two. I am not prepared for the absolute Six Flags Over the Dead Witch I find there.

I get a map and stroll, counting the different witch spots: the Salem Witch Museum, the Witch History Museum, the Witch Dungeon, the Witch House, and the Witch Village. They also have the Peabody Essex Museum, the Museum of Myths and Monsters, and the Spellbound Museum. Vampires wouldn't feel out of place here. Between the Pirate Museum, the Poe's Witch Mansion, and the Hollywood House of Wax, they have all kinds of villains. The only thing I can't find is a Frankenstein exhibit—until I spot the Frankenstein's Laboratory right next to another wax museum. I cancel my plans and spend the next twenty-four hours trying to hit every attraction I can find.

I visit Mollie Stewart, a "licensed ghost hunter with the International Ghost Hunters Society," who runs two shops in town as well as a ghost and vampire tour. Sitting in the Ghostly Parlour as the room goes dark, I hear Stewart's voice come over a speaker to tell me in low tones about some tale of murder and revenge at an old plantation down on the bayou, approximately 1,500 miles away. As the tale unfolds, spotlights illuminate objects on the wall. Light shines through pictures and mirrors, revealing various spooks and specters. The story itself is actually pretty good. Some of the effects are a little overdone, but I walk out of there feeling like I'd heard a good yarn.

Next I visit her Spellbound Museum, where I find a couple of voodoo-related items as well as a vampire slaying kit assembled by my old buddy "Ernst Blomberg."

"Some vampire experts claim that the kits were common among travelers to eastern Europe, particularly the Carpathians," a sign tells me, "and could be requested from the concierge desks of hotels." I've heard something like this before, so I don't doubt it's a widely circulating story. But I'm skeptical. It resembles the kits sold by Sotheby's and on eBay.

I wander down to the harbor and check into my hotel, anxious for dark. I came here primarily to see the tour, and I can't wait. Near dusk, I go back to the meeting spot, where a small crowd is gathering as the mist begins to settle.

Stewart is here, but her assistant Mike Vitka takes over the tour. A wisecracking, sharp guy with blocky black Elvis Costello glasses, he leads us past several spots where ghosts have supposedly lingered. One site, a graveyard, is allegedly haunted by the spirit of Giles Corey, an eighty-year-old man who was pressed to death with heavy stones in 1692.

Vitka gives an impassioned and eerie rendition of the tale of the poor old bastard being piled high with rocks while they tried to get him to confess to witchery. If you died a confessed witch, Vitka explains, supposedly you couldn't pass on your property to your family. The idea is that it gives people a reason to finger you. (A pamphlet I pick up later says this part of the story is not true, however. According to *that* account, Giles just refused to confess because he knew he was dead anyway.)

Along the way Vitka encourages us to take plenty of pictures and look for orbs. They're supposedly the energy left over by spirits. But snapping shots with a flash camera in the dark and rainy night, each picture of mine is absolutely filled with glowing orbs. You can supposedly tell the real orbs from the bits of dust and moisture because real orbs are perfectly round and solid. But my orbs are all different shades and shapes, depending on how the light hit the particles and droplets in the air. The shots I take seem to be powerful evidence that orbs are nothing more than the light from a camera's flash bouncing off something you can't see with the naked eye. Still, I'm having a good time.

At some point during the tour, Vitka tells us an apocryphal story about the historical Vlad Țepeș actually dipping a piece of bread into blood during one of his impalings. Then Vitka segues into an account of vampires in New England, such as Mercy Brown.

It's a really small part of the tour to be calling it a vampire and ghost hunt. (I tell Elizabeth Miller a few days later about the story of the bread dipping. She thinks it didn't really happen.) However even though the vampires don't really lurk in Salem, they're not that far away. A case of reported vampirism happened in Jewett City, just over the border in Connecticut. Back in the 1850s, a man and his sons died mysteriously, prompting authorities to dig up the bodies and burn them so they wouldn't feed on the living. It was reported in the May 24, 1854, edition of the *Norwich Weekly Courier* and recounted in folklorist Michael Bell's book *Food for the Dead*. So the vampires they talk about in their tour are actually more "real" than Dracula ever was.

The next day, I take a tour of the different history museums, some shockingly bad. Many seem to be big musty cellars filled with store mannequins made up to look like the girls of Salem, the slave who steered them wrong, the witch hunters, and all the extras tangled in that nasty hair clog in the drainpipe of American history. And the more politically correct exhibits talk about the story of Wicca and how it's been maligned, comparing the persecution to the McCarthy era or the demonization of AIDS victims.

I'm all in favor of not demonizing folks. But it's hard to take it seriously in a town where every third shop is a New Age emporium. The publicity not only failed to drive the witches out of town. It did the opposite. Where there were no witches in Salem, now you can walk into any one of a number of spots and get yourself enough tarot decks, crystals, and incense to score on a date with Stevie Nicks. If this is victimization, I want some. There were victims here, obviously. They just weren't these guys.

I've seen this kind of thing before. I live near Fredericksburg, where 18,000 people died fighting in 1862. The downtown is filled with shops selling Civil War memorabilia, and the battlefield site has beautiful, lush fields and forests today. It's a great place to take a drive or jog. The most awful things happen in our history and we turn their memories into a merchant area or a park. And sometimes it seems like the one unforgivable thing we do is to keep going. But we do. We must.

In our next chapter, we will retrace the literary journey of Jonathan Harker in the first pages of *Dracula* to see how the Transylvanians have treated the Count and Vlad and the connection between the two. But it's clear how we see them. It's how we see everything. Above all in the West, the Dracula industry is about change. We take the gripping image and tweak it until it becomes the best product it can possibly be. No one wants a lawn statue of a bloodthirsty medieval prince or a dated Hungarian actor . . . They want Mickey. And just as garbage bags magically grew twist ties, a flexible weave, and even a chemical floral scent as the years have passed, the consumer Dracula has to change with the times. Just like the shops in downtown Fredericksburg or Salem. We take the past and use it for our own purposes.

"Who among us has not feasted on death?" wrote Walker Percy in his novel *Love in the Ruins.* Back home in my suburban tract house near the Civil War battlefield, the tourist pamphlets of Salem scattered around my room as I write these words, I still can't answer that question. And don't blame yourself for it, friendly reader, but neither can you.

Lost Treasures of Dracula

"In the very heart of much keened Transylvania . . .
you are just about to find vivid the story
of a prince whose soul you can keep into immortality."

It's less than a week before the fiftieth anniversary of the 1956 Hungarian Uprising when my plane touches down in Budapest. I'd noticed the calendar before I arrived and wondered if I'd be in the city during the ceremony. But I don't think much of it. That will come later. For now, my aim is to follow Jonathan Harker through the first pages of *Dracula*. I want to retrace his journey to the mythical Castle Dracula in the Borgo Pass—to take my own survey of a country hidden for so long.

On the nine-hour flight out of JFK airport in New York City, I sit next to a Hungarian radiologist who's some kind of computer consultant. His name is Tibor. He's an amateur photographer who's

Deep in Transylvania on the hunt for Stoker's monster.

traveled all over the world. He talks about his wife and kids back in Jacksonville, Florida. Then he boots up his laptop and shows me pics of his travels in New Zealand. The brilliant blue water, stark fields, and mountains blow me away.

During the flight, I envy Tibor's uncanny ability to fold himself up and actually get sleep on the plane. Who can sleep on a plane? Despite taking full advantage of the airplane bar and eating all my dinner, I'm unable to drop off. I stare dully down the corridor to the little curtained doorway where the stewardesses are preparing the meals and drinks for the first-class crowd. The night stretches to 2:00 a.m. Eastern Standard Time—like I've stayed up late at a party or have been working on a project—but at that point, we've made it deep into central Europe, and it's 8:00 a.m. there. Through the window I can see the sky lightening, and it gives me that familiar rush of jet-lag wakefulness like a slug of coffee.

The plane lands at 9:00 a.m. local time. I pull my backpack from the luggage return and hoist it onto myself. I find my way to the bus and then take the metro to Pest, just across the Danube River from its ancient twin, Buda. I get out and wander northwest along the river toward the Széchenyi Iánchíd.

"Count Széchenyi's bridge over the Danube linking Buda and Pest was built between 1854 and 1873," according to the notes in the Norton Critical Edition of *Dracula*, edited by Nina Auerbach and David J. Skal. Called the Chain Bridge, it is the span Jonathan Harker remarked on in the first paragraph of Stoker's novel:

The impression I had was that we were leaving the West and entering the East; the most Western of splendid bridges over the Danube, which is here of noble width and depth, took us among the traditions of Turkish rule.

Though named after a Hungarian political leader, it was actually designed and built by a Brit, Tierney Clark, who designed bridges in Hammersmith, Shoreham, and Marlow. The bridge I walk across isn't the same one Harker describes, however. That bridge was destroyed in World War II and then rebuilt. But it's 666 feet long, which seems perfect for a mention in *Dracula*, but kinda unlucky to drive over. They couldn't have just put an extra foot of clearance? Haven't these people seen *The Omen*?

As I walk toward it, I can see the massive Buda Castle on the high hill. Off in the distance I spot the Liberation Monument, a bronze statue of a woman standing on a pedestal. It's a tribute to the recovery of the city after WWII.

Along the Danube next to the boardwalk are several moored ships that have been converted into cool pubs and nightspots. A particularly hip-looking place called Spoon seems to have a menu packed with desserts and after-dinner drinks. It's not open, but I don't even really feel hungry. I actually don't know what I feel like at this point because I'm exhausted, but I can't sleep.

I cross the Chain Bridge on foot. Up ahead is a beautiful hill-climbing trolley called the Buda Castle Funicular. It costs a couple bucks for a ride up a steep, 300-foot hill. Unlike other kinds of trains, a funicular operates with an ascending train on one side hooked by cable to a descending train on the other. The down car helps pull the up car. In a fit of machismo, I decide to skip it and start climbing through a series of hilly sidewalks winding their way through a park. How hard can it be?

One slope leads into another. And then another. The park is crawling up the hill, and the trail seems to take forever. Sweat is pouring out of me. Finally, I reach a clearing and see the trail lead into what looks like the back entrance of a church or castle tower. I climb several more flights of stone steps through a wide cloister hall, and I emerge onto a plaza in the middle of the Castle District, right next to Matthias Church. Built in the thirteenth century, the church was captured by Turks and converted into a mosque in the sixteenth century and then recaptured by Habsburgs and reconverted back into a church in the seventeenth century. There is a column nearby that was erected to commemorate the people buried in mass graves from four different outbreaks of the plague that hit the city in the eighteenth century. If I were mayor of this town, I'd paint a giant bull's-eye right on this square.

A mob of elderly German tourists mills around here, and behind them I spot the sign to my hotel. I stumble in a few hours before check-in, but the front desk clerk takes pity on me—or maybe he thinks I have some kind of glandular disorder because of the fact that I'm soaked in sweat, and he's afraid I will die in his lobby. He lets me have my room. I go up, strip to my underwear, pop open a mini-fridge beer, and pass out watching incomprehensible local Hungarian news that somehow seems exactly like incomprehensible local American news. It's a parade of pretty people presenting ugly people who've had terrible things happen to them.

Waking around four in the afternoon, I walk down from the plaza to find a good restaurant. At Trio, a small place, I order something called "fried knuckle of pork" along with a "poultry soup." I have a Budvar—a beer from the town of České Budějovice in the Czech Republic. The company tried to market its suds under the German name for its town, "Budweis," calling it "Budweiser Budvar," which landed the company in court with Anheuser-Busch. American Bud's lawyers argued that it had developed a copyright since 1876, while the European company said it had been producing beer since the thirteenth century, long before America even existed.

Today Budvar goes under the name "Czechvar" in America, but its website claims it has "achieved important victories in the legal trademark disputes . . . in Great Britain, Australia, Japan, South Korea, Greece, Portugal, Denmark, Sweden, Finland and New Zealand." Budvar also gained trademark rights in China, their site says, when the Beijing high court threw out the American company's objections.

Let me wade into this. I'm no trademark scholar. And I'm not hostile to American beers. I love Sam Adams and Yuengling and even Miller High Life. But Budvar is clearly better. It's thick and rich, not over-processed crud that gives you a weird aftertaste, a sharp sense of desperation, and wicked gas.

Nobody, nobody at all, thinks American Budweiser tastes good. The people who own the company know it sucks. The people who buy it know it sucks. Bud is bad. Bud is what you drink when you're out of Nyquil and paint thinner. My advice is to Google Czechvar, find where it's sold, and go get yourself a taste. Then peel off the label, send it to Anheuser-Busch's corporate office, and tell them they make a bad beer. Tell them to manufacture chemical weapons or bolt guns for cattle slaughter or substandard child safety caps—anything but what they're doing now.

The poultry soup is heavily spiced with dill, greasy as hell, and filled with unidentifiable bird meat. It's one of the tastiest things I've ever ingested. It's hard to describe how bad it is for you. Eating it, my body instinctively knows it's wrong, but it tastes so right.

The knuckle of pork is a huge chunk of glistening crispy meat, surrounded by fried onions—the kind you sprinkle over your cold green bean casserole at Thanksgiving if you are, like me, a redneck. On the side, potatoes have been chopped up and *violated* with grease and fire. If the soup has the health benefits of a pack of Camels, the main course is an eight ball and unprotected sex. I throw some money at the table and head out into traffic, holding my belly and groaning softly. Back at the Castle District, the sun is setting, as red and orange shadows stain the buildings across the Danube like cathedral windows.

The next morning, just as the sun rises, I find myself staring up at the grand architecture of the Keleti train station from a sunken plaza dotted by small kiosks selling pastries, espresso, and porn magazines. I load up on the first two and surreptitiously eyeball the third while waiting for my train to arrive. The station is old and charming, but a nearby platform couldn't be more garish and futuristic if it came from a PlayStation game.

At 9:35, the train pulls out of Keleti, and I'm on my way to the Romanian border. I will start from Timişoara, the historic settlement dating back to the Neolithic period in the Banat region. From there I will take a rental car along the roads that squeeze between the western and southern Carpathians—called the Apuseni Mountains and Transylvanian Alps, respectively. These famous vamp-related peaks carve a backward C across the eastern part of the country, with a good dollop of mountains in the middle. And according to an associate professor at the University of Virginia, Stoker set his tale here with a purpose.

"Victorian readers knew the Carpathians largely for its endemic cultural upheaval and its fostering of a dizzying succession of empires," Stephen D. Arata writes in his essay, "The Occidental Tourist." "By moving Castle Dracula there Stoker gives distinctly political overtones to his Gothic narrative." The region would unnerve Stoker's audience, English folk, because its "upheaval" would make them think of their own precarious empire. And the idea of an undead nobleman turning good, solid Brits into his blood-servants would call up an even darker fear—one that Arata calls "reverse colonization," a kind of mirror image and poetic revenge for what the English themselves were doing to people all over the world.

I will eventually reach the city of Cluj-Napoca in the heart of Transylvania. From there I will drive to Bistriţa, or Bistritz, the town where Jonathan Harker spent the night at the Golden Crown before journeying east toward the Borgo Pass to visit the Count.

The train rumbles over flat farm country toward the border. There's less industrial blight than I found in Wallachia, but still a fair number of unused building materials alongside great heaps of junked machinery. The guy sitting across from me in the compartment has a scruffy beard, an iPod, and a cell phone that keeps going off. He seems like a typical friendly, hyperconnected youngster. And he tries to adjust the heat with an ancient gauge on the wall above us, but he can't get it to work. We both chuckle at this. Friendly and polite, neither of us talk much. We pass through many little towns without stopping.

Sometime after we cross the border, a spasm of coughing grips me as I feel dust in my lungs, and I honestly think there is a noticeable change in air quality. I leave my compartment and walk up and down the train trying to catch my breath. Finally I settle down just before the train rolls into my destination. From a distance, I can see the stark, gray, industrial buildings of Timişoara.

Trying to find a bathroom in the station, I follow a WC sign down a flight of dark steps tucked behind the main room. There I see two people sitting in a booth with turnstiles, and I realize I don't have any Romanian cash, so I can't enter. But I do get a glimpse of what must be the Most Terrible Job Ever: Romanian public restroom attendant. The boredom, the darkness, and the smells of the damned wafting over you as you collect tiny bits of worthless money from all who enter.

I trudge down the street as the industrial district gives way to a cute, bustling business area. Hotel Timişoara is at the north end of Victory Square, right next to the opera house where thousands of demonstrators gathered on December 16, 1989, to protest a crackdown against an outspoken local priest. Over the next several days, tanks had rolled into the square, and the regime gave the army an order to fire on protestors. But the army eventually retreated, and protests spread to Bucharest, resulting in chaos, revolution, and the downfall of Ceauşescu. I'm standing at the fault lines of the 1989 Revolution that destroyed the Soviet empire and brought a decade of wild capitalism, freedom, despair, and hope to millions. And I really have to piss.

After checking into my room and unloading my pack and my bladder—the place is neat, slightly boring, and exactly what I want—I walk farther north and reach the second plaza, Union Square. Union is big, wide, and beautiful, with the Roman Catholic cathedral on one end and a Serbian Orthodox church at the other. According to one of my guidebooks, the column in the center is the Plague Column, and it's dedicated to the victims of the Black Death, which struck from 1738 to 1739. Nearby, I spot a picture of Frank Sinatra on a sign for a business club. There is a tent and equipment for an outdoor party that they evidently host in honor of the Man from Hoboken.

I find Don, a restaurant that has steps leading down to an underground, vaulted area festooned with pictures of scenes from *The Godfather* along with a couple shots of real gangsters from the 1940s, '50s, and '60s. There are no shots of the modern mafia, though. No John Junior hanging out in Ozone Park in a horrid track suit.

The place serves a mix of Italian and Romanian food, with an emphasis on pizza. I order a pie and it comes with a side of ketchup, and since I kinda miss my wife and our time together in the wilds of Wallachia, I actually have some this time. And you know what? It tastes *kinda good*. The ketchup is a little spicier than the regular bottled stuff back home, and it contrasts in a weird but nice way with the tomato sauce from the pizza. After that, I go to Java, an Internet café. It looks like one of those old, polished wood bars you can find in every American city, but it has a small flight of stairs in back with a bank of computers and a thick, dank smell of cigarette smoke and stuffed ashtrays scattered around. I check my e-mail while some guy behind me rocks out to a violent fantasy warfare game. Then I walk past Liberty Square, which has another plague statue—I've now seen three plague monuments since I got here, with two of them in Timişoara alone. Liberty Plaza is sandwiched between Union and Victory, and it's smaller, dingier, and more crowded than either of them. And it's also the site of the brutal torture and execution of Gheorghe Doja, who led peasants in a revolt throughout the area in 1514. His captors supposedly heated a metal throne and crown until they were glowing and sat Doja down for a gruesome and excruciating "coronation." Then they carved him up like a Christmas Butterball and forced his followers to feast on him—before their own executions.

Club-hopping later, I pass a giant artillery gun with the piece of graffiti—"Respect '89"—stenciled on it, maybe to keep the spirit of revolution alive. And late at night I pass Makaveli, a hip shop with a picture of Tupac Shakur in the window. Also in the window is a skateboard on which is printed a Texas flag and the slogan "Don't mess with Rodrigo, TX."

Soon after that, I get hassled by a hooker.

She's wearing an insulated *Back to the Future*-style jacket and tight jeans. Her hair and clothing seem filthy—brown or dust colored. I pass her and two men, and she says something to me in Romanian. I keep walking without comment because at first I don't realize she's talking to me. But as I continue, I see a shadow on the stones coming up from behind to my left. Then she appears at my elbow.

"Fired," she says, twice. I immediately think she's a street person, about to tell me she's gotten fired and needs money. But then she shows me a pack of cigarettes.

"Fire. Fire."

I tell her I don't have a match, feeling guilty I ignored and misjudged her.

"Where are you going?" she asks me, and my suspicions come back.

"Club 30."

"We go together."

"Aha!" I think. "Not a civilian." But I'm still nervous, because hookers usually leave you alone if you're not interested, and she's being pretty aggressive. (I used to work near Times Square, so I know hooker protocol.) I leave.

"Wait. Talk to me," she says.

"No. Sorry."

I walk on and instinctively pull up the collar of my jacket, not because it's cold, but as a defensive reaction. She follows me for a bit, but I pick up stride and make no eye contact.

Club 30 is my last stop of the evening. It's a small room down a flight of stairs. A DJ is playing house music and there is a projected film clip of some bit of Japanimation. Two break dancers do lame pop and lock moves in the middle of the room. People are scattered around on the plush furniture, languidly eyeing each other. The cover charge—about $10—seems steep for this bullshit. I feel ripped off, hassled, and tired. But somehow this is comforting. Homey. This place is becoming more westernized by the minute.

Friday I wake up to the sound of church bells playing a delicate melody from just on the other side of my softly glowing white curtain. I go downstairs and ask the desk clerk where the sound's coming from.

I thought it was the Orthodox church on the opposite end of the plaza, but he tells me it must be the Serbian Orthodox and Catholic churches facing each other across Union Square. Packing up to go later, I look out my window and it turns out he's right. Even though those churches are a few blocks farther away, the surrounding buildings are old and low, and you can see their bell towers clearly from the window. I'm charmed to be waking up in the kind of place where you hear church bells and not know the source.

I'm in a really good mood, and in the shower I'm mentally composing a whole section about how economically vibrant Timişoara is. And there's something inspiring about how Romania seems to be really coming back to life after some dark years. I'm idly wondering if Transylvania and Banat—the north and west of the country—were always doing better than Wallachia or if this is because the entire country has turned a corner since the 1990s. I think it might be both. But the youth culture here—the sharp-dressed, friendly, good-looking kids yapping on their cells and club hopping—makes me think that the revolution started in 1989, but it continues today. I am on the point of coming up with some huge, fluffy, over-generalized piece of crap about how Romania is wonderful and everything in the world is going to be fine. But then I forget it all because I go down to the parking lot and my car never shows up.

I stand out there and tell the attendant that I am waiting for a rental. And I ask a couple of people coming into the hotel if they're here to deliver a car. I'm worried that I'm insulting them, but unable to do anything else. Is this just a casual approach to time, and I should pull the pole out of my ass and relax? Or is it an indication that my car is not coming? I scan cars and faces, making eye contact with the attendant, wondering if he's on the lookout for my car as well. It's an ambiguous situation. This is supposed to be part of the adventure. How far could I get? Could I reach my destination in this country, or would crazy things happen to prevent me? Now that the adventure is happening, I don't like it. Just as I'm giving up, a harried, attractive, brown-haired woman runs into the hotel lobby and asks the clerk right next to me for me.

"I'm Paul," I tell her.

"Sorry," she says. "The car you were going to rent has been in an accident. We have a smaller car for you, I'm afraid." I tell her that's fine.

"Have you been driving on Romania's roads?" she wants to know.

"No," I say. And I see a glint of real fear in her eyes.

"Please, be careful," she tells me solemnly.

She sits down at a desk and gives me a sheet of paper with a different company name than the rental place I'd signed for. She tells me the person I've been dealing with is actually in another city. Then she says the card I registered with—AmEx—won't work, and that I need to use a MasterCard for the deposit. And for the actual rental, they will need cash up front.

"Do you have lei, euros, or U.S. dollars?" she asks. A different time, different car, different company name, different people, and a different method of payment. My spider sense is tingling. Then again, they knew where I was, and the paperwork has a cell phone number of mine that I haven't been giving out to anyone except the car rental place. And in the end, I have this curiosity about what is going to happen. I run out to an ATM, return with cash, and sign the papers. I figure if the thing dies on me in the hills, and if they charge my card for thousands to buy bogus airline tickets, I'll have a good story to tell.

The car is a small, five-speed Daewoo. Dull gray, blunted, and round, it is shaped like a tin can. And I've coughed up stuff bigger than it. I squeeze myself in and hang my lucky green pair of fuzzy twenty-sided dice on the rearview mirror.

"When would you like to drop it off?" she says to me through the open window.

"9:00 a.m. Monday?"

"Fine."

"I'll bring it to the airport?" I ask.

"Yes," she says.

"Is there a drop-off counter in case I get back early?" I want to know.

"It's better if you just meet us at the airport," she says. Do they have a counter? Or, have two random people just given me use of a dodgy car for $200 cash? Eh, what the hell. I'm committed.

The engine putters, a little rough and whiny. And the stick shift feels like overcooked pasta—I can bend it wherever I want to, but engaging the right gear is hard. The "check engine" light blinks at me for a few seconds, which means it probably needs some maintenance.

But it's not like I'm traveling to the far reaches of some foreign country where I won't have any way of calling a tow truck if I break down. It's not like I will have to sell my clothing and buy a small tent and start a new life as an itinerant peasant laborer.

The car starts, and I'm off. I hurtle into traffic toward the town of Lugoj. But almost immediately I get confused by the signs and lost on a traffic circle. I start going down every road that leads out of the circle, a few kilometers in each wrong direction, trying to find the right way. At some point I'm in the tiny, crowded back roads in the sprawl just outside Timişoara. Cars are constantly honking at me. They're driving fast, and I'm driving slow, blocking their way. Mad and scared, I start talking to myself with every wrong turn I take.

"No signs! No signs!" I'm cackling. "Oh here's the exit. Let's not put a sign here to show the way. Yes. Thanks! *Thank you for that.*"

At some point, I stop at a gas station and get a Romanian highway map. Slowly, I begin learning all the names of all the towns I am supposed to be heading through. I pull over by the side of a road in a traffic circle just to scan down the list of names on the street signs—my engine running, my foot on the brake, and my hazards flashing as my eyes dart from the sign to the map and then from side to side to make sure I'm not about to get hit or carjacked.

I finally isolate the road leading out and I find the way. And soon I'm flying down the highway. Even the highways only have two lanes. You have to pass at high speed into the oncoming lane if you want to get anywhere. You pop out and pop back in, barely dodging a truck. Sometimes the road becomes a one-laner with wagon carts, slow-moving trucks, and massive potholes. There are spots where the pavement just breaks off. I whiz by a driver and team of horses. And then a moment after, a stray black horse bolts out into the road and runs straight at my car. I swerve into the oncoming lane to dodge it, and I'm rattled when I return. A few kilometers later, traffic heavy and fast, I glance to the side and see a guy driving right beside me against the traffic for what seems like a suicidally long time—and he is doing it with the car going full speed *in reverse*. My mind goes blank. I actually start *giggling*. These conditions have gone from bad to surreal. I don't know what kind of people could drive in this place. I have no idea what's going to happen to me.

The Romanians drive like they're a spiritual people. It's astounding and inspiring to see someone in a giant truck hog the center lane and force you off the road—someone who has that much faith that our souls are not snuffed out at the end of our earthly lives. Surely such a person believes that what lies beyond this veil of tears is better. The Romanians are ready to go to that next world. And if that world has cars, the Romanians will probably scare the crap out of drivers there, too.

I zip by Deva, built next to a thirteenth-century fortress and the top of a volcanic hill that was created, according to the legend, by a massive battle between warring armies of djinn, or spirits. Another story says the builder of the fortress walled his own wife up into its structure so that it would be indestructible. The map lists countless different castles, forts, and other sites on the road from Lugoj to Cluj, and I'm hurrying past them to get to a castle that doesn't even exist. But I don't want to be caught on these roads at night.

My eardrums are popping as I descend the steep hills into the depression in the land that holds Cluj. As the roads lead into it, I see a haze over the city that might be pollution or fog, and I can't tell which. But the dark is thickening, and sharp white and yellow lights are coming on all over the city, as I take the old, dirty streets to the heart of the city.

Cluj is a fascinating place. Hip and urbane since Emperor Hadrian declared it a city back in the second century A.D., it's saturated in the Hungarian culture that's still strong in Transylvania. Transylvania was Hungarian until 1920, when it was awarded to Romania after the breakup of the Habsburg family empire.

I make a large circle through the streets and alleys in the shadow of St. Michael's, a massive Gothic church in the middle of the town. And tucked in the back of a small group of shops, I enter a restaurant with so many decorations on the walls colored in the red, green, and white of the Hungarian flag that it looks like Christmas blew up in it.

I sit down and listen to a live band play old folk tunes while a woman sings one sad song after another. It's so beautiful that I break out clapping. The band looks at me and smiles politely. They play *Strangers in the Night*, and I'm wondering vaguely if it's because they can tell I'm American—it seems like a uniquely American song. (But I look it up later, and it was Ivo Robić, from nearby Croatia, who composed it.) The flags and decorations and songs of this people here in a country that is and is not their own feel rebellious and intriguing. This place doesn't appear so different from Budapest or Timişoara. But it seems like a long way from Wallachia.

The next day is the final push toward my destination. I am leaving for Bistriţa, the place where *Dracula* opens. It is still dark when I leave the hotel, and I need gas. I also sample one of the joys of the Romanian highway system. They don't have good paving, they drive like maniacs, and they obviously have no warning signs in English. (There's nothing quite like the feeling you get from flying down the road and seeing a giant billboard announce something incomprehensible with an exclamation point at the end of it.) But in every two-bit gas station across this great country, you can throw a couple bucks on the counter and get a shot of fresh, piping-hot espresso that's the best thing you've ever tasted in your whole road-tripping life.

I leave with a full tank and a double shot of joe, and I hit thick fog on the road to Bistriţa. The road twists and turns, and as the sun comes up, the mist seems to get even creepier, like a horror movie smoke machine.

Bistriţa is a town of about 90,000 people built by Saxons sometime before the middle of the thirteenth century—although most of the Saxon population vacated after World War II, leaving behind merchant houses and the Saxon Evangelical Church at the center of the downtown. I get out of my car and walk around the area, eventually finding Harker's hotel, the "Coroana de Aur," or "Golden Crown."

"The hotel is outstanding in Romania and in the world, as it was described in the well known novel 'Dracula' by the Irishman Bram Stoker," the brochure reads. "One of the main characters in the novel, the lawyer Jonathan Harker, was also a guest of the hotel and he felt there as comfortable as at home."

I don't really know if he felt comfortable with all those people warning him about demons and vampires. Plus, he didn't actually stay anywhere—except maybe in Bram Stoker's addled noggin'—because he didn't exist. But the hotel looks comfy. It's like an upscale HoJo's—big and modern, with plenty of parking and clean, nondescript rooms equipped with phones, minibars, and color televisions. I try to get someone to take my picture next to the Jonathan Harker room. A middle-aged Romanian guy in an NYPD baseball cap volunteers to help.

"You lived in New York?" I ask him. He nods.

"What borough?" He nods.

I realize his English isn't that good. Maybe he's just responding to the words "New York." Still, if you're a Brooklyn cop taking a vacation in Dracula-land, you might want to stop by the Golden Crown. You've got a fan in Transylvania.

I head out west on the road for the Borgo Pass, the very site where Dracula's ghostly carriage was supposed to have picked Harker up for a short jaunt to the castle. And what a road it is.

"In this respect it is different from the general run of roads in the Carpathians," Stoker writes, describing the area, "for it is an old tradition that they are not to be kept in too good order. Of old the Hospadars would not repair them, lest the Turks should think that they were preparing to bring in foreign troops, and so hasten the war which was always really at loading point."

Whether by accident or because of his research, Stoker's description is apt even today. The road begins to break up with huge stretches of unfinished pavement. Whole sections of one lane are blocked off with temporary stoplights at either end. You wait your turn while the traffic from the other end rolls by, and when the light turns green, you gun it and hope that nobody from the opposite side decided to ignore the light (and they do, sometimes).

When the highway occasionally enters a little town, the road gets so bad that you have to cut your speed in half and then in half again. I find myself surrounded on both sides by tiny dilapidated houses with crowds of people milling around and sometimes darting across my path. Wagons roll ahead of me. And it occurs to me that the piss-poor conditions of the road are actually good for these little towns. Because they need motorists like me to cut their speed down to nothing. The cracks and ditches and potholes are a crude but effective speed bump system. Without a warning sign or a speed limit sign or a Romanian cop lying in wait, the Transylvanians have forced all the crazy tourists to keep it to a minimum.

Still, I'm terrified I'm going to hit someone. For some reason, I get nervous and I find myself talking out loud again.

"Don't hit anyone," I tell myself helpfully. "Don't hit the people. They're not like cars. They won't survive a little tap. Not even a little tap." I don't know whether this helps my driving, but it calms me so I can focus. It occurs to me, though, that the day this area gets revitalized and people build the roads up will be terrible for these towns. On the upside, people like me will be able to shave a half hour off our trips out to visit Drac. The downside is that every once in a while, someone's kid will get killed.

If they had any power, these people would never build good roads through this area. This is the problem with globalization, perhaps. Everyone gets a new road. Everyone gets dangerous and annoying things they don't need and didn't ask for.

The road lifts up as I skirt past the base of one of the highest mountains in the eastern Carpathians, Mount Caliman, rising almost 7,000 feet into the air. The road begins to curve one way and then the other, dipping and rising like a roller coaster. There is no shoulder and ridiculously little clearance. Sometimes I catch a glimpse off the side of a hill and it feels a little like that scene in Coppola's *Dracula* in which Keanu rides in the carriage looking down that deep, fatal drop.

After a few miles, though, the area flattens out a little. There are dramatic foothills here, and the grade is impressive, but there aren't the kind of steep craggy spires of rock you'd expect. The Poinari castle down in the south looks more like the movies. And Vlad had very good military reasons to build it that way.

And at the top of a green sloping hill is a huge, modern-looking building. "Hotel Castel Dracula," the sign reads. There is also an insignia of a big *D* made by the stylized outline of a dragon. A half dozen cars and a tour bus have parked out in the lot. There's a large, spooky gate, and dramatic stone steps inside make the courtyard look like the castle in *Nosferatu*—or it would if there weren't lumber and construction equipment lying all around. They're doing renovations, the clerk tells me. He also says I can't have a meal in their restaurant—there's a luncheon. Down by the dining hall, a guy steps out to have a smoke. I ask him about his group, and he tells me they're all Romanian prosecutors. (I thought of making a joke here about Transylvanian lawyers. But it's too easy.)

I browse through the glass case in which souvenirs and knick-knacks are displayed for sale, and I buy a copy of *Dracula A surviver's guide to Transilvania Romania.* (This is how the title is really written. The graphics are all messed up and it's difficult to figure out exactly what it's supposed to be.) The book is published by the Transylvanian Society of Dracula Romania. Outside, just off the parking lot, is a giant flea market-style lot filled with T-shirts, ornamental knives, a skeleton, and sweaters. It is as big and tacky as the gift shop they have in the entry room of a Cracker Barrel, where you can buy penny candy, gift books, and those little wooden puzzles with golf tees. I get a knife for one buddy back home and a bust of Vlad the Impaler— the historical figure with the mustache, only with a pair of bloody fangs etched into his mouth—for another. I walk about, admiring the hilly country and checking out the chairlift that disappears into the distance.

"This paradise of silence and recreation offers excellent condition for practicing winter sports," the Hotel Castel Dracula brochure tells me. It promises the "region has a tonic, stimulating climate and a strong ozonized air with the highest level of the iodine from Romania. This and other natural factors create a unique healing environment for the exhausted persons, hyperthyroidism convalescents, Basedov illness invalids, improving the general health condition."

In the shadow of the tour bus, I spot a small graveyard filled with families. Most of the people died at least twenty years ago. There is a plot for a married couple here—a husband named Julius who lived from 1903 to 1985. And though his wife, Florica, has 1921 listed as her birth date, the space for the death date is blank. The plot waits for her, now in her eighties, to join her husband. Adorning the stone is a small picture of the two of them together—a man with a mustache and dark hair and eyes standing next to a woman in a shawl. This area is a vampire tourist magnet, where lawyers come from around the region to lunch. It's a beautiful place to vacation and to buy a T-shirt and to tell people you visited the spot where Stoker set his fictional villain. But couples and families are growing up and growing old all around here. It's a home for them. That small spot of land just a few hundred feet from the hotel is the only ground Julius can lay claim to. There are flowers all around the yard, so people must come to visit their loved ones, idly watching the tourists come in their endless buses. What must they think of us?

Back in Bistriţa, I stop one more time to get a couple more pictures of the Golden Crown; the hotel has a small freestanding building next to it that's quite cute. While fiddling with my camera, I hear a voice.

"My friend! My friend!" It's the middle-aged guy with the NYPD hat. He's calling to me from the small building's basement window, and he's waving me in. I look around the building and find a side door I hadn't noticed. And there in the replica of the inn where they warned Harker not to tempt fate by traveling on to Castle Dracula, I find a small casino with video games and an electronic roulette wheel. A few bored locals are sitting around the thing losing their money, but NYPD guy seems cheerful enough. He takes my picture sitting at the games.

I have reached the spot Stoker etched into countless readers' minds as the mysterious place where the natural and supernatural worlds collide, and . . . ah, hell, it's just a place to blow money on roulette. It's a bit of a letdown, I have to admit. I wanted it to be spookier. I wanted it to be something. Instead, I sit there with the machines ringing and beeping, the NYPD fan grinning at me in a friendly and utterly uncomprehending manner, and I can't keep some kind of crazy alternate version of *Dracula* from spinning through my head:

This is the very casino where Jonathan Harker blew all his money on Transylvanian hookers and Victorian-era poker and sweet, sweet balls of opium. He hid out in Greece for a few months, then concocted some ridiculous story about how a foreign Count he'd never met was really a magical creature with terrible powers. Of course Harker hardly expected to be believed. But his friends back in England became terrified of a mysterious nobleman, dragging him out of his bed one night and viciously stabbing him to death with an arsenal of crudely made pointy sticks.

Maybe that's crossing the line. But what can I say? Though I've spent all this time—this whole book, in fact—trying to get to the truth behind the Dracula legend, I also have a secret, kinky desire to find something that actually is . . . legendary. And of course this place isn't. Nothing ever is. Legends just don't hold up. They break your heart again and again because something in you just can't stop believing in them. I can't help feeling bad about it even now.

Harker married his fiancée. They lived together contentedly for several years, before she discovered he'd somehow infected her with gonorrhea.

Okay, I'll stop.

On my way back from Castle Dracula—or the spot where it should be—I spend one more night in Cluj, where I walk about paying attention to the streets and sites. The sheer volume of competing Hungarian and Romanian names seems obsessive. The city seems to be caught in a war of monuments, with the two factions struggling to slap a name or label on everything made of stone.

Tensions have flared up between the two groups. In 2002, the BBC reported on the case of a young couple who had to file a suit in court to say "Igen" or "Yes" to their wedding vows in their native Hungarian, after the registrar walked out during the service when they uttered the offending language. They won their case.

I walk down a street and across the river to where the Belvedere hotel stands on the high hill. During the Ceauşescu reign, according to my guidebook, it was the informal headquarters of the Securitate, Romania's feared secret police. Twelve people were shot here during the 1989 revolution. And next to the hotel stands a cross monument. When I reach the top of the hill, there is a crowd of frumpy, middle-aged people in tuxes and gowns spilling out of the hotel ballroom with bad eastern European pop thumping in the background. Someone tells me there's a wedding going on. One of the men looks haggard and spent, his tie is undone. He staggers around with a blank, scared look. I figure him for the father of the bride, the one who is getting stuck with the bill. And in the shadows around the monument, a hoard of teenagers and young adult couples have paired off together to admire their beautiful city from across the river and do all the things young couples do. All the things that result in exactly the kind of wild, chaotic party where you have to invite your relatives and foot a scary, scary bar tab plus expenses for the Romanian equivalent of Kool and the Gang.

Wandering through this scene, I find myself remembering my own wedding—and the honeymoon that first brought me to Romania. And I'm also filled with an incredible sense of optimism. After all the ugliness that a bad century could chuck at Romania, kids are still finding dark spots to neck, teenage girls are still getting knocked up, and folks are still marrying each other off. This former secret police HQ and a religious monument are now magnets of familial love and obligation, drunkenness, and good old-fashioned lust.

Take that, commie bastards.

The Rough Guide to Romania also says that unlike many large cities, Cluj has no civic center at the heart of its downtown. Instead, like many of the small towns I've been traveling through, it's wrapped around a church. My optimism is a little bit tempered. I'm astounded by the persistence of religion and ethnicity as a way to organize society in the face of communism, but it's also something that persists in the face of globalism, capitalism, and other kinds of ways we have of arranging the world to make everybody play nice. We've seen books and essays assuring us that borders will melt away and people will ignore their differences and spend the centuries text-flaming one another instead of going to war. In the past few years, most of us have realized that such notions are dumb. Strolling back through the maze of streets, spangled with their different nationalist names like the shields and banners of warring tribes, I find myself wondering if globalism could ever someday be remembered like communism—like another proselytizing faith that thought it could wipe out the differences among people.

Then again, I pass a guy in an Iron Maiden T-shirt. People everywhere are drinking Cokes and American booze. I spot a Ford ad next to a picture of the American flag next to an umbrella with the Coca-Cola logo, and I impulsively take a picture.

And smoking! Oh, the smoking. In all the cities in which I've traveled, I've never seen a strange unidentifiable brand of cigarettes. Nothing but Marlboros, Winstons, Pall Malls, and Lucky Strikes. In U.S. bars, the display cases feature booze and energy drinks like Red Bull. Here there are display cases for cigarette brands—big, slowly revolving things, shiny as jewelry cases.

Eastern Europe is not just a viable market for American cigarette companies, but a young market—the last place they can openly try to get new people hooked on smoking. And cigarette brands—like Dracula—depend on style, glamour, and image for their value. If you've ever had to soak cigarettes in the sink when quitting because you knew you'd just fish them out of the wastebasket later or cobbled butts together into a Frankensmoke, you know that you're not trying to get to Flavor Country when you light up. Image and distribution are everything. The lessons I learned watching all those bad vamp movies until I scorched my retinas are finally coming in handy.

I walk back to my hotel room, and lay down on the bed clicking through Romanian channels and waiting for sleep to come. I miss my wife and family. It's been seven years since my first trip to this country. Part of me thought it would be easier to go back alone. My wife and I were not good travel companions there. Now, two kids, a dog, a cat, and a mortgage later, I realize I can't go anywhere without her.

The next day on the road back across Transylvania toward Banat, I see a sign for some other "Hotel Dracula" in Turda. I stop and pull over. My guidebook tells me Turda was a prosperous salt-mining town in the Middle Ages as well as the site of a sixteenth-century edict that recognized equally the Calvinist, Lutheran, Roman Catholic, and Unitarian churches. It was a rare spot of religious tolerance in Europe at the time. But I still can't say the name without giggling. Go ahead. *Turda*. Hee hee. I follow the signs to a hotel just outside the main square. It's a cute, Gothicy thing with a beautiful courtyard. It's also called the "Hunter Prince Castle" on some signs, but clearly the name "Dracula" is a draw. The lady there lets me take photos of the interior—which boasts a lot of cool stonework and a small wooden statue of Vlad.

"Placed somewhere on the boundary between centuries . . ." its website reads, "in the very heart of much keened Transylvania . . . you are just about to find vivid the story of a prince whose soul you can keep into immortality." *(Much keened?)*

I think the folks who run the place have the right idea. If the Borgo people can have a hotel on a literary site that has no real significance—and certainly no connection to the real Dracula—why can't they set up their own Dracula hotel anywhere they want? If I ever get a publisher for my novel about the real story of how

Jonathan Harker lost all his money gambling and smoking opium, I'm going to plop the castle right down in the middle of, uh, Turda. (Note: I discover later that Turda actually does have a historical connection to the life of the real Vlad. When Matthias Corvinus finally let Vlad launch his last push for the Wallachian throne, it was in Turda that Vlad set up camp. And, according to McNally and Florescu, one of the commanders of the army was Stephen Bathory, the great-uncle of Elizabeth Bathory, the Blood Countess.)

I pass Romanians selling glassware from the side of the road. I see quite a few of these people on my trip. And some of the same vases appear over and over—making it seem like I'm being stalked in some weird Pottery Barn–themed version of *The Hitcher.* I'm wondering if this is how Romanians buy their table sets. How do they prevent breakage when the sales force has to dodge trucks and wagons just to close a deal? Also, is this stuff appropriate for weddings?

"Thanks for RSVPing. The bridal couple is registered at Macy's, Williams-Sonoma, and I-95."

I also notice a growing number of hitchhikers at stops and villages along the way, and this makes me feel guilty, too. These aren't western-style backpacking kids trying to bum a ride. You see old babushka ladies wrapped up in black like wizened ninjas. You see whole families. I zip by one teenage kid who is brazen. He waves at me in a friendly way, then puts his hands together in a prayer, and, finally, as I pass, he instantly turns around and gives me the finger. He goes from friend to supplicant to pissed-off punk in seconds. People seem to use passing cars as a sort of informal taxi system. I tell myself if I see someone who doesn't look like he will butcher me and feed off my flesh, I'll pull over.

Near a field I have to put the brakes on as a whole flock of sheep spill out into the road. Several shepherds are trying to get them all on the other side, but they're curious and obstinate. Dozens of them are going the wrong direction, their cute little petting-zoo heads poking up next to my driver's-side window and all around my car, *bahhing* incessantly.

Just 35 kilometers north of Lugoj, I stop by a large cargo plane turned into a café and painted with the Coca-Cola sign. According to one of the guys who helps run the place, the plane is a Russian-made AN-24. A 75-foot light-transport craft, it came off the line in the early 1960s, and the first mass-production model was, ironically, called the AN-24 COKE. According to this local, it was the plane that ferried Gheorghe Gheorghiu-Dej around. Taking power in 1948, he ran the country for almost twenty years until his death, when Ceaușescu took over.

"Like Air Force One for Romania?" I ask.

"Yes, like Air Force One," he tells me.

The guy complains to me that a member of his family, I think his sister, had serious difficulties getting a visa. He's been to San Francisco. We talk about how nice it is. How expensive.

I wave good-bye and get back on the road. I notice that by now I have acclimated to the suicidal traffic in a frightening way. I have actually become desensitized to oncoming cars and even trucks. A few more weeks of this and I'll have the nerves of a bomb disposal tech.

I reach Lugoj and drive into the center of town looking for a monument to Bela. Lugosi is known as a Hungarian actor because the town itself was part of Hungary when he arrived into the world. I find a few monuments to various Lugojans I've never heard of—the town is home to poets, opera singers, and composers. But no Bela. I find more monuments a few blocks away, but no Bela there, either. I walk around the place and eventually get into my car and drive down along a river where there are monuments aplenty. I find more than a dozen statues and busts of other folks . . . But I can't find a single one dedicated to a guy who became internationally famous—we're talking John-Lennon-bigger-than-Jesus-famous—playing Dracula. Quick, name a person besides Bela who comes from Lugoj. One. Just one. Can you? Didn't think so.

"I have never heard of any Lugosi monument in Europe," Dracula expert David J. Skal tells me. "The only one I know of is his Hollywood Walk of Fame star . . . And, of course, his gravestone."

"When I visited Budapest, I kept looking for something on Bela in the 'famous Hungarians in history' exhibits I saw everywhere," UVA professor Paul Cantor tells me. "Franz Liszt, Edwin Teller, Bela Bartok—big deal! But nothing on Bela. Finally after a week in Budapest, I saw at least a photo of Bela in a memorabilia shop—on my last day there. But really, he is not getting the recognition he deserves. The most famous Hungarian of the twentieth century—no questions asked."

Someday, when Britney Spears dies, you know that whatever Louisianan backwater she came from is going to have a massive replica of her twenty-year-old ass and charge visitors $8 a pop to smack it. Why? Because the town leaders know that she is and always will be the only thing to come out of that place that will be recognized by Maori tribesmen and Japanese schoolgirls and even my mom. A giant bronze ass. And I will go to see it, and I'll probably use it for a book, and you'll buy it, too.

A few miles outside of Lugoj, I finally pull over for a hitchhiker. An old babushka lady stands by the side of the road waving at me, and the rain is just beginning to come down in the middle of the afternoon. If she has a band of thugs waiting to whack me, they must be far away. She gets in and tells me, "Timişoara," which is just where I'm going. She chats at me cheerfully, and I shake my head and smile and tell her I don't speak Romanian. And I chat at her, and she shakes her head and tells me (I think) that she doesn't speak English. Pretty soon I realize we're not going to be able to communicate at all. She settles in comfortably, and we don't make an attempt to speak. I realize that hitchhiking isn't something they must give much thought to. In America it's a big deal, a good deed, and a little bit of a risk to take on passengers. Here I think they're more casual about it, because if you live in a village, and you don't have a car, how else are you going to take those few trips a year? And if you are a driver, why not let someone help you pay for fuel? At the end, she matter-of-factly asks "banii?" and makes the international money finger-rub-signal. And since it's probably inappropriate to tell her she can pay with cash, grass, or ass, I just wave her off.

Back in Budapest the next day, I tell the lady at the train station's tourist booth that I want to get a hotel room nearby so I can explore things on the opposite side of the river from the Castle district. But she doesn't think that's a good idea.

"There are fights all over that area," she tells me. And she tries to sell me on some hotel room a few miles away, but I'm not buying. I figure I'll be careful, and I'm not scared if Budapest has a few rough neighborhoods.

What I don't understand is that she's not talking about a few rough parts of town. I've arrived on October 23, 2006, the fiftieth anniversary of the day that tens of thousands of Hungarians spilled out into the streets to demand an end to the Soviet-backed government and the return of their Prime Minister Imre Nagy. And by early November, Soviet tanks rolled in and crushed the revolt.

Locals expected tension at the 2006 anniversary celebration. Hungarians had been protesting against the government since mid-September, when the prime minister was caught on tape admitting to lying about the economy to win an election. Weeks before the celebration began, rioting had erupted that injured more than a hundred police and dozens of civilians. A later *Chicago Tribune* article would report cops using tear gas, water cannons, and rubber bullets to disperse angry crowds on the day I arrived. Dozens were injured. Then came the tank hijackings.

"In one of the main showdowns on Monday near Deak Square, the city's main subway hub, hundreds of police behind three water cannons slowly advanced on a few hundred rioters. The protesters threw bottles and rocks at the police who fired tear gas and rubber bullets back at them as a police helicopter circled low over the crowd," the *Tribune* reported. "Then one of the protesters seized a tank that was part of an exhibit in the square to commemorate the revolution. He drove it among the protesters until he was pulled out by police who rushed the vehicle. A second tank in the exhibit was pushed by the rioters toward the police."

I find a hotel just across the street from the train station and ask the clerk there for a good place to get some traditional Hungarian food nearby. That's going to be a problem, she says, because the locals don't want tourists coming in to eat. She tells me the whole story.

"There were police shooting into the air," she adds. She says that some of the fighting broke out in this very area. Things are a lot quieter, but it hasn't quite settled down.

Now, I'm not really a brave man. But I am a reporter. So whenever someone gets clunked over the head, shot at, or steals a tank, it's my job to try to get in the middle of it. I'm a scavenger of human misery. Someone's got to do it.

"I don't want to get into any trouble," I say solemnly. "Tell me *exactly* where I shouldn't go. Here, can you mark it on the map?"

I reach one of the sites where the demonstrations were held and make my way into the middle of a crowd. Orchestral music blares out over speakers and flags wave in the air—some are copies of the Hungarian tricolor with a hole in the center that the 1956 revolutionaries flew after tearing out the Communist symbol. A media helicopter is sweeping overhead. But for all the commotion, the crowd seems to be just commemorating their history. I spot proud old people and couples with young kids. I spot teenagers and young adults having a good time. I suspect that the vast majority of people were just here to mark the day and that some knuckleheads tried to make it ugly.

One guy walks by with his wife—both in their sixties—holding a sign in Magyar. And it shows a series of pictures of a red star assembling into a symbol of the new socialist government.

The phrase from his sign, he tells me, is "I turn it out, I turn it in . . . Bunda a Bunda." Bunda is a coat, he adds. The sign means that a coat is a coat, whether you turn it out or in. Or to put it another way, meet the new boss—same as the old boss. I ask him if he remembers the 1956 revolt.

"I was fourteen years old. My father was very much involved," the man says. "Every time that day comes, I have an inclination to cry." I ask him if I can quote him with his name.

"Today it's very risky," he says, demurring. "Write that down."

Some of the people are waving flags with horizontal red and white stripes—exactly like an American flag without the blue box in the corner. I spot a couple of them who have shaved heads, and I wonder if they're skinheads intent on taking over the demonstration.

"It's a misused symbol," the old man tells me. "The fascists made it dirty, but it's a very old symbol." He says it's not a fascist symbol per se. But he and his wife say they wouldn't fly it because they have Jewish friends. So clearly some people take offense. And some people fly it to *give* offense.

I ask whether it's a generational thing—whether younger people might fly it without really understanding the feelings it brings. They agree with me. Every tricolor has been misused, he says.

"Many of the protesters were from far-right groups," BBC would report later, "and some carried the red-and-white striped flag of the Arpad dynasty—a centuries-old symbol of Hungary that was also used by the nationalist pro-Nazi government during World War II."

This Arpad dynasty goes back to the tenth century, and the flag itself is eight hundred years old. But during the 1940s, the fascist Arrow Cross party, which murdered thousands of Jews in Budapest alone, appropriated it. The Arrow Cross symbol is banned, according to newspaper accounts I read. And that makes it hard to tell what it's supposed to symbolize.

"Because it's shorn of the Arrow Cross, it's impossible to know exactly what the flag-wavers mean, or if they comprehend the crimes committed under the flag against fellow Hungarians six decades ago," reported the *New Jersey Jewish Standard*. During the demonstration, I do see some people who are obviously dressed in the skinhead uniform, with big puffy jackets, boots, and suspenders hanging past their asses. In fact, an hour or so later, I'm walking back to the hotel surrounded by stragglers who are going home, when I hear the rumble of motorcycles and suddenly find myself surrounded by a dozen skinheads on Harleys.

They've clumped together in the middle of the street, and one of the riders moves a couple of police barricades across a lane so they block traffic. A few cars come to a screeching halt when they reach the obstruction. They honk horns, and one guy hits the accelerator, pops up on a curb, and screeches through. For a moment I really think the skinheads are going to pull him out of his car and beat him. But they don't. I casually make my way out of the middle of the group and watch with some onlookers from the side. I don't say anything. I'm not sure how their little paranoid right-wing worldview classifies Americans, but I suspect it's not good.

I know not all skinheads are racists. I know many of them are nice, tolerant straight-edge punks from Ohio or Virginia Beach. They listen to Henry Rollins, and the only political principle they're willing to get angry about is the fact that skateboarding is not a crime. These guys are not those kinds of skinheads. They have more Arpad flags, and one of the cyclists has a German-style World War II helmet and an iron cross symbol on his jacket. He's chubby, and the getup makes him look like Sergeant Shultz from *Hogan's Heroes*. Suddenly, some of them strip the license plates off their bikes or cover them with bandanas—and within a few minutes, they all roar off down the long street to find something to do. Within an hour, a few ambulances follow, sirens blaring.

The weird thing about skinheads is they're ultra-nationalists who want to protect their country's culture, but the skinhead uniform is an international one. Their outfits and Kojak hairstyles make them look like they could be hoods from Hungary or Germany, rednecks from the Deep South or the Midwest, or skate punks from So Cal.

Skinheads themselves might argue that what they're trying to preserve is some multinational and ancient "white culture" from all the pasty corners of the earth. But they're doing it by flattening out European culture and defining it down so that it's something simplistic and stupid.

I'm proud of my ethnic culture—Irish and French—and I'm definitely proud of being an American, home of George Washington and Elvis, Jack Daniels and Harley Davidson. But all this craziness makes me realize culture is like currency. It has value only if you give it away. You don't hoard piles of money if you're smart. You increase your savings by investment. Cultural power works the same way. If these skins ever get their wish and create some isolated, secure, homogenized racial homeland—Honkeyvania, let's call it—that place will almost instantly become the most boring and forgettable spot on earth. Their women will look uglier and their kids will start fleeing the moment they get their driver's licenses. It will have all the cachet of a highway rest stop.

American culture has power as a cause and effect of the fact that Tupac's face is appearing in Timişoara along with Frank Sinatra and Coca-Cola. As for Dracula, it's a mark of his power—and the source of it—that he can be stolen, changed, and transferred and pop up in a million different places as a million different things. It's power the skinheads don't understand and can't use. And despite how scary they are, I feel sorry for them.

And it's power for the Romanians. I started this book thinking these Romanians were getting ripped off by the West, but it doesn't have to be that way at all. If Dracula can be transformed into a Transylvanian count, a Hungarian actor, a kinky '70s symbol of kitsch and sex, a felt hand puppet, a breakfast cereal spokesman, or a symbol of love after the age of AIDS, he could probably be transformed into anything at all. And maybe, just maybe, he could even be transformed back into a fifteenth-century Wallachian prince. He could be a historical figure. And he could be a gateway to a wild and beautiful country that has no real need of movie stars.

Here's my advice, for what it's worth, to you folks in the Romanian tourism industry: Design a massive ad campaign around the historical Vlad. Don't tangle with Universal's lawyers. Don't try to dress him up as a pop culture figure. Make an ad campaign that is as clear as possible that you're offering people a chance to look at the birthplace, government palaces, castles, and possible death and grave of a real person who lived, loved, and impaled. Don't avoid speculation that he wasn't buried in Snagov. Encourage it. Offer tours to alternate burial sites. Put more money into the museums displaying his real relics and documents and into sites with tourist-friendly information that spells out as completely as possible what we know as fact, what we guess at based on evidence, and what we accept as merely legend. Imagine giant posters that say in bold letters: "Dracula Never Wore a Cape" or "Dracula Never Had Fangs" or even "Come Meet Dracula for the First Time."

He can be anything. Why can't Dracula be turned back into the real thing? You'd be offering history instead of Hollywood. Hollywood, we have plenty of. The sites and the culture you have in Romania are irreplaceable, and the horror flick hacks could never do them justice.

Of course—and I say this with love—you *really* should rebuild that staircase up the side of Poinari. Damn thing's a deathtrap.

Conclusion

Planet Vlad

Cook a Hungarian dish called Paprika Hendl, and it will tell you everything you need to know about *Dracula*. Back home in Virginia after my trip, I prepare it for my wife—grabbing the recipe off the Web and cooking it with some dumplings. It includes a sauce of onions, butter, tomato juice, and sour cream, with plenty of garlic and paprika. The sour cream gives it a smooth, mellow taste slightly offset by the tang of Hungary's favorite pepper.

"I had for dinner, or rather supper, a chicken done up some way with red pepper, which was very good but thirsty (Mem., get recipe for Mina)," writes Harker in his journal about this meal.

He's not a bad guy once you get to know him.

Anne and I drink a rich Pinot Noir from a company called Vampire with our dinner. I was leery of buying it—I remember it from my patent search, and it seemed like a novelty. But the wine store clerk recommended it, and it turns out to be good. Imported from Transylvania, it's available at my local shop, which means you can buy it absolutely anywhere.

Many people smarter than me have talked about how Dracula is a tale of foreign theft and invasion; the vampire from Transylvania steals land and women from the English. But interestingly, the novel opens with a kind of cultural theft committed by Jonathan Harker. He copies a recipe, demonstrating how the spread of communication and travel technology make it possible to take a national dish and re-create it back at home. And the fact that the theft is connected to the act of eating is particularly weird.

Later, at Drac's house, the Count brags that he has a library with books on the English cultural and political system. Before we talk about blood and gene pools and soil in this horror novel, we're talking about the central weakness of culture. That it's based on data, and data can never be fenced in. In fact, as information replicates itself—I tell you a fact and you know it, but I don't stop knowing it—it spreads, like, well, a vampire. It's something a couple of people can do with recipes on their websites, and I can make my own version, and you can too, because information not only flows freely, it can mutate as it jumps from source to source. Until it becomes impossible to distinguish a foreigner from a native, because we all know the same things and copy the same folkways.

In a modern world, it becomes impossible for one culture to safeguard itself. Stoker predicted this almost exactly one hundred years before the spread of the Internet made it obvious to everyone who's ever seen that guy do his rendition of the Numa Numa dance on YouTube. And even stranger, the themes in Stoker's novel mirror exactly what the novel—and its movies, plays, MP3s, video games, and TV shows—did to the historical figure of Dracula. Once he became pure information—a character in a story instead of a historical figure—Dracula could constantly shift his shape, just like this Paprika Hendl recipe. We brought Dracula in from his homeland and helped him stash hiding places all over the West. He went native over here.

Where Stoker got it wrong is the last scene, where the Count tries to get home, and we kill him as the last rays of sunlight are caressing his castle. He did no such thing. He never went home, because what he became is not really welcome there.

We never killed him, either. Arata's essay pointed something like this out, but when you colonize a country—militarily or culturally—it can colonize you right back. You bring back its treasures and it haunts your dreams. We've seen how the phenomenon of Dracula can tell us about retail business and religious belief, intellectual property and political squabbles. It can tell us about the memories of that first great summer job and the horrors that descend on overworked costume shop staffers every fall. Up on the screen, his story is a flickering copy of our own. And back in our beds at night, the Count has visited all of us at one time or another. Here in our bizarre land, he is at home.

For the data is the life.

Acknowledgments

Writing a book is every bit as thrilling, baffling, and exhausting as hunting down a vampire. And it takes a team of dedicated stalwarts. My Professor Van Helsing was John Talbot at the Talbot Fortune Agency, whose enthusiasm and advice kept me alive during this struggle. Julian Pavia at Three Rivers Press was the perfect Dr. Seward, providing guidance and multiple transfusions. Kennan Gudjonsson, who accompanied me to Wildwood, New Jersey, played two-fisted Texan Quincey Morris. And unlike poor Quincey, Kennan braved the gunfire and survived.

Jason Pinter used his royal connections and wielded a hammer and stake as Lord Arthur Holmwood. And the editor at *Maxim* who first helped me dig this story up was Charles "Renfield" Coxe. The bright, endlessly charming Lucy Westenra was Jeanne Youngson. And her sinister "Bloofer Lady" counterpart was Elizabeth Miller, who knows more about this stuff than I will probably ever learn.

The garlic-toting villagers were my family who read the odd chapter and listened to me worry, complain, and brag—Mom, Dad,

Sue, Chris, Sarah, and Annette Graham. Thomas Veech and Thomas Lipscomb made for great wolves, David Henry turned into a bat on command, and Sean Devereux was riveting as the dead captain lashed to the wheel of the *Demeter.* The London constables were Officers Carl Swanson and Juanita Felton. Flitting into the scene as the Count himself was Jonathan Coleman, the best writing teacher a guy could have.

And if I'm Harker, my Mina was, and always will be, my wife Anne.

About the Author

Paul Bibeau has been a lifelong vampire enthusiast, possibly because he was born in the same town as Stephen King and attended the same college as Edgar Allan Poe. He was an editor and writer for *Maxim* and has written for the *Washington Post, Mademoiselle*, the *New York Observer, Cosmopolitan*, and the *New York Post*. He does not own a cape. His wife won't allow it.